The
Essential
Nostradamus

The
Essential
Nostradamus

Translation, Historical Commentary, and Biography by

RICHARD SMOLEY

JEREMY P. TARCHER/PENGUIN
a member of Penguin Group (USA) Inc.
New York

JEREMY P. TARCHER/PENGUIN
Published by the Penguin Group
Penguin Group (USA) Inc., 375 Hudson Street, New York, New York 10014, USA • Penguin Group (Canada),
90 Eglinton Avenue East, Suite 700, Toronto, Ontario M4P 2Y3, Canada (a division of
Pearson Penguin Canada Inc.) • Penguin Books Ltd, 80 Strand, London WC2R oRL, England •
Penguin Ireland, 25 St Stephen's Green, Dublin 2, Ireland (a division of Penguin Books Ltd) •
Penguin Group (Australia), 250 Camberwell Road, Camberwell, Victoria 3124, Australia (a division of
Pearson Australia Group Pty Ltd) • Penguin Books India Pvt Ltd, 11 Community Centre, Panchsheel Park,
New Delhi–110 017, India • Penguin Group (NZ), 67 Apollo Drive, Rosedale, North Shore 0632,
New Zealand (a division of Pearson New Zealand Ltd) • Penguin Books (South Africa) (Pty) Ltd,
24 Sturdee Avenue, Rosebank, Johannesburg 2196, South Africa

Penguin Books Ltd, Registered Offices: 80 Strand, London WC2R oRL, England

Most Tarcher/Penguin books are available at special quantity discounts for bulk purchase for
sales promotions, premiums, fund-raising, and educational needs. Special books or book excerpts also
can be created to fit specific needs. For details, write Penguin Group (USA) Inc. Special Markets,
375 Hudson Street, New York, NY 10014.

Library of Congress Cataloging-in-Publication Data

Smoley, Richard, date.
The essential Nostradamus/translation, historical commentary, and biography by Richard Smoley.
p.   cm.
Includes bibliographical references and index.
ISBN 978-1-58542-794-9
1. Nostradamus, 1503–1566. 2. Prophecies (Occultism). I. Nostradamus, 1503–1566. Prophéties. English
& French. II. Title.
BF1815.N8S64   2010   2010000610
133.3092—dc22

Printed in the United States of America
1   3   5   7   9   10   8   6   4   2

Frontispiece painting dated 1846, oil on canvas, Réunion des Musées Nationaux/Art Resource, NY

BOOK DESIGN BY NICOLE LAROCHE

Contents

Acknowledgments

While there are many people whose insights have helped me navigate the turbulent waters of mysticism and prophecy over the years, there are two who most deserve my thanks specifically in the creation of this project. Mitch Horowitz, my editor at Tarcher/Penguin, deserves the credit for conceiving this book and suggesting it to me back in December 2003. Without his guidance and suggestions, this book would not exist. In addition, I would like to thank my agent, Katherine Boyle, for her help and support in negotiating the waters of contracts and rights, as well as Mark Birkey for his excellent work in copyediting, and David Fuller for his map.

Introduction

Would you like to write a book on Nostradamus? All right; I'll tell you how. First, cobble together a translation of some of his prophecies. (You don't have to know French; in fact it can be helpful not to know French too well.) Then sit down and use them to prove that the world will come to an end in ten years.

Of course the world won't come to an end in ten years. But it won't make any difference. By then you will have long since made your money, and your erroneous predictions will have been forgotten. If you're the cheeky type, you can repeat this exercise two or three times over the next couple of decades. This will even establish you as an authority on Nostradamus, utterly regardless of the failures of your previous prognostications.

Books like this must be easy to write; certainly there are enough of them. And they are so consistently popular that they must meet some need among the reading public. Nevertheless, this is not the sort of book I have set out to write. For me, it would require more than a small amount of intellectual dishonesty, nor does it seem particularly interesting as an exercise.

And yet Nostradamus and his prophecies retain their fascination. Why, after all, should his name remain a household word more than four hundred years after his death? Could he really see the future? What draws us back to his prophecies so consistently that they have never been out of print since they first appeared in the sixteenth century?

Nostradamus's current popularity in the English-speaking world goes back to World War II, when passages in his *Prophecies* with the name "Hister" were believed to foretell the rise of Adolf Hitler. (See *Prophecies* II.24, IV.68, V.29, VI.49. Hitler's propaganda machine also made use of Nostradamus; see *Prophecies* III.57–58, VI.51, X.31.)* Since then, the French seer has been constantly invoked as the prophet of most of the great upheavals and disasters of our time.

How seriously can we take this interest? No doubt there are people who believe in Nostradamus's predictions as reported in *The Weekly World News,* but I suspect they are fairly few. On the other hand, the self-styled "skeptical inquirers," who dismiss out of hand the idea that the future can be known, are in some ways just as credulous as the believer. The latter at least acknowledges that there is more to the world than we see or perhaps *can* see, that it contains mysteries and magic that elude easy formulation. The skeptic, however, "knows" the truth. It is all solid and self-evident and has no secrets left to offer, except for a few small details that science is sure to sort out in ten or twenty years. This is even more naive, given that science changes its mind over and over (as is its right) and will no doubt disrupt our settled views of the cosmos many times in the future, just as it has in the past. The skeptic, for all his pseudoscientific bravado, is, in the end, something of a flat-earther.

I believe there is a middle ground to be found here, and for all the intense interest the occult and paranormal have aroused and continue to arouse, it remains largely unoccupied. I am speaking of the position between an unenlightened credulity and an equally

---

*In 1555, Macé Bonhomme, the original publisher of Nostradamus's *Prophecies*, decided upon a format for his quatrains that has remained in use since: each of the quatrains is divided into groups of one hundred, which are called "Centuries." There are ten Centuries in all. When I refer to a specific quatrain, I will use a numeration that cites the Century followed by the number of the quatrain. Hence the first quatrain of the first Century would appear as I.1.

unenlightened skepticism. I believe a figure such as Nostradamus can be intelligently and seriously examined without taking him at face value: we do not have to assume that he was a semidivine prophet in order to sift through his haunting and obscure utterances and find truth in them—as well as some insights about our own worldview.

Nor is this fence-straddling. The material demands it. Anyone who has investigated the world of the occult and the paranormal with any depth would, I think, agree that it occupies a shadowy liminal space in reality. No sooner do we dismiss it than some piece of evidence rises up, forcing us to reconsider what we had just ruled out. And yet as soon as we start to believe in an alternate reality, the evidence seems to evaporate, leaving us wondering just what it was we saw or imagined we saw.

So with Nostradamus. Perusing his dense, obscure prophecies, one is often tempted to throw down the book and dismiss it as nonsense. Just at that point one usually encounters some glimpse of insight, some hint that perhaps Nostradamus really could see into the future. If this teasing ambiguity was part of the game he played— oracles have been famous for ambiguous messages since antiquity— it is a part of the game of prophecy itself.

What, then, is prophecy? To answer this question, let me begin by recalling that man is an animal that can foresee the future. You know that someday you are going to die; your cat probably does not. Our capacity in this regard is, it is true, limited and imperfect. I can say for certain that someday I will die, and I can even go further and say everyone breathing on this earth right now will die, but I cannot be more specific: I do not know exactly when this will happen for myself or for anyone else.

Here is the dilemma: we can see and know certain things in the future, some of them quite precisely. Tonight we will go to bed fairly well assured that the sun will rise tomorrow. Other things are totally concealed from us. It is this capacity, so sharp and yet so defective, that constitutes both the genius and the torment of humanity. Some strains of the esoteric tradition say that the serpent in the garden in Genesis, the cause of all our woes, symbolizes forethought.

Another characteristic of the human race is that we constantly attempt to surpass our own limitations. Our eyesight, compared to that of some species, is not particularly good, so we've designed telescopes and microscopes to expand our visual possibilities. We build machines to do work that is too cumbersome or wearing for our rather frail bodies. And, over the past generation or two, we have even invented machines that can "think" (or, at any rate, calculate) faster and more accurately than we can.

Today we are using these machines for calculating in order to peer into the future, to determine, for example, when the Dow will hit 20,000 or the world will run out of oil. But this approach is extremely new. For most of human history, we have relied on a different process—delving into our own minds, using capacities so mysterious that many people today do not even believe they exist, in order to see what is about to manifest in material reality.

This, in essence, is prophecy. In Old Testament times, it was so common that there were not only prophets but "schools of the prophets," in which visionary powers were cultivated and developed. The prophets' frequent refrain "Thus saith the Lord" certainly indicates that they believed they had access to the mind of God. Iamblichus, a philosopher and magician of the fifth century A.D., evidently felt the same way. In his work *De mysteriis Aegyptiorum* (III.7), he writes of divination: "Its entire validity pertains to the gods, and is conferred by the gods." Echoing Iamblichus, Nostradamus writes, alluding to his own prophetic method, "Divine splendor! The divine one seats himself nearby" (*Prophecies* I.2).

Despite its proximity to the gods, a great deal of prophecy has simply proved false. To use comparatively recent examples, the psychic Jeane Dixon gained nationwide fame for predicting the assassination of John F. Kennedy, but she also predicted that Russia would be the first country to land a man on the moon. Edgar

Cayce, the famous "sleeping prophet," made enormous numbers of accurate medical diagnoses while in a state of trance, but he also forecast major "earth changes" between 1936 and 1998, including the rising of Atlantis near the island of Bimini in the Bahamas and the sinking of Japan as well as much of Europe; in addition, he predicted that "the waters of the Great Lakes will empty into the Gulf of Mexico."[1] A 1991 book on Nostradamus tells us that Prince Charles will inherit the throne of Britain before the end of the twentieth century and that the Hollywood studios will be destroyed by earthquake in 1993. If you are interested in prophecy and the issues it raises, I would suggest going to a used-book store and paging through some volumes of predictions dating from ten or twenty years back. You will be amazed—but not at their accuracy.

The spottiness of prophetic accuracy has led humanity to turn to scientific and quasi-scientific methods of prediction based on statistics and current trends. And yet mystical and quasi-scientific forecasting have more similarities than may first appear. They can both be easily turned to work on behalf of hidden agendas, and both often rely on mumbo jumbo as an out for failures and mistakes. If you look at books written by futurologists a decade or two in the past, you will not necessarily be impressed by *their* accuracy either. Like the works of occult prophecy, they usually say far more about their creators' assumptions than they do about the future.

All of this is germane to the question of prophecy on Nostradamus's scale, which focuses not on the destinies of private individuals but on the rise and fall of nations. Nostradamus, like all of us, lived in a specific time and place, and, again like all of us, he absorbed his assumptions and ideals from that context. Sometimes they misled him, leading him to confound his predictions with his hopes and fears. At other times, we can observe him seesawing between one outcome and another, as events themselves do. And there are still other instances in which his prophecies do bear some resemblance to what actually happened. Take this quatrain, for example:

New law to occupy new land
Near Syria, Judea, and Palestine.
The great barbaric empire to crumble,
Before Phoebus completes his age.
                              Prophecies III.97

This apparently alludes to the collapse of the Ottoman Empire, the "barbaric empire" that ruled Syria and Palestine in Nostradamus's day—although the empire itself would not crumble until after World War I. In this case, the "new law" would be the British and French mandates granted over Syria and Palestine by the League of Nations, which would eventually lead (not entirely fortunately) to the "new land," the states of the Middle East as we know them today.

In this book I will provide a selection of Nostradamus's most compelling prophecies. I have focused on those that are of most relevance to the English-speaking reader today, although, given that Nostradamus was a sixteenth-century Frenchman, naturally most of his predictions focus on his nation and his own time. I have done my best to treat them objectively and impartially, attempting neither to vindicate Nostradamus nor to discredit him. Where I have been able to find reasonably close parallels between his predictions and later events, I have mentioned them; on the other hand, I have done my best to avoid forced associations. Afterward I will step back and discuss my own impressions and suggest what Nostradamus and his work may say to our age. In this way I hope to give the reader some idea of exactly how accurate Nostradamus's prophecies were and how seriously they should (or should not) be taken.

First, however, I will begin with a short biography of Nostradamus, not only because he was a fascinating character in his own right but also because he embodies an archetype that is extremely important to our time—that of the sage or magus. An archetype, in the sense given to it by the great Swiss psychologist C. G. Jung, is a center of psychological energy that exists in the human mind both individually and collectively. For an individual, the archetypes (which are countless, although for Jung there were only five or six that were central to the human experience) are the basic building blocks of the psyche. They make their appearances in dreams, in the images we project upon others, even in daydreams and fantasies. Each of us is a unique combination of these principles, which we make manifest in our own particular ways.

The archetypes also make themselves felt in a culture as a whole—in literature and art, in religious symbolism, even in popular culture. Certain archetypes are more pregnant and powerful in a given age than others. One example, discussed by Jung himself, was the flying-saucer myth that reached its peak in the 1950s. In a famous essay on this subject, Jung refused to commit himself about what UFOs are in a factual sense (all he would say is "something is seen, but one doesn't know what"—a statement that still holds true fifty years later), but he did claim that these round objects, "things seen in the skies," were symbols of what he called the "Self"—the transcendental wholeness that lies at the core of every human being. Whatever they may mean from a factual point of view, UFOs express this longing for inner wholeness and completion. It is significant that the flying-saucer myth came to public attention soon after World War II, which, following a depression and a previous world war, had left Western culture broken and gasping for wholeness. The myth endures—even grows—today, indicating that we as a civilization are still groping toward this lost wholeness.

Another example of an archetype in mass consciousness brings us to the subject at hand. Jung spoke of the Wise Old Man who symbolizes the transcendent wisdom that speaks to us from the depths of our own souls. One form this takes is the sage or magus or magician. Like all the archetypes, this figure is practically universal in the human race, but in the West, it took its present form during the Renaissance and the early modern era—precisely the time when Nostradamus lived. That age produced Renaissance men in the true sense—men whose knowledge was not merely intellectual, but who had pushed their inquiries further, into the inner dimensions of the spirit and psyche.

Magi of this kind include Marsilio Ficino, head of the Medicis' Academy in fifteenth-century Florence; the mystical sixteenth-century physician Paracelsus; John Dee, the court astrologer to Elizabeth I of England, who was probably the inspiration for Shakespeare's Prospero; Cornelius Agrippa, whose *De occulta philosophia* ("On Occult Philosophy") served for centuries as the primer of this elusive art; and the legendary Doctor Faustus, who supposedly sold his soul to the Devil for knowledge and power.[2] Johann Wolfgang von Goethe, who wrote the greatest interpretation of the Faust legend, has his hero redeemed in the end by this very thirst for knowledge. The figure of Faust has been so potent in the Western mind that Oswald Spengler, in his *Decline of the West,* a classic account of the rise and fall of world cultures, contended that Western civilization as a whole was the expression of "Faustian man."

If Goethe's Faust seems rather remote to us in early twenty-first-century America, we need only to turn to popular books and films to see the archetype of the magus expressed in other forms: Gandalf, the white wizard of Tolkien's *Lord of the Rings*; the (mostly) benevolent masters of Hogwarts in the Harry Potter books; and, in a more futuristic mode, Obi-Wan Kenobi in *Star Wars* and Morpheus in *The Matrix.* Nostradamus himself, the subject of tabloid prophecies and TV programs on the History Channel, takes his place among them. The archetype of the sage lives in our minds and hearts, and he will not allow himself to be forgotten.

But as I have suggested above, an archetype comes especially alive in the collective imagination when it is *absent* from collective expression. On a personal level, you are more likely to dream about food if you are hungry, and you are more likely to have erotic dreams if your sexual needs are not being met. Psychologically, you're more likely to dream about an archetype if you are not living out this aspect of your own nature fully in waking life.

From the collective point of view, there is a tremendous hunger in the West for the figure of the Wise Old Man or Woman precisely because of the widespread (and often correct) suspicion that our old men and women—that is to say, the leaders to whom we instinctively look for guidance and perspective—are not always wise or benevolent. To use the language of one currently popular myth, we are so many Harry Potters, trapped in a world run by Muggles and longing for the wisdom and power of Hogwarts.

Many in America today are concerned about the role and status of old people (now often called "seniors"), and we can assume that this concern will only increase as the baby-boom generation crawls toward old age. Some say we do not value our seniors properly, that ours is a youth culture that discards people when they are superannuated instead of giving them the honor they would receive in a more traditional society.

This is partly true, but only, I believe, partly. I have had the privilege of knowing a few seniors who do live out the archetype of the Wise Old Man and Woman. Far from being discarded as useless or superannuated, they receive a tremendous amount of respect from younger people, who honor them and look up to them as mentors. As Valentin Tomberg, author of the classic *Meditations on the Tarot*, has written, "Name for me a country or a time for which the youth—who are truly 'young,' i.e. living for the Ideal—has not had its imagination haunted by the figure of a wise and good father, a spiritual father, a hermit, who has passed through the narrow gate and walks the hard way—someone whom one could trust without reserve and venerate without limit."[3]

Such figures are rare in every era, but they seem even rarer in our own, when the values of society as a whole seem to run so counter to those of such spiritual fathers and mothers. I am not, of course, suggesting that our senior citizens don flowing gowns and conical hats and pore over ephemerides and magic mirrors to tell us what is to come. I *am* saying that there is a terrible hunger for genuine wisdom from those who have endured many of life's buffets and can give us some perspective on our future as well as on our past. The archetype of the Wise Old Man will never die, because he resides in the structure of our psyches; he is part of what makes us up. But he is submerged, honored and active only, it seems, in fantasy books and films. As he is remembered and resurrected—as he is again and again—he will come to the service of our civilization, and, I am confident, his reappearance will heal many of the ills that we now so despairingly take for granted. In this sense, if in no other, Nostradamus speaks to our future.

July 2005

A Prophet's Life

Michel de Nostradamus was born in St.-Rémy-de-Provence, France, on December 14, 1503, in a modern world that was itself just beginning to be born.

A visitor going back in time would no doubt be struck more by the differences than by the similarities between that era and our own. Much of the technology we take for granted would of course be missing: the way of life was predominantly agricultural, overlaid with thin strata of craftsmen, merchants, nobles, and clerics. Literacy, although becoming more widespread, was still a specialized skill. Trade and travel had picked up in earnest—signs that the modern world was being born—but were difficult and dangerous: sailors would not venture forth on the sea during the winter if they could possibly avoid it. Sanitation was poor, and epidemics were frequent if erratic visitors.

The intellectual climate of the early sixteenth century was equally alien. Then as today, the themes and ideas of Christianity were widespread, but in Nostradamus's day the faith was all-pervasive and more or less obligatory. Learning as a whole meant learning in literature, logic, and theology. Educated men (and they *were* practically all men) were throwing themselves with enthusiasm on the texts from Greek and Roman antiquity that were only then being rediscovered. They were fascinated by the classical ruins that had long been part of the landscape in Nostradamus's corner of the world (Provence, in southern France, had long been a part of the Roman Empire) but which, it seems, had been observed without curiosity in the thousand years between the end of classical times and the Renaissance.

In this atmosphere, freedom of thought was not a right even of the educated. Knowledge of all kinds had to be vetted by the Catholic Church, the supreme—indeed sole—spiritual and intellectual power in Western Europe. Anything believed to conflict with Catholic doctrine was suppressed, often viciously. Science as we know it was embryonic. Knowledge of the natural world was passed on by study of ancient texts instead of direct experimentation or observation.

The political structure was strictly hierarchical. The king and the Church stood at the top of the pyramid, serving as guarantors of the spiritual and temporal orders. Below them were the noblemen; below these, the merchants, tradesmen, and peasants. Social boundaries were not utterly impermeable: then as now, talent and enterprise could bring success, but the obstacles were much greater, and the vast majority of people could expect to die in the class in which they had been born. The ideas of democracy and representative government were known from classical texts, but few thought they could or should be applied to that era.

Such was the legacy of the Middle Ages. This order was beginning to break down when Nostradamus was born, and by the time he died, in 1566, it would have broken down still further. One of the greatest shocks had come in the mid-fourteenth century, when the Black Death coursed through Europe, wiping out perhaps a quarter of the population. (Although this was by far the greatest epidemic, the plague made appearances periodically in many places until much later, when improved sanitation brought it under control.) Further shocks would come in Nostradamus's time. In the early sixteenth century, what is known as the Little Ice Age brought

decades of bad weather, poor harvests, and the resulting social turmoil. In 1517, Martin Luther launched the Protestant Reformation
in Germany. Though far from the first challenge to the supremacy
of the Catholic Church, it was the first to succeed.

In this world, which, like our own, its denizens found dangerous and unstable, Michel de Nostradamus was born. He came into
the upper middle class of his day: his father was a scrivener and
attorney.

Nostradamus was not his name at birth. In one document,
Nostradamus's father signs his name *Ja. de Nostradomin,* "Jacobus
de Nostra Domina," or "James of Our Lady." Like many things in
that era of rapid and disorienting change, names were fluid. The
surname, long the preserve of the elite, was just beginning to be
regarded as a necessity for all social classes.

The surname of this family was a peculiar one. Nostradamus's
grandfather's surname had been Gassonet; his great-grandfather's,
Venguessonne. The "Ven-" prefix may be a mutation of the Hebrew *ben-,* or "son of," indicating that Nostradamus's ancestors
were Jews. His grandfather, Guy Gassonet, had taken the name
"Pierre de Nostredame," "Peter of Our Lady," when converting to
Christianity around 1455. Their famous descendant would Latinize
it further—a common affectation among the learned of his time—
to the familiar "Nostradamus."

Conversion in those days was often a matter of necessity. The
Jews could count on uneasy toleration at best and were often sub-
jected to civil penalties, pogroms, or expulsion. In 1488, King
Charles VIII ordered the Jews of Provence to convert to Christianity. His son, Louis XII, stiffened this order by issuing an edict
in 1501 commanding the Jews to convert or leave Provence immediately. Some Jews continued to practice their original faith in
private—an act that could prove dangerous if discovered.

There is much speculation about Nostradamus's Jewish roots
and how much they influenced his work. The question is a reasonable one. Jews were at the time believed to hold occult knowledge,
particularly as embodied in the esoteric tradition known as the

Kabbalah. In Nostradamus's case, however, there is no real evidence that his Jewish background left much of a mark on his prophecy. His works show the imprint of astrology, classical learning, and Christian apocalyptic works that had been circulating for centuries, but little if any direct influence from Judaism or the Kabbalah as such. He strove to stay on the good side of the Church—a politic move in an age when accusations of sorcery and heresy were rife—and his references to Jews are lukewarm and occasionally negative. In his prophecies, he sometimes calls them *les saturnins*—"the Saturnians"—from the then prevalent idea that the Jewish nation was ruled by the planet Saturn (see VI.17).

We know a considerable amount about Nostradamus compared to most men of his time, but that is still remarkably small compared to more modern figures. For his biographers, his childhood has provided a field for the exercise of imagination rather than scholarship, since there are no real records of what it was like. He had several brothers, who would grow up to be landowners, merchants, and professionals, and at least one sister, who never married. There are few details about his early education. One clue is provided by the brass astrolabe that was handed down to him from his great-grandfather, Jean de St.-Rémy, and which he would hand on in turn to his son, César. The astrolabe is a device for calculating the positions of the stars in the skies; its status as an heirloom indicates that there was some tradition of astrology in the family (in those days astrology and astronomy were still indistinguishable) and that he may have learned some of his astrological skills from his forebears. In the *Epistle to Henri II* (§7), he mentions "a natural instinct" for prognostication "that was given to me by my forefathers," so it is possible, and even likely, that he inherited a family interest in occultism.

Nostradamus went to the University of Avignon in 1519, at the age of fifteen. His disciple Jean-Aymé de Chavigny would later say that even then Nostradamus's affinity for the stars would earn him the nickname of "little astronomer." (Like many of

Chavigny's assertions, this one must be taken with some caution, as he frequently inflated Nostradamus's achievements.) In any event, Nostradamus's stay at Avignon did not last long. An outbreak of the plague forced the university to close in late 1520, and he returned home.

For the next few years the evidence is scant. Nostradamus tells us that he "spent most of my young years from the year 1521 to the year 1529 . . . on pharmaceutics and the knowledge and study of natural remedies across various lands and countries, constantly on the move to hear and find out the source and origin of plants and other natural remedies involved in the purposes of the healing art."[4]

There is no reason to doubt him on this point. In those days it was common for those wishing to learn medicine to embark upon years of wandering, partly in study, partly in practice. In all likelihood it was the best way to gain some knowledge of healing, given the state of medicine in those days. Doctors learned their profession chiefly by reading the works of the second-century Greek physician Galen; they were only beginning to examine the human body empirically. The best medical practice of the time was of dubious efficacy and in many if not most cases did more harm than good. Folk remedies at least gave the journeyman an indication of what worked in the field.

In 1529, Nostradamus returned to more formal education and enrolled at the University of Montpellier; his handwritten enrollment is still in existence. Unfortunately his fieldwork stood him in bad stead: the registry book also shows his expulsion on the grounds that he had practiced as an "apothecary or quack." Whether he was readmitted is a subject of debate. Most of his biographers maintain that he was, and was eventually awarded a degree and a position on the faculty. But Peter Lemesurier, perhaps the most cautious and scholarly of Nostradamian experts, asserts that "there is absolutely no record of his readmission." Later, Nostradamus himself would admit that "I found myself unable perfectly to attain the summit of the supreme doctrine" of academic medicine, so he probably returned to his peripatetic study in the field.[5]

In 1531, Nostradamus moved to the town of Agen in southwestern France, where he was befriended by the great classicist Julius Caesar Scaliger. (Like Nostradamus himself, Scaliger Latinized his name in the erudite fashion of the era; his original name was Giulio Cesare della Scala.) Nostradamus also married a woman named Henriette d'Encausse and had a son and a daughter with her.

For a brief time the young Nostradamus was comfortably settled at Agen, but it was not long before his world here began to fall apart. Scaliger broke with him for unknown reasons (Scaliger's well-known belligerence very likely prime among them), and Nostradamus lost his wife and both children by 1534. Although we do not know the causes, we can surmise that they died from the plague. This dealt Nostradamus a catastrophic blow in the loss not only of his wife and children but of his own prestige as a physician, since he proved unable to save his own family. His in-laws sued him for the recovery of her dowry.

Another misfortune that befell Nostradamus around this time was due to a disparaging remark he made about a brass founder's image of the Virgin Mary. The details of the story are vague, but Nostradamus appears to have called the statue the "devil's work," referring to the craftsmanship, not to the nature of the image; bad art was no doubt as common in his day as it is in ours. Even so, the remark caused him to fall afoul of the Inquisition at Toulouse, which ordered him to appear before it.

This story opens an interesting window onto the mental climate of the time. The Catholic Church had long endeavored to keep close watch over the minds and thoughts of its communicants. Historian Paul Johnson has described the Catholic medieval social order as an attempt at a "total society." Johnson writes, "Men had agreed, or at least appeared to agree, on an all-enveloping society which not only aligned virtue with law and practice, but allotted to everyone in it precise, Christian-orientated tasks. . . . There was total agreement and total commitment. The points on which men argued were slender, compared to the huge areas of complete acquiescence which embraced almost every aspect of their lives."[6]

This attempt at a "total society" was never entirely successful. Human beings are by nature too insouciant and rebellious to be kept down permanently, and in the 1530s the ideas of the Reformation were permeating France itself. But the incident shows how totalitarian the religious climate of the age often was both in spirit and in practice.

This combination of misfortunes at Agen inspired Nostradamus to go on the road again. The next ten years for him were ones of wandering, of visiting cities in France and possibly also Germany and Italy in search of medical knowledge. At this point he may have already begun to gain a reputation as a prognosticator. One charming though quite possibly apocryphal anecdote set in this period hints at the future source of his fame. At one point Nostradamus was staying with a noble family while treating the lord's grandmother. The head of the household, one M. de Florinville, while taking a stroll in Nostradamus's company, spied two suckling pigs, one black and one white. He asked Nostradamus what would happen to these pigs. Nostradamus replied, "We will eat the black one and the wolf will eat the white one."

In order to give the lie to Nostradamus, de Florinville ordered the white pig to be slaughtered and served for dinner. While the pig was being prepared, a tame wolf cub kept as a pet gnawed on the carcass. Not wanting to present a disfigured entrée, the chef had the black pig slaughtered and served.

At the dinner de Florinville, unaware of this development, said to Nostradamus, "Well, sir, we are now eating the white pig, and the wolf will not touch it here."

Nostradamus replied, "I do not believe it. It is the black one that is on the table."

De Florinville summoned the chef, who confessed what had happened. As the seventeenth-century source that has preserved this story puts it, the incident "provided the company with another more agreeable dish."[7]

The next known appearance of Nostradamus was in Aix-en-Provence in 1546, whose city fathers engaged him for the sum of ten gold crowns to combat an outbreak of the plague. Nostradamus recounts, "It started on the last day of May and lasted nine whole months, and from it died an extraordinary number of . . . people of all ages, such that the churchyards were so full of dead bodies that nobody knew of any further consecrated ground in which to bury them."

Like other such epidemics, the plague wreaked its toll on the social fabric as well as on life and health. As Nostradamus goes on to say, "Fathers took no care of their sons, and many abandoned their wives and children as soon as they realized that they had been infected by the plague. . . . Among the most amazing things I saw, I think, was a woman who, even while I was paying a visit on her . . . [was] sewing herself unaided into her own shroud, starting with the feet." Attendants charged with the duty of removing plague victims found her dead, "with her sewing half-finished."

Incidentally, it is not clear, in this instance or in many others, exactly what the disease was. It may have been the Black Death—that is, the bubonic plague—but it may have been another illness. One of the most curious aspects of medical history is that diseases change their symptoms and manifestations as the bacilli and the human organism constantly adapt to each other, so it is frequently difficult to say exactly what a particular pestilence hundreds of years ago actually entailed.

For this epidemic, whatever it was, Nostradamus admitted that he had no real remedy. His only recourse lay in the realm of confections (a lifetime interest of his). He prepared a type of lozenge made out of rose petals and spices. The lozenges served not only as breath fresheners ("if the breath has been stinking, whether as a result of the teeth being rotten or because of bad smells emerging from the stomach, . . . keep a little of it in the mouth without chewing, and it will give out such a good odor that nobody will be able to tell where it is coming from") but also as a protection against the plague ("for there is no fragrance better for keeping away the bad and pestiferous air)."[8] In Nostradamus's day, contagion was imperfectly understood. People realized that diseases spread from one person to another, but they did not know how and usually thought infections came through bad air or noxious fumes. Preventatives against plagues thus often involved pomades of agreeable fragrances.

Although Nostradamus himself admitted that none of his remedies really worked, he performed his duties as a plague doctor well enough to be engaged afterward for the same services by the city of Lyon. When this epidemic was over, he moved to the town of Salon in Provence, which would be his base of operations for the rest of his life. In November 1547, he married a rich widow named Anne Ponsarde Gemelle—probably not for love, since he embarked soon afterward for a two-year trip to Italy and possibly other destinations in search of more recipes for cosmetics, confections, and medications.

By 1550, Nostradamus was back in Salon. At some point early in his marriage, he had taken a step that many newlyweds take when they can: he had his house enlarged. A top floor was added to his house in Salon to serve as a study and observatory. It was common for astrologers of the day to have some venue where they could look at the stars, but even apart from his astrological interests Nostradamus always had a deep attraction for gazing at the heavens; indeed he called himself an *astrophile*, a "lover of the stars." Some Nostradamians speculate that the remodeling was part of his motive for going to Italy: the work could be done while he was away.

The image of the Renaissance scholar's study, familiar from Rembrandt's paintings and etchings, remains a powerful one. It is often imagined as dark, secluded, and cluttered with ancient and dusty volumes as well as magical sigils and possibly flasks and burners for alchemical research. In spirit, at least, it is a place set at some remove from the world, where the scholar could contemplate the supernal realms in peace and serenity. Nostradamus's top-floor chamber must have had at least some of this atmosphere.

What were Nostradamus's own spiritual practices? From his later work, it is obvious that he had a long-standing interest in the occult sciences of his day, including magic, alchemy, astrology, and similar arts. Given Nostradamus's well-documented interests in astrology and divination, it is hard to imagine that these esoteric pursuits did not form at least part of the impulse for his years of wandering, particularly since occultism had not yet been entirely divorced from medicine or chemistry, the chief arts he practiced in those days.

The central ideas of this philosophy can be found in the first chapter of *De occulta philosophia* ("On Occult Philosophy"), a seminal work by Henry Cornelius Agrippa, another Renaissance magus, that was published in 1531:

> Seeing that there is a threefold world, elementary, celestial, and intellectual, and every inferior is governed by its superior, and receiveth the influence of the virtues thereof, so that the very original, and chief Worker of all doth by angels, the heavens, stars, elements, animals, plants, metals, and stones convey from himself the virtues of his omnipotency upon us: wise men conceive it no way irrational that it should be possible for us to ascend by the same degree through each world, to the same very original world itself, the Maker of all things, and First Cause, from whence all things are, and proceed: and also to enjoy not only these virtues, which are already in the more excellent kinds of things, but also besides these, to draw new virtues from above.[9]

This dense passage contains many ideas, but the essential one to consider here is the doctrine of correspondences, which at its core states, "As above, so below." There are three worlds, or dimensions of existence: the world of matter; the world of the stars and planets; and the unseen, spiritual (here called "intellectual") world. (Often a fourth world, the realm of the divine, is added.) The higher levels transmit the power of God down to the lower ones, in the process transmuting it into denser and more palpable forms of energy.

Here lies the idea behind astrology. If the stars and planets transmit divine power to the earth, it stands to reason that earthly events would correspond to the positions of the planets at any given time. Since we know quite clearly the positions of the planets in the future, we should be able to infer what earthly events will happen as well.

This is the theory by which Nostradamus worked. Much of what he did is today called "mundane astrology," which concerns itself with global and political affairs. In those days, most nations were ruled by monarchs, so the birth charts of the king, queen, and their offspring would also be examined.

Some of the results in Nostradamus's prophecies came from his astrological calculations, some from his own insight. In his *Preface to César,* §22, he describes the means of making predictions:

> One comes by infusion, clarifying the supernatural light for the person who predicts by means of the stars and prophesies by inspired revelation. The other comes from a certain participation in the divine eternity. By this means the prophet comes to judge what his divine spirit has given to him through God the Creator and by his natural instigation.

Nostradamus is saying that there are two ways of ascertaining the future. One is by observing what Agrippa calls the "celestial" world: the stars and planets. The other is by participating in the spiritual or what Agrippa calls the "intellectual" world by means of a higher cognition, usually attained through meditation or contemplation. Nostradamus speaks of these practices in the first two quatrains of his *Prophecies.* These verses allude to the teachings of the fourth-century Greek philosopher Iamblichus, so they do not necessarily describe the practices that Nostradamus himself used, but they at least give the spirit of what he was attempting.

But in 1550 the *Prophecies* themselves still lay in the future.

Nostradamus began his prophetic career by producing a type of work that was extremely popular in his own day and long thereafter—an almanac. As I have said, the early sixteenth century was an era of dramatic and alarming climatic change, with decades of below-normal temperatures. In those uncertain times farmers wanted some idea of what the growing season might offer, so they consulted any of a large number of almanacs that would supposedly tell them.

Long-range weather forecasting remains a highly imperfect art, and in the sixteenth century it was totally a matter of guesswork and folklore. To the extent that there was any method to it, the method was astrological. If the stars foreshadowed events on earth, they should enable an experienced practitioner to predict the weather as well. This aspect of astrology has fallen into disuse in modern times, but for many centuries it formed a major part of the discipline. A look at one of the seminal astrological texts, the *Tetrabiblos* of Claudius Ptolemy, written in the second century A.D., reveals that many characteristics of the zodiacal signs have to do with their place in the seasons and with their real or imagined influence on the climate.

Thus Nostradamus the astrologer produced his first almanac in the year 1550. Almanacs are highly ephemeral works—people throw them away when the year has passed—so no copies of this first almanac have come down to us. Some samples, however, have been preserved:

> The bodies aloft threaten great bloodshed at the two extremities of Europe, in the east and in the west, and the center shall be in most uncertain fear.
>
> In the autumn, heavy rains, which shall be the cause of many setbacks, shall even confound some very great enterprises.
>
> At the same time there shall be a great change of condition, almost from top to bottom, and the opposite from bottom to top.[10]

As these specimens show, the predictions tended to focus on both weather and political events. They were quite general and often hardly required much prophetic insight. In the west, for example, wars between France and the Hapsburg Empire had been going on for years and showed every sign of continuing, as indeed they would; in southeastern Europe, the Christian powers were attempting (with uneven success) to hold off the onslaughts of the Ottoman Turks. Nonetheless, the almanac did well enough that Nostradamus continued to write subsequent editions in the years to come.

For Nostradamus, the early 1550s were times of increasing influence and creativity in other ways as well. He became involved, financially as well as personally, in a long-term project managed by the architect Adam de Craponne to construct an aqueduct to improve the water supply in Salon. Before he died, Nostradamus would have invested some 688 crowns—a substantial sum for the time—in the project, which actually did come to fruition, beginning to provide water to the town in 1557.

In 1552 Nostradamus wrote his *Traité des fardemens et des confitures* ("Treatise on Cosmetics and Preserves," published in 1555), which includes his recipe for rose lozenges. Nostradamus's interest in these products was no doubt partly commercial, but it also fit in with his esoteric pursuits. In the passage quoted above, Agrippa points out that celestial influences have correspondences in certain plants. According to the occult philosophy, a given plant was thought to be governed by a planet—and hence to convey some of its influence—if it shared some characteristics of the planet as it was traditionally conceived. Elsewhere in his opus, Agrippa associates roses with the beneficent planet Venus, probably because of their pleasant fragrance and their associations with love. By this theory, rose lozenges would imbue the user with some of the favorable traits of Venus and not only mask unwholesome fragrances but also ward off the "bad airs" of plague. Whether Nostradamus had Agrippa's associations in mind when he devised his lozenge recipe, this gives at least some idea of the reasoning he was likely to use.

In 1552 Nostradamus and his wife celebrated the birth of Madeleine, their first child. Over the next nine years they would have five other children, notably their eldest son César (probably named after Scaliger, against whom Nostradamus apparently held no grudge), who was born in 1554 and to whom the initial preface to his *Prophecies* is addressed, although César was less than a year old when they were published in 1555. Nostradamus had his second family at an age that would be considered late in life in our time and was still more so in his: men of fifty and sixty were considered advanced in age. His youngest daughter, Diane, was only five when he died at the age of sixty-two.

Around 1554, Nostradamus befriended Jean-Aymé de Chavigny, who would remain his friend and amanuensis for the rest of his life. (Some sources say Chavigny did not apprentice himself to the magus until 1560 or 1561.) Chavigny was obviously a man of considerable ability; he held doctorates in both theology and law and had been mayor of his native city of Beaune. At some point, however, he decided to throw over these worldly pursuits in favor of esoteric knowledge and attached himself to Nostradamus as a pupil and assistant. He would remain with Nostradamus for the rest of the latter's life (although sources differ on whether their connection was continuous or interrupted during this time), and later he would serve as Nostradamus's editor and the most fervent champion of his memory.

Chavigny gives us the most vivid portrait we have of Nostradamus the man:

He was a little under medium height, of robust body, nimble and vigorous. He had a large and open forehead, a straight and even nose, gray eyes which were generally pleasant but which blazed when he was angry and a visage both severe and smiling, such that along with his severity a great humanity could be seen; his cheeks were ruddy, even in his old age, his beard was long and thick, his health good and hearty (except in his old age) and all his senses acute and complete.

His mind was good and lively, understanding easily what he wanted to; his judgment was subtle, his memory quite remarkable. By nature he was taciturn, thinking much and saying little, though speaking very well in the proper time and place: for the rest, vigilant, prompt and impetuous, prone to anger, patient in labor. He slept only four to five hours. He praised and loved freedom of speech and showed himself joyous and facetious, as well as biting, in his joking. He approved of the ceremonies of the Roman Church and held to the Catholic faith and religion, outside of which, he was convinced, there was no salvation; he reproved grievously those who, withdrawn from its bosom, abandoned themselves to eating and drinking of the sweetness and liberties of the foreign and damned doctrines, affirming that they would come to a bad and pernicious end. I do not want to forget to say that he engaged willingly in fasts, prayers, alms and patience; he abhorred vice and chastised it severely; I can remember his giving to the poor, towards whom he was very liberal and charitable, often making use of these words, drawn from the Holy Scriptures: "Make friends of the riches of iniquity" [Luke 16:9].[11]

Chavigny's portrait requires some modification. Nostradamus's professions of allegiance to the Catholic faith were, like much in his life and work, not entirely what they seemed. Jean Dupèbe, editor of a recent compilation of Nostradamus's letters, makes these observations about the magus's correspondence with Lorenz Tubbe, a young law student:

In his letters to Lorenz Tubbe, who was a Lutheran, he [Nostradamus] speaks with total confidence and conceals neither his sympathies nor his hatreds. Without being Reformed, he inclines toward Reform. He displays more understanding for the cause of the Protestants, whom he oftens calls "Christians," than for that of the Catholics, the "Papists," whose fanatical violence he detests. . . . Nostradamus's duplicity is obvious, and his protestations of orthodoxy are gestures of prudence and opportunism. To Lorenz Tubbe, he has revealed the basis of his piety: a more or less Lutheran evangelicalism with a farrago of Neoplatonism bizarrely mixed in.[12]

And yet even this perspective is not entirely complete. Like the Apostle Paul, Nostradamus tried to be "all things to all men" (1 Cor. 9:22); no doubt he emphasized his sympathies with Protestantism in his letters to a Protestant. In the end, Nostradamus probably was loyal to the Catholic Church, while deploring its corruptions and excesses and recognizing the need for reform. The "farrago of Neoplatonism" we find in him is not a bizarre admixture, but the occult philosophy of the Renaissance that formed the core of his thought, as it did for the other great magi of his age, from Cornelius Agrippa to John Dee.

The period 1554–55 opens the last phase of Nostradamus's life, in which he would establish himself as a prophet and magus whose fame would extend far beyond the borders of France.

The prime impetus for this change seems to have come from the mood of France itself. The restiveness of the times, the religious fragmentation, and the bad weather all seemed to portend the end of the world. To this alarming situation another sign was added: the births of monsters and deformities. In 1554, Nostradamus's son César would recount much later, "hardly had January come to an end than a monstrous child was found alive and kicking at Sénas with two heads, which the eye could scarcely behold without some kind of horror." The next month a kid (that is, a baby goat) was born with two heads.

César goes on to describe the conventional view of such creatures in his day: they foreshadowed "disasters and divisions . . . the bloody Wars of Religions that followed shortly afterwards, given that they always happen contrary to the order and ways of nature—not, certainly, as causes, but as true signs and extraordinary and certain presages of dark and baleful events."[13]

Here too we see an echo of the doctrine of correspondences. The sixteenth century was unaware of the genetic nature of mutation; the only possible thing it could mean was that something was deeply wrong in the world of nature, which had to have a parallel in human events as well. In that era, such portents were the subject of numerous broadsides and pamphlets—the equivalents of our tabloids—and, along with the general unrest, led many to believe the Last Judgment was nigh.

For Nostradamus, these omens warned of "signal mutations and changes which were to occur universally throughout Europe, and also the bloody civil wars, and the pernicious troubles fatally approaching the Gallic realm," as Chavigny would write years later.[14] It was in this period that he embarked upon the work that has guaranteed his fame from his age to our own: the *Prophecies*.

The *Prophecies* were not the only product of Nostradamus's pen. We have already encountered the *Traité des fardemens et des confitures* as well as the almanacs, some of which survive. In addition, we have some letters; a treatise on the *Horapollo* (a spurious work on Egyptian hieroglyphics dating from late antiquity); and a translation of a work by Galen. Finally, there are works of doubtful authenticity, the *Sixains,* or six-lined verses (the *Prophecies* are written in quatrains, or four-lined verses) and some dubious supplementary quatrains for the *Prophecies.* But these are of secondary importance. It is the *Prophecies* that are principally associated with his name. Whenever someone quotes Nostradamus, it is almost always one of these quatrains that is being cited.

The first installment of the *Prophecies* was published in 1555. This edition contained the first four "Centuries": the idea of publishing verses in Centuries, or groups of one hundred, was evidently the idea of Nostradamus's first publisher, Macé Bonhomme of Lyons. Nonetheless, the fourth Century was incomplete, so that the earliest edition of Nostradamus contains only 353 quatrains. The rest of the quatrains were published in 1557–58, along with a dedicatory epistle to King Henri II of France. No copies of these latter editions have come down to us; the first complete edition of the *Prophecies* dates from 1568, two years after Nostradamus's death, and was compiled by Chavigny, with the assistance of Nostradamus's widow. Because of its comparatively late date, some scholars have doubted its fidelity to the original, suspecting that Chavigny doctored some of the verses to make them fit subsequent events. But this cannot be proved one way or the other.

What prompted Nostradamus to write the *Prophecies*? Undoubtedly the success of the almanacs, in part, and the fame that had begun to accrue to him as a result. Certainly Nostradamus's prophetic works won him a wide readership and popularity in many classes of society. By 1560 the poet Pierre de Ronsard could write of Nostradamus, "Like an ancient oracle, he has for many years / Predicted the greater part of our destiny."[15] A cynical observer might see nothing beyond purely commercial motives for Nostradamus's work, and there is no doubt that he did profit from writing books that filled such a demonstrated public need. On the other hand, one can go too far in casting aspersions on his motives. Probably Nostradamus did believe that the times were approaching some sort of climax and that he could serve a real need by sounding a warning.

There are several reasons for drawing this conclusion. First, it is usually only a sociopath who can pull off a fraud that he regards as a fraud. Most people, even when they are committing acts of deceit—dishonest salesmen, say—probably persuade themselves that they are doing so for the victim's own good or justify their actions in some other way. A good number even manage to believe what they are saying, at least while they are saying it. Usually it is much easier to deceive one person than many, even if that one person is yourself.

Second, the *Prophecies* stand very much in the mainstream of apocalyptic, a literary form that has persisted from the earliest times of Christianity to the present. Many of the first Christians thought the Second Coming of Christ was imminent—a belief that pervades the New Testament, for example in 1 Thessalonians—and while this hope faded somewhat as time passed, it never vanished.

In the history of Christianity from then to now, there have been few if any generations that did not believe theirs would be the last.

Such expectations were heightened by major events or key dates—the fall of the Western Roman Empire in the fifth century, the coming of the year 1000, the "Babylonian Captivity" of the Papacy in the fourteenth century, when the popes moved to Avignon for almost seventy years. Although these hopes (or fears) were constantly disappointed, they continued to arise. We see the same thing in our own day, when the beginning of the third millennium and various wars and upheavals are seen as presages of the end.

I will have more to say about this question in the last section of this book, "Nostradamus and the Uses of Prophecy," but for now let me simply say that this apocalyptic tradition, which Nostradamus knew and mined heavily for his own prophecies, served as a kind of guarantor of authenticity for his own work. From his point of view, he was simply following in the line of many holy men and women who had made similar predictions and whose testimony certified that these things would come to pass. If this conclusion seems curious in the light of their actual success rate, we should bear in mind that tradition and authority carried much more weight in Nostradamus's time, especially since many of these prophecies were merely trying to elaborate on the hints found in Scripture itself.

For instance, Nostradamus foresaw the coming of a universal Christian monarch who would overcome the enemies of the faith and establish a reign of peace on earth (cf. I.4, IV.77). Although the theme of a universal Christian monarch does not appear in the Bible itself, it has pervaded Christian prophecy ever since the Christianization of the Roman Empire in the fourth century, when it was tied into predictions of a millennial age found in Revelation 20:2–3. Here is one example, from an apocalyptic work called the *Tiburtine Sibyl,* probably also dating from the fourth century:

Then will arise a king of the Greeks whose name is Constans. He will be king of the Romans and the Greeks. He will be tall of stature, of handsome appearance with shining face, and well put together in all parts of his body. His reign will be ended after one hundred and twelve years. In those days there will be great riches and the earth will give fruit abundantly so that a measure of wheat shall be sold for a denarius, a measure of wine for a denarius, and a measure of oil for a denarius. . . . He will devastate all the islands and the cities of the pagans and will destroy all idolatrous temples; he will call all pagans to baptism and in every temple the Cross of Christ will be erected. . . . Whoever does not adore the Cross of Jesus Christ will be punished by the sword. When the one hundred and twelve years have been completed, the Jews will be converted to the Lord, and "his sepulchre will be glorified by all." [Isaiah 11:10][16]

The text goes on to prophesy the coming of Antichrist next—another common theme in Christian apocalyptic and in Nostradamus as well.

Finally, Nostradamus was right in seeing turmoil ahead. In his time France was becoming increasingly split between the Catholics and the Protestant Huguenots. The first of several wars of religion would erupt in 1562; they would continue off and on for a generation. Only when King Henri IV issued the Edict of Nantes in 1598, guaranteeing freedom of worship, would the strife finally come to an end. The first half of the seventeenth century would see equally bloody warfare between Catholic and Protestant, this time centered on Germany, which was the battleground of the ruinous Thirty Years' War from 1619 to 1648. If, as we shall see, Nostradamus was often wrong about details, his constant invocation of approaching "blood, fire, iron" was, broadly speaking, on the mark.

Besides the first installment of the *Prophecies,* the year 1555 marked another signal event for Nostradamus—his invitation to the French court. The queen, Catherine de' Medici, was fascinated with astrologers, occultists, and magi and collected a retinue of them around her; his invitation was doubtless due to her. Nostradamus left Salon in mid-July 1555 and arrived in Paris only a month later—a journey so rapid for the time that some have speculated that the royal posting service was put at his disposal.

Unfortunately, when Nostradamus reached the end of his journey, he found that the court had gone to its summer residence. Given 130 crowns to cover his expenses, he was lodged at the residence of the Archbishop of Sens, where he was promptly stricken by an attack of the gout. After two weeks' indisposition, during which he managed to conduct private consultations, he went to meet the royal family at their residence in Blois.

The purpose of Nostradamus's visit was to read the horoscopes of the children of Catherine and her husband, Henri II. Apparently the magus foretold that their four sons would all be kings. If so, he would prove only partly right: the three eldest sons would rule France as François II, Charles IX, and Henri III (all briefly and ineffectively), but the youngest, Hercules, Duc d'Alençon, later renamed François, would die in 1584 at the age of thirty before he could attain the throne. In any event, Catherine was to all appearances satisfied with the prognostication, and she was to remain Nostradamus's patron and supporter for the rest of his life.

This journey to Paris gives other, less appealing glimpses of the magus's character. Laurent Videl, a rival astrologer, published a pamphlet excoriating Nostradamus in 1558. In it he tells of seeing a woman in Lyon (through which Nostradamus had passed on his way to Paris) vainly beleaguer Nostradamus to refund the money she had paid him for a worthless prescription. As Videl says, "She called after you, 'Give me back my ten crowns, for your prescription is no good.' And like a charlatan you said, 'It's all right.'"[17] (To be fair, I have never heard of a doctor of any sort refunding money for a remedy that did not work, except perhaps under the duress of a malpractice settlement.)

In another incident from this journey, Nostradamus borrowed money from Jean de Morel, a member of the queen's household, in order to pay his hotel bill. Morel wrote to Nostradamus, asking to be repaid but got no response for a long time. Nostradamus finally replied to him in a letter dated November 29, 1561, six years later. Apologizing for the inconvenience, he tells Morel that he had mentioned the loan several times to the queen and adds that he had never received any of Morel's previous letters asking for repayment. Nostradamus also points out that the trip did not pay for itself: "His Majesty the King paid me a hundred crowns. The Queen paid me thirty. And that's a fine sum for having come two hundred leagues!—having spent a hundred crowns, I made thirty."

Nostradamus's reply to Morel contains another interesting detail. He had to leave Paris in haste, he says, because he had been warned "that the Lords Justices of Paris were proposing to come and see me in order to ask me by means of what science I was predicting what I was predicting." Rather than defending himself against possible charges of sorcery, Nostradamus found it expedient to go home at once.[18]

Nostradamus's increasing reputation—the result of his *Prophecies* and his popular almanacs—naturally led to diverse opinions about his work. An anonymous Latin epigram began to circulate:

Nostra damus cum falsa damus, nam fallere nostrum est:
Et cum falsa damus, nil nisi nostra damus.

The verse hinges on an untranslatable Latin pun—*Nostra damus* literally means "we give our own"—but here is a literal rendition:

We give our own when we give the false, for it is ours to
   be false,
And when we give the false, we give nothing but our own.

Evidently Nostradamus has always had his share of detractors.
The years 1556 through 1558 were spent completing the 942 quatrains of the *Prophecies,* which, as we have seen, were published in 1558, although the earliest extant complete edition dates from 1568.

The now lost original last installment appears to have contained the last three Centuries (the fourth through seventh had been published in 1557) as well as the dedicatory *Epistle to Henri II*.

The *Epistle* is a strange but revealing document. It begins with a long and adulatory address to the king, which to our ears sounds obsequious but was simply a matter of convention at the time. ("The Epistle Dedicatory" to James I, published at the front of many editions of the King James Bible, has a similar flavor.) Nostradamus then goes on to lay out a chronology of biblical history dating from the Creation. As he himself bafflingly admits, this does not accord with *another* chronology that he presents at the end of the letter.

Nostradamus also discusses his own method of working. As in the *Preface to César,* he says it comes from two sources, from "God and nature," and that he has not "mixed in anything that proceeds from fate" (§12). This is a curious statement in a letter full of curious statements, especially since he also says he is using astrological calculations, and the ancient esoteric science taught that the planets govern fate. He may be trying to avoid the accusation that he believes in an immutable fate that could interfere with free will as conceived by Catholic doctrine. But as with many of his utterances, what he is trying to say is far from clear. Elsewhere in the letter (§11), Nostradamus insists he has "put nothing ambiguous or of double meaning" into his verses, a statement that is difficult to accept.

The main part of the *Epistle* lays down a series of obscure predictions that are meant to proceed from his day to the beginning of the apocalyptic millennium, when "Satan will be cast and bound into the abyss of hell in the deep pit." Here he will remain for a thousand years until he is released as a prelude to the Last Judgment (cf. Rev. 20:2–7).

The predictions in the *Epistle to Henri II* are largely incomprehensible, incorrect, or possibly both. To take one example, Nostradamus writes, "God will look upon the long sterility of the great lady, who then afterwards will conceive two principal children." Of these, the daughter will die by the age of thirty-six and "will leave three brothers, and one female; two of these will never have had the same father" (§13). The identities of this woman and her offspring are unclear (indeed the wording of the *Epistle* leaves it uncertain whether it is the first woman or her daughter who will have these three sons). Although the three brothers are often connected with several verses in the *Prophecies,* here, too, their identities are unknown: we may dismiss the modern identification of them with John, Robert, and Edward Kennedy (cf. VIII.17; IX.36), if only because Nostradamus says "two of these will never have had the same father" (that is, all of them would have had different fathers). To my knowledge, no one has seriously questioned that Joseph P. Kennedy was the father of all the Kennedy brothers. Sometimes the "great lady" is taken to be Mary, Queen of Scots, who was then married to the future King François II of France. Sometimes she is equated with Catherine de' Medici herself, who remained barren for the first nine years of her marriage. But neither figure fits the predictions: Catherine had seven children, all of them born by the time this text was written; Mary, one. If Nostradamus foresaw these futures for these women, he was wrong.

Later, Nostradamus predicts that "the year 1792 will be regarded as a renewal of the age." This is generally seen as a correct prophecy, because the French Revolutionary calendar (used between 1793 and 1806) began its dating from the establishment of the First Republic on September 22, 1792. Indeed this prophecy was cited in at least one contemporary journal when the short-lived new calendar was promulgated.

But Nostradamus goes on to say about this era: "Afterward the Roman people will begin to rise again, and to chase away some obscure darknesses, recovering some small part of their ancient fame, not without great division and continual changes. Venice afterward will raise her wings with great force and power, almost to the level of the powers of ancient Rome" (§42–43). Actually the opposite happened. In 1796, Napoleon put an end to the moribund Venetian Republic, then over 1,100 years old. The French did proclaim a Roman Republic in 1798, but it was little more than a French puppet. It lasted until 1799.

In *The Epistle to Henri II,* as in the *Prophecies* as a whole, Nostradamus has cobbled together predictions from a number of sources and supplemented them with his own astrological calculations and prophetic insights. Such sources included the *Mirabilis liber* ("The Wonderful Book"), a compendium of prophecies published in Lyon in 1523 and (according to some sources) edited by Nostradamus's father; the predictions of the twelfth-century Italian prophet Joachim of Fiore; and Richard Roussat's *Livre de l'estat et mutations des temps* ("Book of the State and Mutations of the Times"), published in 1549–50.

That Nostradamus's forecasts are cryptic and often confusing should not surprise us: his sources were much the same. He did not for the most part plagiarize these sources or copy them outright, but he took their themes and concerns and combined them in a fashion that made sense to him in light of his own expectations. Modern apocalyptic prophecies—in which, say, the establishment of the state of Israel and an expected rebuilding of the Temple in Jerusalem are viewed as preludes to the Second Coming—use biblical texts in the same way. It is not strange that people cast their visions for the future in light of the past and the present; what *is* strange is that they have done this so consistently when events have almost never borne them out. For the last two thousand years, apocalyptic has been a constant exercise in crying wolf.

Yet Nostradamus would never have gained his renown without making some ostensibly accurate predictions. The year 1559 saw an event that was to certify his reputation. It would happen in connection with festivities for the double wedding of Marguerite, sister of King Henri II, to the Duke of Savoy and of Elizabeth, Henri's elder daughter, to King Philip II of Spain. The celebrations included a mock tournament including a joust, in which Henri himself took part. His opponent was the Comte de Montgomery. The first bout ended in a draw, and the king asked for a rematch. In the second round, Montgomery's lance hit the king's shield, splintering.

One of the splinters went up through the golden visor of Henri's helmet, pierced his eye, and entered his brain.

Henri was a man of great stamina. Andreas Vesalius, the celebrated anatomist and physician who attended him, wrote, "Upon receiving the wound, the king appeared about to fall first from one side and then from the other, but eventually, by his own effort, he managed to keep his saddle. After he had dismounted and was surrounded by spectators running forward from the crowd he showed loss of consciousness, although he later ascended the steps to his chamber with hardly a totter."[19] But given the state of surgery at the time, the wound was sure to prove fatal. Henri took eleven days to die.

The Constable of France, Anne de Montmorency, was heard to remark, "Cursed be the divine who predicted it so evilly and so well."[20] Montmorency was probably thinking of another prognosticator, Lucas Gauricus, who had warned Henri to avoid single combat until the end of his forty-first year (the king was forty when he died). But news rapidly spread that Nostradamus had predicted the weird accident. César—whose testimony is not always trustworthy—even claimed that mobs in the Paris suburbs burned Nostradamus in effigy on the night of Henri's death.

Usually the verse that is applied to this event is I.35, which speaks of the "young lion," Montgomery, overcoming the "the old," Henri. But Nostradamus himself claimed to have made the prediction in III.55, which speaks of "the year when one eye in France shall reign"—"one eye" referring to the king's loss of an eye in the joust. Regardless, the idea that Nostradamus had foreseen the king's peculiar death confirmed his status as the premier prophet in France.

Rumors at the court spread about Nostradamus's other prophecies. Courtiers whispered that one verse, X.39, had predicted the death of the sixteen-year-old King François II, successor to his father, Henri II, in 1560. Another concern was raised about Nostradamus's alleged prophecy to Catherine de' Medici that three of her sons would all be kings (a variant on his earlier pronouncement, in which he predicted this destiny for all four). While this may sound favorable at first glance, it would also mean that the elder two, at least, would have to die young so that the third could inherit the throne. This time he was right. François II reigned a little more than a year; Charles IX, his brother, reigned for fourteen years and died before turning twenty-four. The third brother, Henri III, would reign for fifteen years before being assassinated in 1589.

The court was both fascinated and frightened by the apparent accuracy of these forecasts. The Spanish ambassador, Thomas Perrenot de Chantonnay, wrote in 1561 that "it would be better to chastise [Nostradamus] than to allow him to sell thus his prophecies, which lead to vain and superstitious beliefs."[21] Learned opinion was equally suspicious. The works of Nostradamus—not only his *Prophecies* but the almanacs he continued to issue each year—inspired large numbers of pamphlets, most of them critical or abusive. In 1557 an anonymous author issued "*La première invective du Seigneur Hercules le françois, contre Monstradamus*" [sic]: "The First Invective of Lord Hercules the Frenchman Against Monstradamus," which described the prophet as a "refined, twenty-four-carat liar."[22] Other pamphlets impugned not only his honesty but his astrological knowledge and made insulting allusions to his Jewish ancestry.

The criticisms of his astrological skill had some merit. Rather than casting horoscopes for the time and place of his client's birth—which is the correct practice—Nostradamus customarily used the planetary positions for noon at whatever place the astronomical tables had been written (usually Germany). In other cases, he asked clients to supply their own horoscopes. The astrologer Laurent Videl charged, "Of true astrology you understand less than nothing, as is evident not merely to the learned, but to learners in astrology too, as your works amply demonstrate, you who cannot calculate the least movement of any heavenly body whatever."[23]

At one point Nostradamus ran up against the censorship of the era, which was growing more and more strict as a result of the intermittent religious warfare of the time. In 1561 he made the mistake of publishing his almanac for 1562 without getting the imprimatur of a bishop—a requisite for published material at the time. The governor of Provence had him thrown in jail and forbade him to write any more almanacs and prognostications. After a couple of months, however, Nostradamus was released and continued his work as before.

In spite of opposition and adversities, the magus kept his share of satisfied customers: people who read the almanacs avidly (as Henri II had done on a daily basis before he died); those who dwelt upon his *Prophecies*; and those seeking personal consultations. His most important admirer remained the queen herself. Despite or because of his prediction of her husband's death, Catherine continued to hold Nostradamus in the highest regard. Chantonnay recorded an interview he had with the queen: "'Do you know,' said she, 'that Nostradamus had affirmed to me that in 1566 a general peace would reign over the world, that France would be peaceful and that the situation would become stronger?' And saying that, she had as confident an air as if she had quoted St. John or St. Luke." (This prophecy for 1566, incidentally, would prove inaccurate.)

In 1564, Catherine, who served as regent for her son Charles IX in the early years of his reign, took him on a two-year royal progress through the realm. The retinue passed through Salon in October of that year. César recounts that Nostradamus greeted the young king with an orotund epigraph: "*Vir magnus bello, nulli pietate secundus*" ("A man great in war, second to none in piety"). César continues:

> Then my father . . . accompanied him [the king], always at his side, with his velvet hat in one hand, and a very large and beautiful Malacca cane, with a silver handle, in the other, to support him on the road (because he was often tormented by that troublesome pain in the feet vulgarly

called gout) up to the gates of the chateau, and again in his own chamber, where he entertained this young King for a very long time, as well as the Queen-Regent, his mother, who had a very benevolent curiosity to see all his family, even to a little baby girl in arms. I remember this very well, for I was of the party.[24]

The royal party left Salon the next day, but soon afterward Nostradamus was summoned to visit them at Aix for further consultation. According to Don Francisco de Alava, the Spanish ambassador who succeeded Chantonnay, the magus prophesied that the young king would marry Elizabeth I of England (which never happened). Nostradamus was rewarded with a present of three hundred crowns and several royal licenses and patents, which would have proved quite lucrative had he lived to take advantage of them.

Now in his early sixties, Nostradamus was in failing health, plagued by gout and arthritis. In June 1566, he dictated his will, dividing his estate among his wife and children, with small benefices for various churches and charities. Around June 25, dropsy (today known as edema) set in, and on July 1 a priest was called to administer the last rites. That evening Nostradamus told Chavigny, "You will not find me alive at sunrise"—a prophecy that *did* prove correct.

The magus was buried at a Franciscan chapel in Salon, where his remains would rest in peace until his tomb was desecrated by a mob during the French Revolution. His bones were carried off as souvenirs until they—or some substitutes—were returned at the behest of the town's mayor.

Of Nostradamus's children, his sons César and Charles became worthy local citizens; César would become an amateur painter, poet, and local historian, and would, along with Chavigny, serve as the most steadfast defender of his father's memory. Nostradamus's youngest son, André, would retire to a Capuchin monastery after killing a man in a duel. Nostradamus's sons had no children; if the mage has any living descendants, it is through his daughters.

ALTHOUGH HE SUFFERED HIS share of life's misfortunes, Nostradamus was in many ways a lucky man. He found a niche that ensured him constant popularity during his lifetime, and he made good use of it. He was especially fortunate in the patronage of Catherine de' Medici, without whom his name might merely be a footnote in history. After his death, posterity was equally kind. Nostradamus's reputation continued to grow (as he himself may have predicted; see III.94). Chavigny made it his life's work to promulgate his memory. Indeed Chavigny was as vital to Nostradamus's fame after his death as Catherine had been while he was alive. Chavigny, along with Jean Dorat, a distinguished classicist who had also been Chavigny's teacher, became the prophet's most accomplished interpreter. Chavigny would edit a collected edition of the *Prophecies* in 1568 (possibly with some alterations to improve their accuracy).[25]

Since then, Nostradamus's *Prophecies* have remained in print more or less continuously—a remarkable record for a book that is nearly 450 years old. Numerous editions have regularly appeared, many or most with agendas of one kind or another. One edition produced in 1649, for example (a counterfeit of the 1568 edition), contains two spurious quatrains aimed at the French statesman Cardinal Mazarin.

Nostradamus had other uses as well. Théophilus de Garancières, a French physician who settled in England and produced the first English version of the *Prophecies* in 1672, claimed that when he was growing up, Nostradamus was the first thing he learned to read after his primer, "it being the custom in France about the year 1618, to initiate children by that book; first because of the crabbedness of the words; secondly, that they might be acquainted with the old and obsolete French; and thirdly, for the delightfulness and variety of the matter."[26] Learning to read using Nostradamus is almost unimaginable in any era, but Garancières's claims must be taken at least somewhat seriously, since he says he has done it himself.

Of the numerous editions of the *Prophecies*, very few have attempted to deal with Nostradamus in a scholarly fashion. Even these usually have more than a small share of eccentricities. In the early eighteenth century a French priest named Jean Leroux tried to show that Nostradamus's peculiar style resulted from his use of literary devices from Greek and Latin—a creditable proposition—but then went on to argue that the *Epistle to Henri II* was really intended for Louis XIV and that Nostradamus's predictions were being proved true on a daily basis.[27]

Few editions of Nostradamus are free from such indulgences. In the eighteenth century, most of these predicted a glorious future for one or another of the contemporary monarchs, but as monarchy fell out of fashion, Nostradamus's editors would take a different tack. One Englishman writing in 1775 used Nostradamus to predict (correctly) that the American Revolution would be successful, and a 1790 work by a man named d'Odoucet claimed that Nostradamus foresaw the French Revolution. Taking the opposite tack, in 1791 a Russian commentator named Shryalmo pronounced that Nostradamus foresaw a counterrevolution coming in the following year. In short, Nostradamus soon became what he has been ever since: a blank slate on which commentators can write the future they want.

Up to the twentieth century, the vast majority of editions of Nostradamus have been in French. It was not until World War II that the prophet would attract a widespread audience in the U.S. Bizarrely, his popularity here is partly due to Magda Goebbels, the wife of Hitler's propaganda minister, Joseph Goebbels. In 1939, she brought to her husband's attention a claim made in a 1921 book by a German postal worker named C. L. Loog. According to Loog, Nostradamus had predicted in verse III.57 that there would be a crisis in Poland in 1939—the year of the Nazi invasion. Using the same quatrain, Loog said that Nostradamus had also foretold that England would be steeped in blood for 290 years, from 1649 (the year King Charles I was beheaded by the English people) through 1939—presumably indicating a major defeat in that year.[28]

Goebbels found the predictions not only intriguing but potentially useful. He tried to find someone to write propaganda based on Nostradamus. Loog declined, so Goebbels eventually settled on a Swiss astrologer named Karl Ernest Krafft, who had used Nostradamus to correctly predict an assassination attempt on Adolf Hitler in November 1939. Krafft produced propaganda booklets using spurious verses of Nostradamus, which German planes airdropped over Belgium and France during the Nazi invasion of May 1940. (For more on Krafft, see the commentary on VI.51 below.)

Around the same time, the Germans also produced a small volume whose main point was to popularize Loog's interpretations of the key quatrains. The book was issued in French under the title *Comment Nostradamus a-t-il entrevu l'avenir d'Europe?*, or "How Did Nostradamus Predict the Future of Europe?" and also appeared in other languages, including English. A similar, though not identical, *What Will Happen in the Near Future?* was written by the pseudonymous "Norab" ("Baron" spelled backward) and published in Stockholm in 1940 (see commentary on III.57–58).*

The Nazis' use of Nostradamus was so successful that the Allies followed suit. The British strewed Nostradamus pamphlets of their own over occupied Europe, and MGM made four short Nostradamus films to boost American morale. Creatively entitled *Nostradamus, More About Nostradamus, Further Prophecies of Nostradamus,* and *Nostradamus IV,* these films launched the U.S. craze for the French seer that continues to this day. In 1940, the Modern Library, an imprint of the New York publisher Random House, hurriedly issued a volume entitled *Oracles of Nostradamus,* whose jacket breathlessly informs us:

---

*The Dutch scholar T.W.M. van Birkel informs me that "Norab" was the pseudonym for Baron Lage Fabian Wilhelm Staël von Holstein. *What Will Happen in the Near Future?* is his translation of a German text, written at Goebbels's command in late 1939 by the propagandist Hans-Wolfgang Herwarth von Bittenfeld.

Nostradamus, Europe's greatest prophet, foresaw three centuries ago events which history has confirmed with uncanny frequency. His "prophetic centuries" forecast the fall of Paris, war in the air, the invasion of Britain. Read the fateful happenings predicted tomorrow for Europe and America by the sixteenth-century soothsayer whom Hitler relies upon today.

Unfortunately, the Modern Library edition was a reprint of a nineteenth-century commentary by an Englishman named Charles A. Ward, with a perfunctory supplement attempting to bring the book up to date. Although Ward makes some interesting applications of Nostradamus's verses to England (a nation for which the sage's predictions were more accurate than most), he of course says nothing about World War II.

Since then, editions of Nostradamus have relentlessly appeared, many mining his verses to show that some cataclysm is imminent. Consequently, Nostradamus's name is invoked in connection with just about any unforeseen disaster. Soon after the 9/11 disaster, the most common search term on the Web was not "New York" or "World Trade Center" or "Osama bin Laden" but "Nostradamus."[29] (For some pseudo-Nostradamian quatrains on this event, see the commentary on VI.97.)

In the early twenty-first century, Nostradamus has continued to appear regularly in the so-called supermarket tabloids. The February 17, 2004, edition of *The Sun,* for example, informs us on the prophet's authority that sometime before the summer solstice of that year, "the greatest 'war of wars' will be brought to a screeching halt by a mystic visitor from the skies."[30] An article in the July 4, 2005, issue cites an otherwise unidentified "long-lost collection of journals written by Nostradamus" that allegedly says, "The stars spin and whirl, leaping beyond their appointed courses and falling upon cities with strange names—Yoruck, Albaquare, Angelus, and Bayjing, Peonjan, Teerihan"—that is, New York, Albuquerque, Los Angeles, Beijing, Pyongyang, and Tehran.[31] Like practically all the material in the *Sun* and its relative the *Weekly World News,* the predictions are not even half serious, so it is not surprising that Nostradamus has become a figure of fun. Comedian Dave Chappelle has featured a semi-regular skit on his popular *Chappelle's Show* spotlighting "Negrodamus."

Though not always in a way he would appreciate, Nostradamus's name remains a household word in the United States, a country whose existence he probably never dreamed of. Does he deserve the fabulous, if somewhat equivocal, reputation he enjoys? To answer this question more fully and fairly, it would be helpful to examine the key *Prophecies* in some detail.

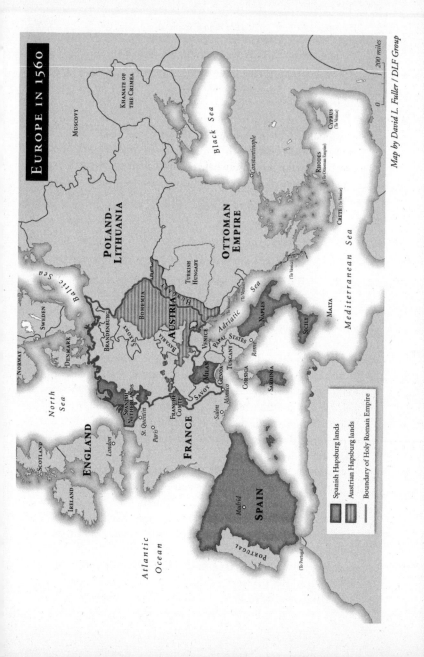

EUROPE IN 1560

Map by David L. Fuller / DLF Group

MUSCOVY

KHANATE OF
THE CRIMEA

POLAND-
LITHUANIA

Black Sea

Constantinople

OTTOMAN
EMPIRE

TURKISH
HUNGARY

BOHEMIA

AUSTRIA

RHODES
(To Ottoman Empire)

CYPRUS
(To Venice)

CRETE (To Venice)

Mediterranean Sea

MALTA

SICILY

NAPLES

Adriatic Sea

VENICE

PAPAL STATES

Rome

TUSCANY

SARDINIA

CORSICA

GENOA

MILAN

SAVOY

Monaco

BAVARIA

SAXONY

BRANDENBURG

Baltic Sea

SWEDEN

NORWAY

DENMARK

SPANISH
NETHERLANDS

FRANCHE-
COMTÉ

Salon

St. Quentin

FRANCE

Paris

North
Sea

ENGLAND

London

SCOTLAND

IRELAND

Atlantic
Ocean

SPAIN

Madrid

PORTUGAL

(To Portugal)

Spanish Hapsburg lands

Austrian Hapsburg lands

Boundary of Holy Roman Empire

200 miles

Historical Note

To understand Nostradamus's prophecies, it is essential to have a sense of the historical situation of his time. He lived in an era when the feudal system of medieval Europe was breaking down and the modern European nation-states were coming into formation. Among these, France itself, in the two hundred years after his lifetime, would become the most centralized and unified. In addition, the age endured the chaos of innumerable religious wars, which would continue off and on until the end of the Thirty Years' War in 1648. Overall, the mood in Nostradamus's time was one of profound disruption, which as usual offered opportunities for some and disaster for others.

France during Nostradamus's lifetime was ruled by the House of Valois. King Henri II reigned during the time the *Prophecies* were written in the 1550s. His wife and queen, Catherine de' Medici, came from the powerful Medici clan, which ruled Florence and also functioned as one of the largest banking houses in Europe.

France's chief rival in European power politics was the Hapsburg dynasty, which had ruled Austria since the thirteenth century but which in the sixteenth century gained control of Spain, the Netherlands, southern Italy, and much of Germany as well. This was accomplished through adroit dynastic marriages, and indeed the entire early modern era was characterized by dynastic power politics.

The greatest of the Hapsburg monarchs was Charles V (1500–58), who had been elected as Holy Roman emperor in 1519. The Holy Roman Empire, as historians are fond of saying, was neither holy nor Roman nor an empire. It was a secular power (usually at variance with the pope), did not rule Rome, and was a confederation of German states, led rather loosely by an emperor chosen by several electors consisting of the most powerful nobles and bishops of the realm. In Nostradamus's time, the Holy Roman Empire included practically all of modern-day Germany, Austria, Switzerland, Belgium, the Netherlands, and the Czech Republic, as well as parts of what are now Italy, Slovakia, Slovenia, and Poland. Most of Germany was carved up into smaller states owing allegiance to the Holy Roman emperor but governed directly by Protestant princes.

In 1556, Charles V would abdicate the throne of Spain in favor of his son, Philip II, who was married to Mary Tudor, queen of England from 1553 to her death in 1558. In 1558, soon before his own death, Charles would hand over his realms in Central Europe to his brother, Ferdinand I. After this time, Spain and Austria would be ruled by separate branches of the Hapsburg dynasty.

The other great power was the Ottoman Empire, which ruled over what is now Turkey as well as Greece and the Balkans and part of Hungary. The Ottomans continued to push into Central Europe, and were only held off with great difficulty by the Hapsburgs in alliance with Hungary and the Polish-Lithuanian commonwealth (then including not only Poland and Lithuania but also modern-day Latvia, Belarus, and the western half of the Ukraine). Although France was a Catholic nation, the French often found it expedient to ally with the Ottomans against their common enemy, the Hapsburgs.

In England, Mary Tudor was succeeded by her half-sister, Elizabeth I (a Protestant, unlike the firmly Catholic Mary), in 1558. England held Wales and Ireland. Scotland was a separate kingdom; the two nations would not be united until 1603, when King James VI of Scotland became King James I of England. England and France had long been enemies, not least because of English dynastic claims on French territories, which went back to the Middle Ages and had led to the Hundred Years' War in the fourteenth and fifteenth centuries.

Italy, like Germany, was a collection of small states that would not be unified until the mid–nineteenth century. The Hapsburgs held the southern third of the Italian peninsula, including Naples as well as Sicily and Sardinia. The popes ruled much of central Italy, including Rome, directly as part of their secular holdings. Florence, formerly a republic, was a grand duchy headed by the Medici dynasty; Venice and Genoa were republics.

This admittedly sketchy account focuses on the regions of most concern to Nostradamus's prophecies. Other parts of Europe and the world, including Scandinavia, Muscovy (the nucleus of modern Russia), and the Americas, were of marginal interest and are only rarely mentioned. Although the discovery of the Americas several decades earlier had opened vistas onto a new world, in this period Spain and Portugal were the nations chiefly occupied with exploring and colonizing them. France would not concern herself with the Americas until the early seventeenth century, several decades after Nostradamus's death.

The
Prophecies

———— ❈ ————

A Note on the Translation

As I have noted, Nostradamus's *Prophecies* are written in quatrains: four-lined verses that rhyme (with one exception: X.91). With some isolated exceptions, which are written in Provençal and Latin, the verses are written in the French of his era, which differs probably somewhat less from modern French than sixteenth-century English does from its modern counterpart. Overall the difficulty with Nostradamus lies not with the age of the language, but with frequent and deliberate obscurity, caused by newly coined words, murky allusions, and broken grammar.

The reader of my translations may object that they are disjointed and often close to meaningless. This is intentional; the French reads the same way. Unlike many translators, I have avoided giving an interpretive rendition of Nostradamus's verse—that is, I am not translating what I *think* he was trying to say, but what he *did* say. Nostradamus was entirely capable of writing clearly when he chose. He very often chose not to.

To take one particularly jarring example, the reader coming across my rendition "Byzantium heart ban" in IX.73 may find it puzzling and nearly meaningless. The French *Bizance coeur ban* is equally so. It would be possible to render it as "*Bizance se courbant*"—that is, "Byzantium submitting"—as some have done.

Given the loose typographical standards of the era and the many errors that crept into Nostradamus's works before publication, this translation is certainly defensible. But it does involve an interpretation that my translation does not.

Much of the power of Nostradamus's quatrains comes from this obscurity. It has enabled people to read many meanings into them. Rather than doing so in my translation, I am hoping to provide as transparent a window as possible onto what Nostradamus was actually saying. (This approach necessarily obscures many puns and double entendres in the original, but these would be lost in any translation; where appropriate, I have drawn attention to these in the notes.) Readers can make their own determinations about the real meaning, although my annotations offer my own suggestions.

The choice of quatrains for inclusion has been based on one simple guiding principle: their interest to the modern reader. These, of course, include predictions that supposedly relate to the present time, but it would be impossible to have a clear idea of Nostradamus and his work without including a large number of verses that deal with his own era. In addition, I have included those that illuminate various facets of Nostradamus's character work, including his prophetic stance (see I.1–2), his writing style, and the relative accuracy (or inaccuracy) of his forecasts. The rest have been omitted usually because either they are too obscure, they repeat prophecies in other quatrains that are included, or they focus on highly specific localities, chiefly in France.

In interpretation, I have tried to be as conservative as possible. In most cases I have favored the reading that makes most sense in the context of Nostradamus's time and the audience he was addressing. I have not entirely avoided speculative interpretations or possible applications to a more remote future, but I have done my best to limit these to cases where Nostradamus's text does not have any obvious relevance to his own time.

The text is based on the first edition of the first four Centuries, published in 1555 and reproduced in Pierre Brind'Amour's edition of 1996, and of the first extant edition of the remaining

Prophecies, edited by Jean-Aymé de Chavigny and published in 1568, as reproduced in Peter Lemesurier's *Illustrated Nostradamus* and John Hogue's *Nostradamus: The Complete Prophecies.* I have based my own text on a comparison of these versions (which differ in a number of instances), as well as on Edgar Leoni's somewhat modernized version of the French in *Nostradamus and His Prophecies,* with some reference to the texts in the works of Erika Cheetham. Spelling and accent marks in the French reflect the usage of the earliest editions.

Century I

1.

Estant assis de nuict secret estude,
Seul repousé sus la selle d'aerain:
Flamme exigue sortant de solitude,
Faict proferer qui n'est à croire vain.

Being seated at night, secret study,
Resting alone on the seat of bronze,
A tiny flame arises out of solitude
And offers what it is not vain to believe.

This verse, a proem to the *Prophecies* as a whole, echoes a description of Delphi by Iamblichus, a Neoplatonic philosopher of the third century A.D.: "The prophetess at Delphi . . . whether she gives oracles to human beings from a subtle and fiery spirit brought up from an aperture, or prophesies in the innermost sanctuary while seated on a bronze stool with three feet, or on a seat with four legs that is sacred to the god, she thus gives herself absolutely to the divine spirit, and is illuminated by the ray of divine fire."[32] In all probability Nostradamus is invoking the spirit of the

Delphic oracle—who was known for ambiguous utterances—rather than describing his own method of divination.

2.

La verge en main mise au milieu des BRANCHES
De l'onde il moulle & le limbe & le pied;
Un peur et voix fremissent par les manches.
Splendeur divine. Le divin près s'assied.

Wand in hand, placed among the BRANCHES,
With the wave he moistens his hem and feet:
Fear and voices tremble through his sleeves.
Divine splendor. The divine seats itself nearby.

Another allusion to Iamblichus, who writes: "As for the woman at Branchidai who gives oracles, it is either by holding the staff first given by a certain god [i.e., Apollo] that she is filled by the divine radiance; or else when sitting upon the axle she predicts the future; or whether dipping her feet or skirt in the water, or inhaling vapor from the water, at any rate, she receives the god."[33] Branchidai, or Didyma, was another ancient oracle, located in Asia Minor. Again Nostradamus is probably invoking classical precedents—a common touch among the writers of his time—rather than describing how he himself works.

BRANCHES, capitalized in the French, seems to be a cryptic way of alluding to Branchidai. *Limbe* is not a word in French. Like many authors of his day, Nostradamus is fond of taking Latin words—here *limbus,* "hem"—and giving them French forms. Sometimes it is mistranslated as "limb."

3.

Quand la lictiere du tourbillon versée,
Et seront faces de leurs manteaux couvers,
La république par gens nouveaux vexée,
Lors blancs et rouges jugeront à l'envers.

When the litter is by the whirlwind overturned,
And faces are buried in their topcoats,
The republic is vexed by new people;
Then reds and whites judge contrariwise.

Certainly one of Nostradamus's more resonant prophecies. The litter was a form of transportation reserved for nobles and royalty; its being overturned hints at revolution. "Faces buried in topcoats" would then mean that aristocrats would try to hide their identity. The republic will be vexed by "new people"—meaning those of lower station, and "reds" and "whites" would indicate rival political parties.

The most obvious historical references would be to the revolutions in France and Russia, when the nobility did have to hide their identity to survive and "new people" did overturn the new order. The last line is particularly striking in light of the civil war that followed the Russian Revolution of 1917, which pitted the Reds (the Bolsheviks) against the Whites (republican and monarchist factions). Some commentators say this line alludes to the white of the French Bourbon dynasty that was overturned by the red of the revolutionaries. But this is far-fetched, since the revolutionary colors of France were the tricolor of red, white, and blue rather than red alone.

It is also striking that Nostradamus uses the term *république*—"republic"—in an age when this form of government was almost nonexistent. Venice and Genoa were the only important states in Nostradamus's time to be governed by republics. But he may be using the term in its more general sense of "state" or "polity."

4.
Pars l'univers sera faict ung monarque,
Qu'en paix et vie ne sera longuement:
Lors se perdra la piscature barque,
Sera regie en plus grand detriment.

> For the universe there will be one monarch,
> Who will not stay long in peace or life;
> Then the fisherman's bark will lose itself,
> Will be guided to its greatest detriment.

It would be hard to apply this quatrain to any specific situation either past or present. It is noteworthy, however, in highlighting one of the key issues in Western history: the struggle between sacred and secular power. Nostradamus is alluding to the ancient myth of the universal ruler. An idealized figure known the world over (known in the Hindu and Buddhist traditions, for example, as a *chakravartin*), the universal ruler was most often imagined in the West as a restored Roman emperor who rules in peace. Dante discusses this figure in his treatise *De monarchia:* "Since it appears that the whole of mankind is ordained to one end, . . . it should therefore have a single rule and government, and this power should be called the Monarch or Emperor."[34] No monarch in history can really be equated with this archetypal figure—nor is anyone in the future likely to match up to this ideal. Nostradamus here suggests that no one will be able to hold this post for long.

Combined with this is a prophecy of difficulty for the Papacy, symbolized by the "bark" of the fisherman Peter. Much of medieval and early modern history was marked by a long struggle between the pope and the Holy Roman emperor. This struggle went far beyond ideology: the troops of Emperor Charles V sacked Rome in 1527, less than thirty years before this prophecy was published. Nostradamus seems to be foreseeing a time when both sacred and secular powers are in crisis. One commentator on Nostradamus, Erika Cheetham, sees in this a prophecy of Napoleon, who ruled most of Europe, though briefly, at a time when the Papacy was at a disadvantage; in fact Napoleon annexed the Papal States to the French Empire in 1810. They were restored to the pope by the Congress of Vienna in 1815.

7.

Tard arrivé, l'execution faicte,
Le vent contraire: lettres au chemin prises:
Les conjurés xiiij. d'une secte,
Par le Rosseau senez les entreprinses.

Late arrived, the execution done,
The wind contrary, letters taken on the road:
Fourteen conspirators from one sect,
Enterprises by the old red-haired one.

This quatrain has generally been applied to the infamous Dreyfus case of the 1890s, in which Alfred Dreyfus, a Jewish officer in the French army, was framed as a spy for the Germans. The case became a cause célèbre and revealed the depth of anti-Semitism in French society. This connection is chiefly based on the fact that the judge in the first trial of Dreyfus was one René Waldeck-Rousseau, an avowed anti-Semite. Beyond this name, the connections with the Dreyfus case are rather vague. Dreyfus was not executed, but sent to Devil's Island, the notorious penal colony in French Guiana, and was later acquitted in a second trial.

I am more struck by this quatrain's evocation of the French Revolution, which was in part inspired by the ideas of the great philosopher Jean-Jacques Rousseau, and that the "late arrival, the execution done" echoes the attempted escape of Louis XVI from the hands of the revolutionaries. But even here the details are not specific enough to make a really good fit.

8.

Combien de foys prinse cité solaire
Seras, chageant les lois barbares et vaines:
Ton mal s'aproche: Plus seras tributaire,
La grand Hadrie reovrira tes veines.

How many times, solar city, will you be taken,
Changing laws empty and barbaric.
Your evil approaches: you will become more tributary;
Great Hadria will reopen your veins.

This quatrain probably refers to events of Nostradamus's own day.
Rhodes is an island off the Ionian coast of what is now Turkey. It
is called the "city of the sun" because in antiquity it was sacred to
Helios, the Greek sun god; it was in fact the site of the Colossus
of Rhodes, one of the Seven Wonders of the World, which was
built in Helios's honor; completed in 282 B.C., it was destroyed by
earthquake c. 226 B.C.

In Nostradamus's time Rhodes often changed hands between the
Ottoman Turks and the Venetians, the two great regional powers of
the day. "Hadria" is a city on the Adriatic, which gave the sea its
name. Nostradamus uses it as a frequent metonymy for Venice. "Laws
empty and barbaric" would in that case refer to Ottoman rule.

9.

De l'Orient viendra le cueur Punique,
Fascher Hadrie et les hoirs Romulides,
Acompaigné de la classe Libycque,
Temples Mellites et proches isles vuides.

From the Orient will come the Punic heart,
To vex Hadria and the heirs of Romulus,
Accompanied by the Libyan fleet;
Malta's temples and nearby islands empty.

Corsairs often harassed Mediterranean shipping in Nostradamus's
day. This quatrain seems to refer to the most dangerous of them.
Known as Dragut or Turghut, he was a Greek by birth and priva-
teered with the connivance of the Ottoman Turks. "Punic" refers to
Carthage, which was located on the north coast of Africa. Settled
by Phoenicians (and thus giving rise to the adjective "Punic"), it
was the greatest enemy of the burgeoning Roman Republic in the

second and third centuries B.C. Here the term alludes to the fact that Dragut had captured a town called Africa in Tunisia in 1550, near where Carthage once had been, and used it as his base of operations.[35] ("Libya" was an antique synonym for the continent of Africa.) The Mediterranean island of Malta was a Christian outpost that took much of the brunt of Ottoman naval aggression. "Hadria," as in I.8, is a metonymy for Venice.

14.

De gent esclave chansons, chantz & requestes,
Captifs par princes & seigneur aux prisons,
A l'avenir par idiots sans testes
Seront receus par divins oraisons.

A slavish race's songs, hymns, and prayers,
Captives for princes and lord in prisons,
In the future by headless idiots
Will be taken as divine orisons.

This is most likely a comment on Nostradamus's own time, when the Protestant Huguenots were reforming the Christian liturgy. In this case the Huguenots would be the "slavish race," since most of them were not nobility but bourgeois. Some commentators, however, like to see in this verse a premonition of the French Revolution, when the nobles and king were in prison as a consequence of popular demands for liberty and equality. If one prefers this sort of explanation, one could see in it a presage of the short-lived rule of the Goddess of Reason set up in Notre Dame cathedral by the Paris mob.

My rendition of the second line is an attempt to reproduce the structure of the French, which, as in many of Nostradamus's verses, is broken and incoherent.

15.

Mars nous menasse par la force bellique,
Septante foys fera le sang espandre;

Auge & ruyne de l'Ecclesiastique,
Et plus ceux qui d'eux rien voudront entendre.

Mars menaces us with bellicose force;
Seventy times he will make the blood spread;
Increase and ruin for ecclesiastics,
And more those who will hear nothing of them.

This quatrain presages the age of appalling religious warfare that would plague Europe for the next century. In France, it would involve a bitter civil war between the Catholics and the Protestant Huguenots that would end only with the sixteenth century. In 1619, more than sixty years after this verse was published, religious strife in Central Europe would provoke the Thirty Years' War, which would bleed Europe white until it ended in 1648.

The verse seems to predict that the power of the churches would increase for a while, then diminish—as in fact happened in Europe over the next two hundred years. "Those who will hear nothing of them" suggests that this struggle would in the end produce people who wanted no more of religion. In fact this is exactly what happened: in the wake of this religious strife came the Enlightenment in the eighteenth century, which gave birth to the secular civilization that we know today.

The last line suggests some of the difficulties that face the translator of Nostradamus. The commentator Pierre Brind'Amour points out that the French word *rien* (translated idiomatically as "nothing" and usually preceded by the particle *ne*) comes from the Latin *res,* or "thing," and so could also mean "something."[36] Consequently, this phrase could have two entirely opposite meanings: "those who will hear *nothing* of them" or "those who will hear *something* of them." Brind'Amour prefers the first reading, as I do, but this case illustrates how Nostradamus's language gives rise to such flexibility of interpretation.

18.

Par la discorde negligence Gauloyse
Sera passaige à Mahommet ouvert:
De sang trempé la terre et mer Senoyse
Le port Phocen de voiles & nefz couvert.

By discord, Gallic negligence,
Shall passage be opened to Muhammad:
Sienan land and sea soaked in blood;
Phoecaean port covered in sails and ships.

The geopolitics of the mid-sixteenth century often made it expedient for the Catholic French to reach some accommodation with the Muslim Ottomans, since both were enemies of the Hapsburg monarchy that ruled Spain and Austria. Nostradamus alludes to a 1543 rapprochement between France and the Ottoman Empire that allowed the Ottoman navy to overwinter in Marseille, the "Phoecaean port." Marseille was founded around 600 B.C. by Greek colonists from the city of Phocaea in Asia Minor.

Evidently, Nostradamus thought this policy of accommodation to the Ottomans would bring disaster to France in the long run and open the way for a Muslim invasion of Europe. He also predicted that it would bring disaster upon Tuscany, a state in northern Italy that included Siena: Tuscan connivance and double-dealing in that period helped complicate the negotiation of a Christian alliance against the Turks.

In fact, none of this transpired: despite French connivance, the Turks did not invade Western Europe. The difficulties encountered by Tuscany came as much or more from its closer neighbors, including France and the Hapsburg dynasty.

25.

Perdu, trouvé, caché de si long siècle
Sera pasteur demi dieu honoré:

Ains que la Lune acheve son grand cycle
Par autres veux sera deshonoré.

Lost, found, hidden for so long an age,
Shall the pastor be honored as a demigod;
Before the Moon finishes her great cycle
By other vows shall he be dishonored.

Many commentators say this verse predicts some future discovery of the tomb of a pope, possibly Peter himself, although this tomb will suffer some sort of dishonor in due course (perhaps because it will have been found to be spurious).

Another view sees the "pastor" (or "shepherd") in line two as Louis Pasteur, the nineteenth-century French scientist who came up with the theory of infection that led to so many scientific advances. As Nostradamus commentator John Hogue points out, since then, Pasteur has been accused of being a rather shoddy self-promoter.

Another equally speculative interpretation is possible. Around 1615, several tracts were published in Germany that proclaimed the discovery of the tomb of Christian Rosenkreutz ("Christian Rose Cross"), an enigmatic adept who is said to have founded the Rosicrucian Brotherhood. It is far from certain that Christian Rosenkreutz ever existed in the literal sense, but it is at least remotely conceivable that Nostradamus knew of this legend, which was at the time hidden, through his esoteric contacts and is alluding to it here: Christian Rosenkreutz would then be the "pastor." After the tracts were published, many seekers (including the philosopher René Descartes) tried to find this brotherhood, but none to our knowledge succeeded. With the coming of the Thirty Years' War in 1619, the "Rosicrucian furor," as the scholar Frances Yates has called it, fell into disrepute.

31.
Tant d'ans les guerres en Gaule dureront
Oultre la course du Castulon monarque,

Victoire incerte trois grands couronneront;
Aigle, coq, lune, lyon, soleil en marque.

So many years shall the wars in Gaul persist
Beyond the course of the Castilian monarch;
Uncertain victory; three great ones will wear crowns;
Eagle, cock, moon, lion, sun in evidence.

At the time Nostradamus was writing, France was involved in a protracted struggle with the Hapsburg dynasty, which ruled Spain (here referred as Castile). He is predicting that these wars will last beyond the lifetime of the king of Spain. This was a safe bet, since the ruler of Spain at the time, the Hapsburg emperor Charles V, was advancing in years and in fact died in February 1558, only three years after this verse was published. Nostradamus is suggesting that the struggle will not leave a secure, obvious winner.

The last line suggests that the great powers of the day—the Hapsburg eagle, the French cock, the moon of the Muslim Ottomans, the British lion, and the sun of the pope will all have their share in these struggles—again not a terribly risky prediction. It is as if a modern prophet were to forecast that the United States, Western Europe, Russia, and China will play a major role in world history in the near future.

32.
Le grand empire sera tost translaté
En lieu petit qui bien tost viendra croistre:
Lieu bien infime d'exigue comté
Ou au milieu viendra poser son sceptre.

The great empire shall be soon transferred
To a little place that soon will grow:
A place ignoble, in a tiny county
In the midst of which he will place his scepter.

"The great empire," in the context of Nostradamus's time, is most likely to mean the Hapsburg monarchy, which, as we have seen, ruled an enormous part of Europe at the time. Nostradamus is predicting that its power will wane and another smaller country will take it up.

The most obvious candidate for this "place ignoble" is England, which at the time was a relatively insignificant power. In 1558, three years after Nostradamus published these verses, Elizabeth I would ascend to the English throne, and by the time she died, in 1603, England had transformed itself into one of the most vigorous and powerful nations in Europe, beginning a long ascent that would reach its zenith some three hundred years later, at the turn of the twentieth century.

Nevertheless, the quatrain is perhaps better understood as an expression of a universal truth: change applies to all things; the great will decline and insignificant ones will be exalted. This idea appears in countless places, for example, in the Psalms: "He poureth contempt upon princes, and causeth them to wander in the wilderness, where there is no way. Yet setteth he the poor on high from affliction, and maketh him families like a flock" (Ps. 107:40–41). This idea is also one of the principal themes of the Chinese *I Ching*, the "Book of Changes." Nostradamus's use of such universal ideas may be one of the chief reasons for his perennial appeal.

35.
Le lion jeune le vieux surmontera
En champ bellique par singulier duel:
Dans caige d'or les yeux luy crevera:
Deux classes une, puis mourir, mort cruelle.

The young lion will overcome the old one
In a martial field by a duel one-on-one:
In a cage of gold his eyes will burst:
Two classes one, then to die, cruel death.

This is one of Nostradamus's most famous prophecies, and the one that, more than any other, made his career. As we have already seen, it is generally taken to prophesy the bizarre death of King Henri II of France. It was fulfilled, if we credit this view, in June 1559, when the French court held a grand celebration for the double wedding of Marguerite, sister of King Henri II, to the Duke of Savoy and of Elizabeth, Henri's elder daughter, to King Philip II of Spain. The festivities included a mock medieval tournament, a form of entertainment of which Henri was extremely fond and in which he liked to participate. In the tournament, Henri jousted with the Duc de Montgomery, who was six years younger (thus a "young lion"). Montgomery's lance shattered against the king's shield, and a large splinter passed through the golden visor of his helmet, piercing his eye and entering his brain. Ten days later, Henri died in agony—certainly a "cruel death."

The reference in the last line, "two classes one," is cryptic. Mine is the most literal rendition, but it is sometimes translated as "fleets" (from the Latin *classis*) or, more commonly, as "wounds." (The splinter entered Henri's head in two places.) In the latter case, the word would be taken from the Greek *klasis,* or "breaking."

Remarkably, this verse was not applied to this misfortune only retroactively. Even before it happened, this murky prophecy was believed to portend the king's death. It solidified Nostradamus's reputation as a seer in the eyes of Catherine de' Medici, Henri's queen, who was much given to occultism and who became a powerful sponsor of the prophet in the years to come. Not everyone took so charitable a view. According to Nostradamus's son César, on the night of Henri's death, a mob in the Paris suburbs burned Nostradamus in effigy as a heretic and sorcerer.

This incident exemplifies the dilemma of the Renaissance magus. If his predictions proved false, he would be dismissed as a fraud; if they proved true, he risked accusations of witchcraft. Few if any of the prominent occultists of Nostradamus's day managed to elude these charges entirely.

40.

La trombe faulse dissimulant folie,
Fera Bisance un changement de loix:
Hystra d'Égypte qui veult que l'on deslie,
Edict changeant monnoyes & aloys.

The false trumpet concealing madness,
Will make in Byzantium a change of laws:
Out of Egypt will issue forth one who would dissolve
The edict changing coins and alloys.

Byzantium—that is, Constantinople—suggests that this refers to
Turkey, or, as it was known in Nostradamus's time, the Ottoman
Empire. Here, as in III.97, Nostradamus is predicting change and
upheaval in this realm, which was at the time the bogeyman of
Europe, much as the Soviet Union was during the Cold War. If so,
the Ottoman Empire took a long time to collapse, as this did not
happen until after World War I, in which it fought on the losing
side. The victorious Allies took away many of its possessions, including Syria, Palestine, and Mesopotamia, and set the stage for
the creation of a new, secular Turkish state under Kemal Atatürk,
which survives to this day. It is remotely possible that Nostradamus's quatrain refers to this event. Most likely, however, this is a
general and not particularly accurate prophecy of the fall of the
Ottoman dynasty at the hands of a usurper from Egypt.

42.

Le dix Kalendes d'Apvril le faict Gotique
Resuscité encor par gens malins:
Le feu estainct, assemblée diabolique
Cherchant les or du d'Amant & Pselyn.

On the tenth of the Kalends of April, the Gothic thing
Revived again by wicked people.

The fire extinguished, diabolic assembly
Seeking the gold of d'Amant and Pselyn.

A verse that seems to point to the resuscitation of some diabolic
activity on March 23 (the tenth of the kalends of April by the old
Roman calendar). Some commentators posit *Gnostique* as a reading for *Gotique* in the first line, which would make this verse apply
to revivals of Gnostic practices. Certain Gnostic sects in antiquity
were accused of licentious orgies in which they supposedly ate
semen, menstrual blood, and aborted fetuses as sacraments. This
would also require emending *or,* "gold," in the last line, to *ords,* or
"ordure." (Some texts give this word as *os,* or "bones.") "D'Amant"
may refer to the Church Father Origen, supposedly known as
"Adamantius." "Pselyn" would then be the Byzantine scholar Michael Psellus; both of these authors described (and denounced)
Gnostic practices.

As must be obvious, these readings require some highly crucial, and speculative, changes to the text. What is clear, at any
rate, is that Nostradamus is describing some kind of lurid and
forbidden rite, whether "Gnostic" or "Gothic" (that is, barbaric).
The obsession with witchcraft in his era made such descriptions
highly sensational and highly popular—rather like the accounts
of supposed Satanic activities that we see in the tabloids of our
own time.

44.
En bref seront de retour sacrifices,
Contrevenans seront mis à martyre:
Plus ne seront moines, abbez, ne novices:
Le miel sera beaucoup plus cher que cire.

Soon there will be sacrifices again,
Those who refuse will be put to martyrdom;
There will be no more monks, abbots, or novices;
Honey will be much more costly than wax.

A prophecy of a return to paganism after the suppression of Christianity. "Honey will be much more costly than wax" because there will be no more need for the latter for liturgical candles. It was (and remains) a common prophetic trope to forecast the persecution of the church as a form of tribulation before Judgment Day, and that is the most obvious interpretation for this verse.

47.

Du lac Leman les sermons facheront:
Des jours seront reduicts par les sepmaines,
Puis moys, puis an, puis tous defailliront,
Les magistrats damneront leurs loys vaines.

Lake Geneva's sermons will cause anger:
Days will be reduced by weeks,
Then months, then a year, then all will fail;
The magistrates will damn their vain laws.

The point of this quatrain is clear: it is aimed at the Reformer John Calvin, who set up his headquarters in Geneva and established a theocracy there. The wording of the second and third lines is murky. Generally they are understood to mean that the Reformer's sermons will be so tiresome that days will seem like weeks, and so on. Others say this is a gibe at Calvin's purging of the ecclesiastical calendar. In any event, Nostradamus is predicting that sooner or later the Genevan city fathers will tire of this regime. In fact, Calvin's theocracy, after experiencing some setbacks, continued to thrive well beyond his lifetime.

Edgar Leoni, another commentator on Nostradamus, relates this verse to the fruitless efforts of the League of Nations, based in Geneva, to prevent World War II in the 1930s. While this is only a remote possibility, the verse does poignantly evoke the empty phrases of that era.

48.

Vingt ans du regne de la lune passez
Sept mils ans autre tiendra sa monarchie:
Quand le soleil prendra ses jours lassés
Lors accomplir & mine ma prophetie.

Twenty years of the moon's reign passed,
Seven thousand years another will hold his monarchy;
When the sun takes up his weary days,
Then will my prophecy be accomplished.

This quatrain alludes to the esoteric idea that each planet rules over the world for approximately 354 years. Since there were seven planets—traditional astrology regards both the sun and the moon as planets—the complete cycle would last 2,480 years. By this theory, the period of the moon lasted from 1533 to 1887; "twenty years of the Moon's reign passed" refers to the time when Nostradamus was writing these verses—that is, in the mid-1550s. After the "moon's reign" ended, the sun's reign would begin in 1887, which was the year 7086 from the year of creation, according to Richard Roussat, a sixteenth-century prophet whose works Nostradamus used as a source. Hence the reference to "seven thousand years." From this it would appear that Nostradamus expected his prophecies to have been fulfilled by the end of the nineteenth century, and indeed it was a common belief in Christian apocalyptic that the world would end seven thousand years after it was created (cf. X.74).

On the other hand, in the preface to his *Prophecies* addressed to his son César (§20),[37] Nostradamus indicates that the reign of Saturn will begin again when the cycle of the sun finishes in 2242. He also says that his prophecies will not be entirely fulfilled until 3797 (*Preface to César*, §19), suggesting that the world will last at least that long. Commentators have exerted much labor to harmonize all of Nostradamus's confusing and often contradictory chronologies, without a great deal of success.

The reference to the sun's "weary days" reflects the traditional belief that the world is old and tired and will soon come to an end.

49.

Beaucoup beaucoup avant telles menées
Ceux d'Orient par la vertu lunaire
L'an mil sept cent feront grands emmenées,
Subjugant presque le coing Aquilonaire.

Much, much before such events,
Those of the Orient, by their lunar might,
Will in the year 1700 make great incursions,
Conquering almost up to the northmost corner.

"Those of the Orient, by their lunar might" would refer to the Ottoman Turks, who as Muslims had the crescent moon as their emblem. Nostradamus is predicting that in the year 1700 they will conquer Europe up to its northernmost part. This would come true to a degree: the Turks, who warred with Austria from 1682 to 1699, would be stopped only at the gates of Vienna in 1683. On the other hand, this would be their last great inroad into Europe, and by the actual year 1700, the situation would be reversed: the peace settlement ending the war with Austria forced the Ottomans to give up most of their lands north of the Balkans. This would set the seal upon a long period of Ottoman decline (see I.40 above).

50.

De l'aquatique triplicité naistra
D'un qui fera le jeudy pour sa feste.
Son bruit, loz, regne, sa puissance croistra,
Par terre & mer aux orients tempeste.

From the aquatic triplicity he will be born
From one who will make Thursday his feast.

His noise, praise, kingdom, power will increase,
Tempestuous in the Orient by land and sea.

In astrology, the aquatic triplicity consists of the three water signs: Pisces, Cancer, and Scorpio. The Nostradamus scholar Edgar Leoni points out that this quatrain could be applied to the United States, which, having its birthday on the Fourth of July, is under the sign of Cancer; it has Venus and Jupiter in Cancer as well. Moreover, the American "feast day," Thanksgiving, falls on a Thursday. Certainly the last two lines could be applied to the U.S., which established itself as the dominant power in the Pacific in the wake of World War II.

51.
Chef d'Aries, Juppiter & Saturne,
Dieu eternel quelles mutations!
Puis pour long siècle son maling temps retourne,
Gaule & Itale quelles esmotions!

Head of Aries, Jupiter and Saturn,
God eternal, what mutations!
Then for a long century his evil time returns:
Gaul and Italy, what disturbances!

Nostradamus is alluding to what astrologers call the "grand conjunction": when Jupiter and Saturn appear to meet each other in the heavens. This was perhaps the most significant conjunction in the astrology of the day, because Jupiter and Saturn were the outermost known planets. Moreover, Jupiter governs rulership and kings (among other things), and Saturn governs structure and law. This conjunction is not all that rare: It happens every twenty-one or twenty-two years. As of this writing, the latest occurrence was in May 2000, when Jupiter and Saturn were conjunct in Taurus, an earth sign. Perhaps the most obvious consequence of this was to bring "down to earth" the inflated stock prices of the 1990s.

Jupiter and Saturn meet in any given sign of the zodiac, however, much more rarely. The conjunction in Aries that Nostradamus mentions is probably the one of December 1702, although it is even more likely to apply to this conjunction as a whole. That is to say, whenever Jupiter and Saturn are conjunct in Aries, there will be disturbances in France and Italy. This verse implies that such tumult will last a century, and certainly the eighteenth century turned out to be such for France: Beginning with the strong and highly centralized Bourbon monarchy, it ended with revolution and the rise of Napoleon.

The commentator Pierre Brind'Amour makes an interesting point about *Saturne* ("Saturn") and *retourne* ("returns"), which do not properly rhyme in standard French. The only way to make them do so would be to pronounce "*Saturne*" in the Italian manner (as if it were spelled *ça tourne*). This suggests that Nostradamus, being from the far south of France, might have spoken with something resembling an Italian accent.

52.

Les deux malins de Scorpio conjoints,
Le grand Seigneur meurtri dans sa salle:
Peste à l'Église par le nouveau Roy joint,
L'Europe basse & Septentrionale.

The two malefics joined in Scorpio,
The great lord murdered in his room:
Plague to the Church from the new joint king,
Europe low and northerly.

Another astrological quatrain. The "two malefics" are Mars and Saturn, which astrologers consider to have mostly baleful influences. Their conjunction in the dark sign of Scorpio, which is connected with intrigue, suggests the murder of a great lord. The Nostradamus commentator John Hogue indicates that the events in this prophecy played out in 1807, when the Turkish sultan Selim

III was deposed, to be murdered the next year. At this time the Catholic Church was under pressure from Napoleon (certainly a "new king"), who had taken away its domains in central Italy, known as the Papal States. Napoleon had also entered into a short-lived alliance with Tsar Alexander I of Russia, temporarily uniting Europe "low and north." Hogue also points out that the next conjunction of Mars and Saturn in Scorpio will take place in October 2012.

53.

Las qu'on verra grand peuple tourmenté
Et la loy saincte en totale ruine:
Par aultres loyx toute Chrestienté,
Quand d'or d'argent trouve nouvelle mine.

Alas! One will see a great people tormented
And the holy law in total ruin;
Other laws throughout all Christendom,
When of gold, of silver he finds another mine.

The Nostradamus scholar Peter Lemesurier plausibly connects this prophecy with the discovery of new sources of precious metals in the New World. It is not clear, however, which "great people" Nostradamus means; he may be thinking of Spain, which was at first the chief beneficiary of these new discoveries. In the long run, the gold and silver of the New World did not contribute to Spain's welfare, but led to its decline as a world power.

Again, however, it is possible to see a more universal theme expressed here: A rise in wealth leads to a decline in virtue. In historical terms, the prophecy can be applied to the birth of the European secular state, which did not exist in Nostradamus's time. Over the next few centuries, however, the nations of Western Europe increasingly detached their allegiances from Christianity to the point where the connection between religion and the state is tenuous at best.

60.

Un Empereur naistra près d'Italie,
Qui à l'Empire sera vendu bien cher,
Diront avecque quels gens il se ralie
Qu'on trouvera moins prince que boucher.

An emperor will be born near Italy,
Who will be sold quite dearly to the Empire.
They will say that he allies with such people
That one will find him less a prince than a butcher.

Whatever Nostradamus may have had in mind when he wrote this, it is hard to avoid connecting this quatrain with Napoleon. Born on the isle of Corsica not far from Italy, he did prove costly to France. He set out on his disastrous invasion of Russia in 1812, for example, with an army numbering 442,000 men and returned with 10,000 (cf. IV.12, V.26, IX.99). From this point of view at least, he was less a prince than a butcher.

63.

Les fléaux passés diminue le monde
Long temps la paix terres inhabitées
Suer marchera par ciel, terre, mer, & onde:
Puis de nouveau les guerres suscitées.

Scourges past, the world diminishes;
For a long time peace, lands inhabited;
He will walk over heaven, land, sea, and wave;
Then again the wars are reignited.

A forecast of a time when humanity, exhausted by war, will rest at peace. The population will decline before it begins to grow again. Although this part of the prophecy has not been borne out to date, this quatrain is interesting in that the third line appears to predict air travel.

64.

De nuit soleil penseront avoir veu
Quand le pourceau demy-homme on verra.
Bruict, chant, bataille, au ciel battre aperceu
Et bestes brutes à parler lon orra.

At night the sun they'll think they've seen,
When one sees the pig that is half-man.
Noise, song, battle, fighting in heaven observed,
And one will hear brute beasts speak.

I cannot avoid seeing in this quatrain an allusion to *The Golden Ass* of Lucius Apuleius. This Latin novel, written in the third century A.D., tells of a man who is transformed into a donkey and back into a man again through mystical initiation. At the climax of this rite the hero-narrator famously says, "*Nocte media vidi solem candido coruscante luminem*": "At midnight I saw the sun shine brightly with white light."[38] The sun shining at midnight is, among other things, a metaphor for mystical perception, which does not rely on the physical eyes or earthly light. Esoterically, to be transformed from a beast into a human means to have one's animal nature placed in subordination to consciousness. Nostradamus here recapitulates Apuleius's motifs of the sun seen at midnight and a creature that is half human, half beast.

Some modern interpreters ingeniously see this quatrain as a prediction of the aerial battles of the twentieth century. The half pig, half human would then be Nostradamus's description of pilots in their masks and goggles.

To view the matter in simpler terms, it was commonplace in Nostradamus's time to see mutants as supernatural portents; talking animals were also so regarded. Such omens were often viewed as a sign of impending apocalypse, which would take the form of a war in heaven (see Rev. 12:7).

67.

La grand famine que je sens approcher,
Souvent tourner, puis estre universelle:
Si grande & longue qu'on viendra arracher
Du bois racine, & l'enfant de mammelle.

The great famine that I feel approaching
To often turn, then become universal:
So great and long that one will come to pull
Roots from wood and the infant from the breast.

A general prediction of a universal famine. Although there have
been countless famines since Nostradamus's time, none can accurately be called universal. Famine was a constant worry in Nostradamus's time, when agricultural production was much less efficient
than it is today and much more subject to the weather. Moreover,
the sixteenth century saw a climatic phenomenon called the Little
Ice Age, decades of cooler weather that wreaked havoc on crops
and was a major cause of the social instability of the time.

81.

D'humain troupeau neuf seront mis à part
De jugement & conseil séparés:
Leur sort sera divisé en depart
Καπ, Θhita, λambda mors, bannis esgarés.

Of the human troop shall nine be set apart
Removed from judgment and counsel:
Their fate will be determined at the start;
Kappa, theta, lambda dead, banished, scattered.

Peter Lemesurier sees in this a reference to the Knights Templar,
fifty-nine of whom were burned for heresy in Paris in 1310, and
nine more in the town of Senlis, whose trials were broken off.
The number fifty-nine derives from the numerology of the Greek,

where letters do double duty as numbers: kappa equals twenty, theta equals nine, and lambda equals thirty, making a sum of fifty-nine. (The letters in Nostradamus's original are written in a mixture of Greek and Roman script, as shown above.) The rest of the Templars were "banished, scattered," and their fates are not clearly known.

Pierre Brind'Amour, on the other hand, finds in the Greek letters an abbreviation of the Greek *kath'olou,* meaning "universal." "Catholic" is derived from the same roots. The verse would then refer either to widespread (that is, universal) destruction or to the persecution of Catholics.

Other commentators are still more adventurous in their conclusions: some see in it a hint of disasters in the U.S. and Russian space programs.

87.

Ennosigée feu du centre de la terre
Fera trembler au tour de cité neufve:
Deux grands rochiers long temps feront la guerre
Puis Aréthusa rougira nouveau fleuve.

Earthshaker, fire from the center of the earth,
Shall make the new city's environs tremble;
Two great rocks for a long time will make war;
Then Arethusa will redden a new stream.

References to the "new city" in Nostradamus are often applied to New York (cf. VI.97, X.49), so that this quatrain would be predicting that a major earthquake will hit that city. (The word for "earthshaker" here is *ennosigée,* from the Greek word *ennosigaios,* a Homeric epithet for the god Poseidon, who was blamed for earthquakes.) Nostradamus commentator Erika Cheetham takes *tour* in its meaning of "tower" and suggests that this speaks of an attack on skyscrapers, which would make it a forecast of the attack on the World Trade Center.[39] As ingenious as this is (Cheetham made her interpretation many years before 9/11), the verse speaks clearly of earthquake and not aerial assault.

A more plausible interpretation connects the verse to Naples, whose original name, Neapolis, means "new city" in Greek. This verse would then predict a major earthquake for Naples, possibly an eruption of nearby Mount Vesuvius, which destroyed Pompeii and Herculaneum in 79 A.D. Naples is in an earthquake zone; major quakes have taken place in the vicinity in 1881, 1980, and 2002.

Nostradamus also predicts that this earthquake will affect Syracuse in Sicily, since Arethusa is the name given to a stream on the island in its harbor. The "reddening" would indicate that this disaster will cause much loss of life. The quatrain also evokes Sicily with its allusion to the "rocks" that "will make war." Nostradamus is probably thinking of the Wandering Rocks, which appear in book 12 of *The Odyssey,* and which were traditionally believed to lie off the coast of Sicily. According to the myth, the rocks clash together to smash approaching ships.

91.

Les dieux feront aux humains apparence,
Ce qu'ils seront auteurs du grand conflit:
Avant ciel veu serain espée & lance,
Que vers main gauche sera plus grand afflit.

The gods will make it appear to humans
That they are the authors of the great conflict.
Before, a serene sky seen, sword and lance;
Toward the left hand shall be the greatest harm.

A cryptic verse suggesting that portents in the sky will herald war (the planets were associated with the gods of classical antiquity). The meaning of "left hand" is not clear; viewed traditionally, from the point of view of an observer facing east, this would refer to the north.

Some commentators see in this quatrain another prophecy of modern aerial warfare, but in Nostradamus's time, it was generally assumed that momentous changes such as wars and dynastic upheavals would be heralded by portents and omens in the skies. Shakespeare's plays—for example, *Julius Caesar,* where "most horrid sights" portend Caesar's death—furnish ample evidence of this belief.

92.

Sous un la paix partout sera clamée,
Mais non longtemps pillé et rébellion,
Par refus ville, terre, et mer entamée,
Morts et captifs le tiers d'un million.

Under one, peace will be everywhere proclaimed,
But not long after, pillage and revolt;
By refusal, city, land, and sea broached,
Dead and captive, a third of a million.

This verse has inspired a number of interpretations. One involves Napoleon I, who proclaimed, *"L'Empire, c'est la paix"*—"The Empire is peace"—but whose reign was marked by continuous bloody warfare. Another view applies it to the Franco-Prussian War of 1870–71, begun when Prussia refused humiliating terms offered by Emperor Napoleon III, and whose French casualties were estimated at a third of a million. The Napoleon I thesis seems to fit marginally better, as France had to fight on both land and sea in those conflicts, whereas the Franco-Prussian War involved land battles alone.

Whatever merits and drawbacks these theories have, the underlying prophetic idea is clear: human rulers will proclaim peace, but will not be able to sustain it.

96.

Celuy qu'aura la charge de destruire
Temples, & sectes, changés par fantaisie,

Plus aux rochiers qu'aux vivans viendra nuire:
Par langue ornée d'oreilles ressaisies.

He who has charge to destroy
Temples and sects, changed by fantasy,
Will harm the rocks more than the living,
With ears captivated by ornate speech.

Nostradamus might be thinking of the Protestant Reformers here, since Protestant iconoclasm did a great deal of damage to statues and churches in his day, but comparatively little to human beings. Nostradamus could also be implying that this destroyer will look more dangerous than he is. By this interpretation, the "ornate speech" would allude to the Reformers' eloquence, as well as to their religious services, which focused much more upon preaching than upon ritual.

Century II

I.

Vers Aquitaine par insults Britanniques,
De par eux mesmes grandes incursions.
Pluies, gelées feront terroirs iniques,
Port Selyn fortes fera invasions.

Toward Aquitaine by British assaults,
By the same ones, great incursions.
Rains, frosts will make terrain uneven,
Port Selyn will launch powerful invasions.

In the Hundred Years' War of the fourteenth and fifteenth centuries, France had only with great difficulty managed to expel the English, who sought to make good on their Norman monarchs' dynastic claims on French territory. Aquitaine, in southwest France, was long an English domain. Nostradamus is predicting another English invasion, with Aquitaine as an objective. He is also forecasting a spate of bad weather (which was, as I have noted, a common feature of the Little Ice Age in the sixteenth century). "Port Selyn" most likely indicates the Ottoman Turks: the Sublime

Porte was the official name for the Ottoman court at Constantinople. "Selyn" is probably drawn from the Greek *selene,* or "moon," alluding to the Ottomans' crescent symbol.

In sum, Nostradamus is predicting invasions of France from both England and the Ottoman Empire. Unfortunately for his credibility, although many nations have invaded France since Nostradamus's time, neither England nor Turkey has been among them. While Britain and France warred in the eighteenth century and into the nineteenth, only briefly, at the end of the Napoleonic Wars, was the fighting ever carried onto French soil, and regaining Aquitaine was not a British objective.

2.

La teste bleue fera la teste blanche
Autant de mal que France a faict leur bien.
Mort à l'anthenne, grand pendu sus la branche,
Quand prins des siens le roy dira combien.

Blue head shall inflict on white head
As much harm as France has done them good.
Death on a yardarm, a great one hung on the branch;
When taken by his own, the king will say how much.

This is principally interesting because of the first line, which predicts conflicts between Muslim Sunnis (white turbans) and Shi'ites (blue turbans; cf. IX.73): Nostradamus himself would explicitly make these associations in his 1566 *Almanac.* It would be tempting to find here a prediction of conflicts between Sunnis and Shi'ites of our own time, but there is no real reason to see a modern reference when Nostradamus's own time witnesses so many of the same struggles. Turkey would spend the last quarter of the sixteenth century in a fanatical war against Persia.[40] The "blue heads"—that is, the Shi'ite Persians—would inflict as much harm on the Turks as the French had done them good. Nostradamus here is giving a veiled warning against French overtures to the Ottomans.

"Death on the yardarm"—*mort à l'anthenne*—is sometimes seen as a reference to the antennae of twentieth-century broadcasting. As ingenious as this is, it does not make the verse any clearer. What is striking is that it predicts that someone high-born will be hanged—an ignominious form of execution. The last line seems to indicate that a king will be taken prisoner by his own men and will beg them to set a price for his ransom.

3.

Pour la chaleur solaire sus la mer
De Negrepont les poissons demi cuits:
Les habitants les viendront entamer
Quand Rhod. et Gennes leur faudra le biscuit.

By the solar heat upon the sea
The fish of Negrepont half-cooked:
The inhabitants will come to take a bite
When Rhodes and Genoa lack their biscuit.

"Negrepont" has two possible meanings: the Venetian colony of Negroponte on the Greek peninsula of Euboea (or Evvoia); or the Black Sea, which is the literal meaning of "Negrepont." This quatrain seems to predict an extreme drought, which will dry up portions of the Mediterranean, causing great famine. It could, however, have a military reference, as "biscuit" in that era was used to refer to army rations. Those who prefer a modern reference could see in these lines a prophecy of global warming (cf. VI.5, VIII.16).

4.

Depuis Monech jusques auprès de Sicile
Toute la plage demourra desolé;
Il ny aura fauxbourg, cité, ne vile
Que par Barbares pillée soit & vollée.

From Monaco nearly to Sicily
The entire shore will remain desolate;

There will be no district, city, or town
But by barbarians pillaged and robbed.

Nostradamus is predicting widespread ravaging of the Mediterranean coast of France and Italy, presumably by the corsairs of North Africa, aided by the Turks (cf. I.9, V.23). The prophecy did not come true, at least not to the scale predicted: Turkish sea power would be broken by a Christian alliance among Spain, Venice, Genoa, and the Papal States at the crucial Battle of Lepanto in 1571, and in the following decades the Turks became a negligible threat in the western Mediterranean. Corsairs continued to harass shipping, but not on the scale foreseen here.

The underlying theme is more interesting than the actual prophecy, because its reference to "barbarian pillage" underscores one of the key concerns of Western prophecy and indeed of Western civilization: a fear, often unconscious, that the fall of the Roman Empire will happen again. This latent anxiety is no doubt part of the background for Nostradamus's predictions, here and elsewhere, that an Ottoman invasion of Europe was imminent. In a more specific sense, as we have seen, the fear was not totally misguided, given Turkish expansionism in that era. Even so, the invasion never took place.

8.

Temples sacrés prime façon Romaine
Rejeteront les goffes fondements,
Prenant leur loys premières & humaines,
Chassant, non tout, des saints les cultements.

Holy temples in the prime Roman fashion
Shall reject their base foundations,
Taking up their first human laws,
Driving away, but not entirely, the cults of the saints.

A prediction of ecclesiastical reform. Some take this to refer to the sect of French Calvinists known as the Huguenots; if so, like Nostradamus's letters to Lorenz Tubbe, this could suggest sympathy with the Protestants. On the other hand, Nostradamus implies that the cult of the saints, which was rejected entirely by the Protestant Reformers, needs to be purified rather than jettisoned. This quatrain points to a need, often stated even among Catholics of the time, to purify and reform the church.

10.

Avant long temps le tout sera rangé;
Nous espérons un siècle bien senestre:
L'estat des masques & des seulz bien changé
Peu trouveront qu'à son rang veuille estre.

Before long, everything shall be arranged;
We expect a century quite sinister:
The state of masks and solitaries shall be changed;
Few will find they want to be in their rank.

A prophecy of a time when the class structure of society is overturned. Some take the word "masks" to mean "courtesans"; others, to mean "courtiers." *Seulz*—"solitaries"—is generally taken to refer to monks or clergy.

Rangé—literally, "arranged"—in the first line is rather unclear; I suspect its meaning is closer to *dérangé*—"disordered." Pierre Brind'Amour suggests that it means "defeated" or "conquered," but I have translated it as it stands. Is Nostradamus, in a veiled way, trying to indicate that the class structure of society as he finds it is itself unjust and in need of rearrangement?

Most interpreters link this prophecy to the French Revolution of 1789, when the ranks of society were indeed overturned and it was far from advantageous to be a cleric or a member of the nobility. But the literal meaning of the verse would point to the seventeenth century, which, with its religious warfare and the continued erosion of the feudal social structure, was unsettled enough.

12.

Yeux clos, ouverts d'antique fantasie
L'habit des seulz seront mis à néant,
Le grand monarque chastiera leur frenesie:
Ravir des temples le tresor par devant.

Eyes shut, open to ancient fantasy,
The habit of solitaries shall be put to nothing.
The great monarch will chastise their frenzy,
To plunder temples' treasure out in front.

A verse that evokes the iconoclasm of the Protestant Reformers. In many areas, churches were plundered, statues destroyed, and treasure taken. In 1536, for example, Henry VIII of England had ordered the dissolution of the monasteries, scattering the monks and appropriating the lands of the abbeys. "Ancient fantasy" would mean the Protestant doctrines, which in the eyes of devout Catholics were merely revivals of heresies from times long past.

It is not clear whom Nostradamus means by "the great monarch." Possibly he means it will be incumbent upon Henri II or another king of France to punish this sacrilege. Or he could see it as the task of the coming universal monarch (cf. I.4) to right these wrongs. The grammar is ambiguous, however: the verb *ravir,* "to plunder," could also have "the great monarch" as its subject, meaning that it would be the monarch who did the plundering. As often in Nostradamus, it is just such ambiguities that give his commentators such wide license for interpretation. The main sense of the verse favors the rendering I have given above.

13.

Le corps sans ame plus n'estre en sacrifice:
Jour de la mort mis en nativité.
L'esprit divin fera l'ame felice
Voiant le Verbe en son eternité.

The soulless body no longer to be sacrificed,
Day of death brought to birth.
The divine spirit will make the soul glad,
Seeing the Word in his eternity.

Rather than speaking of world events, this verse seems to refer to the state of the righteous soul after death. At this point the body will no longer endure the "sacrifice" of mortal existence, and the soul will be born anew in heaven on the day of death. The Beatific Vision—"seeing the Word in his eternity"—will give joy to the soul.

19.

Nouveaux venuz, lieu basti sans défense
Occuper place par lors inhabitable.
Prez, maisons, champs, villes, prendre à plaisance,
Faim, peste, guerre, arpen long labourable.

Newcomers, place built without defense,
To occupy a space previously uninhabitable.
Nearby, houses, fields, towns to take at pleasure,
Hunger, plague, war, an acre long to work.

Nostradamus may be referring to the New World, which had been discovered less than a century before his time, and which offered such rich and easy prey for the conquerors. Everything in this quatrain fits the situation: the relative ease of occupation by the Europeans, their belief that it was previously uninhabited (although a large number of people had already been living there), and the accompanying war, disease, and hunger that were to vex both colonists and natives.

22.

Le camp Asop d'Eurotte partira
S'adjoignant proche de l'isle submergée:

D'Arton classe phalange pliera,
Nombril du monde plus grand voix subrogée.

The Asop faction shall leave Eurotas,
Reconvening near the submerged isle:
The fleet of Arton will fold its phalanx,
The greatest voice of the world's navel invoked.

One of the most fascinating aspects of studying Nostradamus is
the ingenious and often far-fetched interpretations that are made
of his verses. This quatrain provides a good example. It is almost
unfathomably obscure, and I cannot see any clear and comprehensible interpretation. *Eurotte* in the first line is often understood to
mean the Eurotas, a stream on whose banks the ancient Greek city
of Sparta was situated; "Europe" is a variant reading. "Asop" does
not mean anything in French; it is sometimes seen as deriving from
the Greek *askopos,* or "unfocused" (*Ascop* is a variant reading), but
most likely it refers to the Asopus, a river in Boeotia in central
Greece. As for the "submerged isle," the most plausible interpretation would place it in the Gulf of Corinth, where there was supposedly some submerged land, according to the ancient Roman
author Pliny the Elder.[41] Similarly, the last line would point to
Delphi, which the ancient Greeks regarded as the navel of the
world, and to which Nostradamus has already alluded in I.1. These
allusions point to some sort of military operation in Greece, which
in Nostradamus's time furnished a battleground for the Turks and
the Venetians.

Nostradamus commentator Erika Cheetham takes "Arton" as a
kind of anagram for NATO (plus a superfluous "R," presumably
to confuse us). The "submerged isle" would be Britain, on the as-
sumption that Nostradamus in IX.31 (an extremely murky verse
that I have omitted from this collection) is predicting that this
island will sink into the ocean. The "navel of the world" would be
Rome. Hence, this quatrain foreshadows a gathering of the NATO
fleet off Britain in a movement coordinated from Rome.

This is not an even remotely plausible interpretation of these lines, but it is worth noting because many uses of Nostradamus in the popular press rely on similarly wild leaps of imagination.

24.
Bestes farouches de faim fluves tranner:
Plus part du camp encontre Hister sera,
En caige de fer le grand fera treisner,
Quand Rin enfant Germain observera.

Maddened beasts to cross streams for hunger;
Most of the camp will be against Hister,
In a cage of iron the great one will have him dragged,
When the German child espies the Rhine.

This verse gives us our first glimpse of one of Nostradamus's most famous figures: Hister (cf. IV.68, V.29, VI.49). "Hister" is an antique name for the Danube River flowing through Austria, but many commentators have seized upon this as a premonition of Adolf Hitler, not only because of the similarity in the names but on the grounds that Hitler was born in a town on the Danube.

Unlike many attempts to fit Nostradamus into the Procrustean bed of recent events, this one actually bears some resemblance to historical fact. Indeed the greater part of the world eventually combined to fight Hitler, and the third line is sometimes taken to refer to his ally, the Italian dictator Benito Mussolini, who did end up in a cage after his fall from power. The last line would then allude to Hitler's march into the Rhineland in 1936, which set the stage for World War II. Another reading of this line goes, "*Quand rien enfant Germain observera*"—"when the German child sees nothing"—which would point to the obliviousness of the German people to Hitler's evil motives.

Nevertheless, the fit is not exact. Hitler was not born on the Danube. He was born in Braunau am Inn ("Braunau on the Inn"), which, as its name suggests, is on the River Inn, which is only a tributary of the Danube. A more likely interpretation would equate "Hister" with the Austria of Nostradamus's time, thus predicting a bloody engagement in which much of Europe is pitted against the Hapsburg monarchy. In fact, this happened during the Thirty Years' War (1619–1648). The first line would then reflect the incredible savagery and depredations of this conflict, from which it took Germany, the principal battleground, a hundred years to recuperate.

27.

Le divin verbe sera du ciel frappé,
Qui ne pourra proceder plus avant.
Du reserant le secret estoupé
Qu'on marchera par dessus & devant.

The divine Word will be struck from heaven,
Who will not be able to proceed further.
The secret of the revealer stopped,
So that one can walk above and ahead.

A prophecy of some secret that an unknown "revealer" will carry to the grave or to the dungeon—this being the idiomatic meaning of being where "one can walk above and ahead." Both Pierre Brind'Amour and Peter Lemesurier take the "divine Word" to be the Host in a monstrance, struck by lightning in a procession and thus an evil omen, but this hardly makes the verse any less obscure. *Reserant* is not a word in French; usually it is taken to be an adaptation of the Latin *reserare,* "to unlock" or "to reveal."

Taken more generally, this verse would seem to indicate a mystical secret that was about to be revealed but was stopped through some act of Providence. In this case, the last line would suggest that this took place as a result of official persecution—incarceration or death.

28.

Le penultime du surnom du prophète
Prendra Diane pour son jour & repos:
Loing vaguera par frénétique teste,
Et délivrant un grand peuple d'impos.

The next to last of the prophet's surname
Will take Diana for his day and rest;
He will wander far with his frenetic head,
And deliver a great people from tribute.

Most interpreters see this quatrain as a reference to some future messiah who will make Monday his sabbath (Diana being the goddess of the moon, and Monday being the day of the moon). "The next to last of the prophet's surname" is generally seen as referring to some descendant of the Prophet Muhammad or possibly even of Nostradamus himself. But none of these choices is particularly plausible.

The most likely figure in history to whom this quatrain could apply is Mani, the third-century Mesopotamian prophet who founded the religion known as Manichaeism. This faith has been extinct since the Middle Ages, but at one time it claimed followers stretching from China to North Africa. Influenced by Zoroastrianism, among other sources, Mani taught a profoundly dualistic vision of the universe: the world is a battleground between light and dark, and humanity was created as a means of liberating the sparks of light imprisoned in the darkness of matter.

One thing that might relate this verse to Mani is the detail about making Monday his sabbath. The Manichaean faithful were divided into two classes: common believers and the elect. The latter had to follow a more stringent code of conduct; moreover, they were to celebrate Monday as their sabbath, unlike the rank and file, who celebrated it on Sunday.

This interpretation would also explain the line saying this figure comes "next to last" in the line of the prophets. Mani lived in the third century A.D., after Christ but before Muhammad. By this view, Mani would be the next to last in the line of the great prophets. Moreover, driven by his "frenetic head," he did in fact travel far afield to spread his new faith. He was martyred by the king of Persia at the behest of the Zoroastrian priests, who did not want a new religion around.

This interpretation makes even more sense when we consider that Nostradamus could have read about the Manichaeans in the works of the Church Father Augustine, who had been a Manichaean himself for several years. Even so, several questions remain, such as: What people did Mani free from tribute? Why is this portrayed as happening in the future rather than in the past? I do not know the answers. The Cathars, a dualistic sect that flourished in medieval Provence but was wiped out by a Catholic crusade in the thirteenth century, showed many affinities with Manichaeism. Some authors claim the Cathars managed to survive underground for centuries after their official suppression.[42] If so, Nostradamus, who also lived in Provence, could have had contact with them and could have been favorably disposed toward them. But this idea remains extremely speculative.

As for the question of portraying the past as future, there is some evidence that Nostradamus viewed his prophecies as cyclic: the situations would recur as similar astrological configurations moved back into similar places, as we have seen in I.51, so it is possible that Nostradamus believed that a prophet like Mani would return at some point.

29.
L'oriental sortira de son siège,
Passer les monts Apennins, voir la Gaule:
Transpercera du ciel les eaux & neige;
Et un chascun frapera de sa gaule.

The oriental will depart from his seat,
To pass through the Apennine mountains, to see Gaul:

He will press through heaven's waters and snow;
And will beat each one with his rod.

Another prophecy of an invasion from the East. In this one, "the oriental"—presumably the Turks—will go overland through the Apennine mountains of Italy to reach Gaul. "Rod" in the last line—*gaule* in French—involves a play on *Gaule* or "Gaul." The prophecy is an odd one, since going over the Apennines is hardly the most expedient way to invade northern Italy or France, as the Allies found in World War II.

30.

Un qui les dieux d'Annibal infernaulx
Fera renaistre, effrayeur des humains:
Oncq' plus d'horreurs ne plus pire journaux
Qu'avint viendra par Babel aux Romains.

One who the infernal gods of Hannibal
Will resurrect, terror of humans:
No greater horrors will appear, journals,
Than what shall come to Rome from Babel.

The gist of this quatrain is clear: it has to do with the resurgence of sorcery. "The infernal gods of Hannibal" are the Phoenician gods of Carthage, which aroused particular horror among the Romans because they demanded human sacrifice. Chaldea, the legendary home of the Tower of Babel, was the reputed source of the "black arts" of magic and occultism. Pierre Brind'Amour plausibly amends *journaux,* "journals," to *fournaux,* "furnaces," which would then refer to the sacrificial furnaces of the Babylonians (Dan. 3:15–28).

Nostradamus would have made a clear distinction between the "white," or benign, occultism he probably practiced and the more malevolent forms he says will reappear. And when he speaks of "resurrecting" the gods of Carthage and Babylon, he does not mean a quaint worship of pagan gods as an aesthetic affectation—a trend popular among some Renaissance intellectuals—but of reviving demonic entities that had been put to slumber after centuries of Christian devotion. The early Christians did not regard the pagan gods as illusions; they considered them to be real demonic entities who had set themselves up to be worshipped in place of the true God. Such an idea seems to lie in the background here.

Nostradamus's prophecy of a resurgence of sorcery mirrors the concerns of his time. The medieval social structure was falling apart, living standards were in decline, and people grew eager to place the blame on unseen powers of spiritual wickedness, as well as on their earthly allies—witches and sorcerers. Consequently, the witch scare throughout Western Europe would reach its apogee between 1580 and 1630: the vast majority of witch trials took place in this era. Nostradamus, who died in 1566, was lucky to have missed the worst of it.

41.
La grand estoille par sept jours bruslera,
Nuée fera deux soleils apparoir:
Le gros mastin toute nuict hurlera,
Quand grand pontife changera de terroir.

The great star will burn for seven days,
Cloud will make two suns appear:
The heavy mastiff all the night will howl,
When a great pontiff changes his terrain.

Two things make this quatrain interesting. In the first place, as we have already seen, there is the theme of portents in the sky that herald major changes among the rulers of the human race. In the second place, there is the theme of the pope changing his territory. Nostradamus here must have in mind what has been called the "Babylonian exile" of the Papacy—the period in the fourteenth century, when, under duress from the kings of France, the Papacy relocated to Avignon. Nostradamus evidently believes something of the sort will happen again in the future. So far this has not taken place. The closest analogy in history is the appropriation of the Papal States—the territory in central Italy ruled directly by the Vatican—by the unified Kingdom of Italy in 1861. But this is not terribly exact, since this quatrain makes it sound as if the pope is moving rather than losing his domains.

46.

Après grand troche humain, plus grand s'apreste,
Le grand moteur les siècles renouvelle:
Pluie, sang, laict, famine, fer, & peste,
Au ciel veu feu, courant longue estincelle.

After great human suffering, a greater one approaches;
The great motor renews the centuries.
Rain, blood, milk, famine, iron, and plague;
Fire seen in the heavens, with a long trail of sparks.

The most striking aspect of this quatrain appears in the second line, which speaks of "the great motor" renewing the centuries (or ages). Nostradamus is stating a common theme in esoteric thought: that there is a cycle of ages, which is dictated by the movements of the planets. This would be the "great motor" of which he speaks. Here he is most likely speaking of the cycle of the moon, which, as we saw in I.48, was thought to have begun in 1533. The second line echoes a famous verse from Virgil: *Magnus ab integro saeclorum nascitur ordo,* "A great order of the ages is born anew." This comes from the Fourth Eclogue, a poem long believed to have foretold the coming of Christ. The last two lines reflect the idea that such climactic moments in world destiny are marked with portents and natural disturbances.

51.

Le sang du juste à Londres fera faute
Bruslés par foudres de vint trois le six.

La dame antique cherra de place haute,
De mesme secte seront plusieurs occis.

The blood of the just in London will be lacking,
Burned by lightning of twenty-three the six.
The ancient lady will fall from her high place,
Of the same sect many will be killed.

This quatrain alludes to religious strife in the England of Nostradamus's day. King Henry VIII had broken with Rome in 1534, but upon the death of his son, Edward VI, in 1553, Henry's daughter Mary ascended the throne and tried to restore Catholicism in England. Her measures were sanguinary, involving intense persecution of Protestants (as suggested by the last line), and she came to be known as "Bloody Mary." But, as Nostradamus suggests in the third line, her efforts came to nothing. She married King Philip II of Spain in 1554, creating a dynastic bond to a major Catholic power, but she died in 1558, to be succeeded by her sister, Elizabeth I, who finally established England as a Protestant nation.

It may seem peculiar that the Catholic Nostradamus should speak so negatively of a Catholic monarch, but in the struggle over the balance of power in Europe, the French found that a Catholic England linked with France's enemy Spain posed more of a threat to French security than would an independent Protestant nation.

Some commentators see in this verse a prediction of the Great Fire of London of 1666, citing the numbers in the second line as evidence. But they have to go through strange mathematical contortions to turn the cryptic number given here—"twenty-three the six"—into 1666.

62.

Mabus puis tost alors mourra, viendra
De gens & bestes une horrible defaite:
Puis tout à coup la vengeance on verra
Cent, main, soif, faim, quand courra la comète.

Mabus then soon will die; there will come
Of man and beast a horrible defeat.
Then suddenly one will see vengeance,
Hundred, hand, thirst, hunger, when the comet runs.

The name "Mabus" is a pseudonym for which no plausible identity has been suggested; like "Alus" in VI.33, he is sometimes viewed as a cryptic Antichrist in times to come. John Hogue has said that he has received many letters asking whether Mabus could be Saddam Hussein, although any attempt at trying to find an anagram for "Saddam" in "Mabus" is clearly far-fetched. Peter Lemesurier sees in this verse a historical connection: the death of a Flemish painter, Jan Gossaert de Mabuse, in 1532, accompanied by a sighting of what later became known as Halley's Comet. Nonetheless, given that this is a book of prophecies, it is hard to see why Nostradamus would have brought up a past event, or why he would have given such emphasis to the death of an artist: his *Prophecies* focus on nations and monarchs.

I have no better suggestion myself, but it occurs to me to wonder whether this mysterious reference in Nostradamus may have inspired the name of a fictional character—Dr. Mabuse, the evil mesmerist portrayed in the 1922 film *Dr. Mabuse, der Spieler* ("Dr. Mabuse, the Gambler"), along with two sequels, by the German director Fritz Lang.

68.

De l'Aquilon les effors seront grands:
Sus l'Océan sera la porte ouverte,
Le regne en l'isle sera reintegrand:
Tremblera Londres par voile descouverte.

From the North the efforts will be great:
On the ocean will the door be open,
The kingdom on the isle shall be reinstated:
London will tremble when the sail is spied.

This verse is remarkable in that it more accurately reflects a future event than anything Nostradamus might have seen in the immediate present. When he wrote this, England was not under threat from abroad: as we have seen, it was peacefully joined to Spain through the marriage of the nations' two monarchs.

The event that best fits this prophecy is the attempted invasion of England by the Spanish Armada in 1588, more than thirty years after this verse was written. In this case, the third line would refer to the Spaniards' attempt to reinstate a Catholic monarchy in England. Certainly there was tremendous apprehension in London at the coming of the armada.

In terms of the final outcome, however, the prophecy does not seem quite so accurate. The third line of this quatrain seems to point to the success of the venture, but violent storms and the attacks of the English navy turned the expedition into a disaster.

75.
La voix ouye de l'insolit oyseau,
Sur le canon du respiral estage.
Si hault viendra du froment le boisseau,
Que l'homme d'homme sera Anthropophage.

The voice of the unaccustomed bird is heard
On the pipe of the air-vent floor.
A bushel of grain will go so high,
That man of man shall be a cannibal.

A prediction of famine. The first line of this quatrain probably refers to the appearance of unusual birds as omens of disaster, but I suspect the "unaccustomed bird" may be a vulture. Commentators have found the second line utterly baffling; I give a reasonably literal translation. Peter Lemesurier translates it as "on the stern law-book and the winding stair," while Pierre Brind'Amour renders it as "on the chimney-flue," which should give some idea of how mutable translations of Nostradamus can be in some instances.

As I have noted earlier, famine was such a persistent visitor to the Europe of those ages that this prophecy is not going far out on a limb. It also seems to echo Revelation 6:5–6, where famine, the Third Horseman of the Apocalypse, appears while an unseen voice says, "A measure of wheat for a penny."

79.
La barbe crespe & noire par engin
Subjuguera la gent cruele & fière.
Le grand CHYREN *ostera du longin*
Tous les captifs par Seline banière.

The beard, curly and black, by ruse
Will subjugate the race cruel and proud.
The great CHYREN will remove from afar
All the captives of Seline's banner.

The key to this quatrain lies in the identity of "the great CHYREN." Like "Mabus," it is a pseudonym, but commentators on Nostradamus generally agree that it refers to Henri II, king of France at the time these verses were written. CHYREN is an anagram for HENRYC, an archaic form of "Henri." The first line also fits him, since he had a curly black beard.

This verse predicts that Henri II, through some stratagem, will liberate Christian slaves held by the Ottoman Turks: "Seline" or "Selyn," as we have seen in II.1, is most likely a reference to the Turks. Curiously, however, in IV.77, VI.27, "Chyren" and "Selin" seem to be the same person—again Henri II.

It makes sense that Nostradamus would predict a moment of glory for the reigning monarch—such praises were commonplace, expedient, and expected in Nostradamus's era. Unfortunately, Henri II did not fulfill the prophecy. That honor would fall to Don John of Austria, commander of the allied forces at the Battle of Lepanto in 1571, in which some 12,000 to 15,000 Christian galley slaves would be freed. It might be tempting to see a reference to

Don John in this verse, but unlike Henri, he did not have a black, curly beard: the portraits of Don John that I have seen show him with a mustache and a dashing, though rather diminutive, goatee.

81.

Par feu du ciel la cité presque aduste:
L'Urne menasse encore Deucalion:
Vexée Sardaigne par la Punique fuste
Après que Libra lairra son Phaëton.

By fire from heaven the city nearly burned:
The Urn threatens another Deucalion:
Sardinia vexed by the Punic fleet
After Libra has let Phaëton depart.

This disjointed quatrain combines a number of themes. The most obvious is in the third line, which predicts that Sardinia will be harassed by North African corsairs—who were, as we have seen, a constant fixture in the Mediterranean in those days. The fourth line would mean that the danger of such attacks would increase after the sun (presumably "Phaëton," the son of the sun god Helios) has left Libra, which happens each year around October 21.

By another interpretation, Libra stands for Austria (said to be ruled by that sign of the zodiac), and Phaëton represents Philip II of Spain, who had this god for his emblem. If so, Nostradamus might be predicting that Philip II will not rule Austria, though it was part of the domains of his father, Emperor Charles V. In that case, Nostradamus would have prophesied correctly. In 1556, the year after this was published, Charles divided his inheritance, and Philip II would rule Spain only.

The second line suggests that Aquarius (here called "the Urn") will cause another flood: Deucalion was the equivalent of Noah in Greek mythology. What planet or planets will appear in Aquarius to produce this result? The verse does not say. A speculative guess might see in it some connection to the Age of Aquarius, whose beginning has been set at dates ranging from the sixteenth to the twenty-sixth century. If so, here again Nostradamus is predicting major cataclysms as a prelude to a new age.

But by far the most interesting part of this quatrain is the first line, with its reference to "fire from heaven." This anomalous occurrence is predicted often in prophecies of Nostradamus's time, usually as an indication of divine wrath. The idea goes back to Genesis 19:24, which says, "The Lord rained upon Sodom and upon Gomorrah brimstone and fire." The modern reader, however, cannot avoid wondering whether this line presages the aerial bombardment of today's warfare. The most rigorous view would say there is no connection—that Nostradamus is taking a figure of speech from the prophecies he himself knew—and this is probably the case. But the presence of such images suggests why people still find meaning and power in his predictions.

91.

Soleil levant un grand feu lon verra,
Bruit & clarté vers Aquilon tendant:
Dedans le rond mort & cris lont orra,
Par glaive, feu, faim, mort les attendant.

Sun rising, one will see a great fire,
Noise and glare turning toward the north:
Within the circle one will hear death and cries,
By sword, fire, hunger, death waiting for them.

Like the previous quatrain, this one shows why Nostradamus remains so popular. No modern reader can look at these lines without thinking of the nuclear attack on Hiroshima and Nagasaki in 1945. Whatever Nostradamus may have been thinking or seeing when he composed these lines (some sources refer to omens of 91 B.C., which augured the start of the Social War between Rome and its erstwhile allies in Italy), they do seem to fit the horrors of our age better than those of his own.

92.

Feu couleur d'or du ciel en terre veu:
Frappé du hault nay, fait cas merveilleuz:
Grand meurtre humain: prins du grand le nepveu,
Morts d'expectacles eschappé l'orgueilleux.

Fire the color of gold from heaven seen on earth;
The high-born one struck, a wondrous thing:
Great human slaughter; the nephew of the great one taken;
Spectacular deaths, the proud one escaped.

Although the first line of this verse reiterates the theme of fire from heaven that we have already seen in II.81 (and possibly II.91), most interpreters apply it to the fall of the French emperor Napoleon III in September 1870. Napoleon had provoked Prussia to war, expecting an easy victory, but the Prussians inflicted a disastrous defeat on the French.

The link between this verse and Napoleon III is found in the last two lines. Napoleon III was the nephew of Napoleon I. When he realized the war was lost, he wandered onto the battlefield, hoping he would be struck by a bullet, but without success: he was captured in the general capitulation in September 1870. Thus the "proud one" escaped the "great human slaughter" inflicted on so many of his subjects.

Century III

I.

Après combat & bataille navale,
Le grand Neptune à son plus haut befroy:
Rouge aversaire de fraieur viendra pasle
Mettant le grand Océan en effroy.

After combat and naval battle,
The great Neptune in his highest belfry:
Red adversary will become pale with fear,
Putting the great ocean in affright.

Many candidates for "the great Neptune" have been suggested: the Turkish navy; Baron de la Garde, commander of the French Eastern Mediterranean fleet; even Admiral Nelson at the battle of Trafalgar.

More plausibly, the "red adversary" mentioned in the third line could refer to Barbarossa, or "Redbeard," among the most dreaded of the North African corsairs, who, in alliance with the Turks, dominated the western Mediterranean in the 1530s and '40s. Barbarossa himself had died in 1546, but the name could serve to

represent corsairs in general. In fact, their depredations reached a
height in the 1550s, when Nostradamus was writing.

If this interpretation is true, Nostradamus would be predicting
that the power of the corsairs would be broken, as it was by the
Spaniards and their allies at Lepanto (cf. II.4; V.23); the "great
Neptune" would then be the Spanish commander or even the fleet
as a whole. What is curious about Nostradamus's prophecies relating to the Mediterranean world is that he seems more sympathetic
to the Spaniards than to the Turks, which makes sense in terms of
his religion but not his nationality: France and the Ottomans were
generally allied during this period.

2.

Le divin verbe donrra à la sustance
Comprins ciel, terre, or occult au laict mystique:
Corps, ame, esprit aiant toute puissance,
Tant sous ses pieds, comme au siege Celique.

The divine Word will give to substance—
Including heaven, earth, occult gold in the mystical milk—
Body, soul, spirit all-powerful,
As much under its feet as at the heavenly seat.

A compressed description of some of the central teachings of esotericism. On the one hand, there is mind, or pure consciousness—also
known as the "Word," "heaven," or "gold." On the other hand, there
are the *contents* of consciousness—what consciousness experiences,
whether it is seen as external or internal. This is known esoterically as
"substance," "earth," and even "mystical milk."

Out of the interaction of this primordial pair come the three
principal levels of existence: spirit, soul, and body, which form the
tripartite structure of human nature as seen by esoteric Christianity. In the last line, Nostradamus is saying that this interaction
between "heaven" and "earth" takes place everywhere, from the
lowest levels of existence to the most rarefied.[43]

Like many esoteric formulations, this verse is reasonably clear if one understands the conceptual framework and the symbolism behind it; if not, it is almost impenetrable.

13.
Par fouldre en l'arche or & argent fondu:
Des deux captifs l'un l'autre mangera.
De la cité le plus grand estendu,
Quand submergée la classe nagera.

By lightning in the casque, gold and silver melted:
Of two captives, one eats the other.
The greatest one in the city spread out,
When the fleet swims undersea.

Peter Lemesurier points out that this mystifying quatrain echoes several prophecies and omens reported to surround the death of Lorenzo de' Medici of Florence in 1492, including lightning that melted silver and gold shut up in a box; two captive lions fighting with each other in their den; and the sinking of the Neapolitan fleet two years later. By this interpretation, Nostradamus is saying that at some point another leading figure in some unidentified city will have his death foreshadowed by these signs.

However this may be (and overall it does not make these lines much less baffling), the quatrain is chiefly interesting for the last line, which seems to prefigure submarines: after all, Nostradamus is not saying the fleet will sink, but that it will *swim* undersea. In this case, as John Hogue suggests, the first two lines would be an obscure description of the nuclear reaction that powers modern submarines. The idea is that Nostradamus would have seen these mechanisms in a vision but would have had difficulty describing them in the language and concepts of his day. Again, these images seem much clearer in our own day than they may have been in his, and help explain his reputation for prescience.

20.

Par les contrées du grand fleuve Bethique
Loing d'Ibère, au regne de Granade:
Croix repoussées par gens Mahumetiques
Un de Cordobe trahira la contrade.

By the lands of the great river Guadalquivir
Far from the Ebro, in the realm of Granada:
Crosses repulsed by Mohammedan folk;
One from Córdoba will betray the country.

This verse can actually be taken as a successful prediction of a historical event: the revolt of the Moriscos of Spain in 1568. The Moriscos were the descendants of the Moorish conquerors of Spain. After Spain was reconquered by the Catholic Spaniards—which was completed in 1492—the Moors found themselves in a precarious position. They were more or less forced to convert to Catholicism, and many did: they came to be called Moriscos. A number of them continued to practice Islam in secret. They were suspected (probably with some justice) of scheming to help the Turks land on the Spanish coast.

In the first half of the sixteenth century, the Moriscos were treated with reasonable toleration, but in 1566 more stringent measures were enforced upon them, provoking them to revolt two years later. The insurrection lasted for several years, and was finally put down by troops under the command of Don John of Austria, whom we have already met as the victor of Lepanto (cf. II.79). In 1609, King Philip III expelled the Moriscos from Spain completely. Like the expulsion of the Jews in 1492, this would accelerate Spain's decline by depriving her of some of her most intelligent and enterprising citizens.

23.

Si France passes outre mer lysgustique,
Tu te verras en isles & mers enclos:

Mahommet contraire: plus mer Hadriatique:
Chevaulx & d'asnes tu rougeras les os.

If, France, you pass beyond the Ligurian Sea,
You will see yourself hemmed in by isles and seas;
Muhammad contrary: also the Adriatic Sea:
Of horses and asses you will redden the bones.

In this quatrain, Nostradamus advises France not to expand beyond the Ligurian Sea. In all likelihood it refers to the French attempt in 1553 to conquer Corsica, then ruled by Genoa. The French initially met with swift success, only to meet a counterattack from the Genoese and the imperial Hapsburg forces a year or so later. By 1555, when Nostradamus was writing these prophecies, the Genoese had more or less reconquered the entire island. The French would not gain final possession of it until 1768, when the Genoese ceded Corsica to France in repayment of a debt.

In the last line, I have kept the reading of the first edition: *rougeras,* "you will redden." Some editors have suggested that this is a typographical error for *rongeras,* "you will gnaw," and this is a likely conjecture. The line would then read, "Of horses and asses you will gnaw the bones," referring to starvation among the soldiery.

28.

De terre foible & pauvre parentele,
Par bout & paix parviendra dans l'Empire:
Long temps regner une jeune femele,
Qu'onq en regne n'en survint un pire.

From a weak land and poor parentage,
By end and peace she will succeed in the Empire:
A long time to reign, a young female;
Never lived one worse in the realm.

This has been widely seen as prophesying the accession of Elizabeth I to the English throne in 1558. England was a comparatively weak country at that time, but Elizabeth's parentage was not exactly poor: she was the daughter of Henry VIII, though commentators argue that Nostradamus is alluding to the comparatively lowly origins of her mother, Anne Boleyn. In this case, the damning fourth line would refer to the fact that Elizabeth established Protestantism as the official religion of her country.

As often happens with Nostradamus, this prophecy does not fit its favorite candidate all that well. One might just as well apply it to Catherine the Great of Russia, whose origins were much humbler than Elizabeth's, and who actually did rule an empire (the British Empire did not yet exist in Elizabeth's time). But this possibility too is wrecked by the last line: like Elizabeth, Catherine was not one of the worst rulers of her country, but among the best.

Another guess might relate this verse to Alexandra, the last empress of Russia, who acceded to the throne in 1894, at the age of twenty-two. Although she was the granddaughter of Queen Victoria, she came from the insignificant German state of Hesse-Darmstadt. She came to be the power behind her ineffectual husband, Tsar Nicholas II, and in 1915–17, during World War I, Alexandra was to all intents ruler of the country, guided by the sinister healer Gregory Rasputin. Alexandra's mishandling of the government at an extremely precarious time destroyed the Russian monarchy, so she could arguably be called one of the worst rulers Russia ever had—at least up to that point.

31.

Aux champs de Mède, d'Arabe, & d'Arménie
Deux grands copies trois foys s'assembleront:
Près du rivage d'Araxes la mesnie
Du grand Solman en terre tomberont.

On the fields of Media, Arabia, and Armenia
Two great forces three times shall meet:

Near the banks of Araxes the household
Of great Solman shall fall to earth.

Nostradamus probably has in mind the wars between Persia and
the Ottoman Turks, which were waged off and on throughout much
of the sixteenth century. He is predicting three clashes that will
bring down the Ottoman dynasty ("the household of great Solman,"
that is, the sultan Suleiman the Magnificent). These did not happen. If he was predicting the downfall of the Ottomans as a result
of their wars with Persia, he was wrong.

One is then tempted to go forward to the time when the Ottoman Empire actually *did* fall: in the wake of World War I, in
which the Turks fought on the side of Germany. One might be
tempted to try to adapt the prophecy to that situation. But here,
too, the facts do not fit the prophecy particularly well. There was
some warfare between the Russians and the Turks in Armenia, and
the Russians generally got the better of the contest. But the real
downfall of the Ottomans came with a British assault from Egypt,
aided by Palestinian Arabs working with T. E. Lawrence, or Lawrence of Arabia. Media—now Kurdistan—and Arabia did not
figure prominently as battlegrounds. We are then left with the more
obvious conclusion: that Nostradamus was incorrectly predicting
that the Persians would destroy the Turks.

32.

Le grand sepulchre du peuple Aquitanique,
S'approchera auprès de la Tousquane:
Quand Mars sera près du coing Germanique,
Et au terroir de la gent Mantuane.

The great sepulchre of the Aquitanian people
Will approach from the direction of Tuscany,
When Mars is near the German corner,
And in the terrain of the Mantuan folk.

This quatrain is sometimes taken as a prophecy of World War II, because the primary threats to the French (here called Aquitanians by synecdoche, that is, naming a part for a whole) come from Italy and Germany. But these were the exact threats in Nostradamus's own day, when the Hapsburgs held Germany and when Italy was mostly hostile to the French.

35.
Du plus profond de l'Occident d'Europe
De pauvres gens un jeune enfant naistra,
Qui par sa langue seduira grande troupe:
Son bruit au règne d'Orient plus croistra.

From the deepest part of Western Europe
Some poor people will give birth to a young child,
Who with his tongue will seduce a great crowd:
His sound will spread to the kingdom of the East.

This prediction is so general that it could refer to a whole host of figures. Hitler and Napoleon are favored contenders. Edgar Leoni observes that it could be applied to Francis Xavier, the Jesuit missionary who converted thousands of Asians to Christianity, had he not died in 1552. Pierre Brind'Amour and Peter Lemesurier, however, point out that Nostradamus uses the term "the deepest part of Western Europe" to mean the British Isles (cf. V.34), which would rule out any of the figures above.

Bruit—"sound"—no doubt figuratively means "renown." If one is looking for modern candidates, one may take it totally literally and think of someone in the entertainment business. It is curious that these lines apply more exactly to British singers such as Paul McCartney or Elton John, who have innumerable fans in Asia, than they do to Hitler or Napoleon.

44.
Quand l'animal à l'homme domestique
Après grans peines & sautes viendra parler:

Le fouldre à vierge sera si maleficque,
De terre prinse & suspendue en l'air.

When the animal domesticated by man
After great pains and leaps comes to speak,
The lightning to the virgin will be so harmful,
Taken from the ground, and hung up in the air.

There are two chief schools of thought on this quatrain. The more cautious, such as Peter Lemesurier, point to the numerous legends of talking animals and miraculous bolts of lightning that filled the books of portents of Nostradamus's day. Presumably Nostradamus would be simply executing a variation on these.

The more daring approach, exemplified by Erika Cheetham and John Hogue, sees in this a prophecy of modern broadcast media. The talking domestic animal would be Nostradamus's way of describing a radio or a television. In the third line, *vierge* would not be read in its obvious sense—"virgin"—but as a derivation of the Latin *virga*, "rod"—that is, an antenna. The third line would then read something like, "The lightning in the rod, so malefic," presumably alluding to the quasi-diabolical power of this device.

As so often happens with these quatrains, the meaning seems to shift back and forth from something relatively ordinary to something quite extraordinary. Here lies part of Nostradamus's genius. He is not a great poet in the conventional sense, but in his strange way he has managed to combine bizarre and incongruous details and fashioned them into a portal onto another reality. It would be a bit much to say that Nostradamus foresaw modern broadcasting, but when one looks at a quatrain like this, one wonders what he really did see.

55.
En l'an qu'un oeil en France regnera,
La court sera à un bien fascheux trouble:

Le grand de Bloys son ami tuera:
Le regne mis en mal & doute double.

In the year when one eye in France shall reign,
The court will be in a most aggravating trouble:
The great one of Blois his friend will kill:
The kingdom placed in evil and double doubt.

This quatrain is noteworthy because Nostradamus, in his *Prognostication* for 1562, claims that in it he predicted the death of Henri II in the joust in which a splinter from his opponent's lance pierced his eye (cf. I.35).

The last two lines could also conceivably refer to Henri's son Henri III, who had the second Duc de Guise stabbed to death in the Château de Blois in 1563. The Duc de Guise, a fervent Catholic, had violently opposed the policy of toleration espoused by Henri III and Catherine de' Medici, the queen mother. The duke's murder was not the first act of religiously inspired assassination in the France of that era, and unfortunately it was far from the last: religious warfare between Catholics and Protestants would tear the nation apart for the next generation.

57.

Sept fois changer verrez gent Britannique
Taintz en sang en deux cent nonante an:
Franche non point par apui Germanique.
Aries doute son pole Bastarnan.

Seven times you will see the Britannic nation change,
Steeped in blood in two hundred and ninety years:
Free not at all, by German support.
Aries doubts its Bastarnian pole.

Various commentators have attempted to fit this quatrain into British history. Two hundred and ninety years from the writing of this verse, which was published in 1555, would bring us to 1845—the early Victorian era, a time of peace and prosperity for the "Britannic nation." It is extremely difficult to make this verse fit into any obvious historical pattern. In 1649, slightly less than a hundred years after Nostradamus wrote these lines, the British people would depose and behead King Charles I; in the Glorious Revolution of 1692, the Catholic King James II would be deposed in favor of the Protestant William of Orange; but since then, transitions of government in Britain have been models of decorum in comparison to practically all of human history.

The third line is sometimes translated "France not at all, by German support." *Franche* would in this case mean "France" and not "free," although I have chosen the more literal rendition. In the fourth line, "Bastarnian" is an obscure adjective applying to Poland, reinforced by the punning reference to "pole" ("Poland" in French is *Pologne,* so the pun still works, although not so neatly as in English). The constellation Aries is usually taken as a reference to a nation that it rules: Poland is among them. The line probably means that the Poles will have some trouble from the Turks to the south. Since there was constant pressure on Poland from the Turks in Hungary at this time, the prophecy is not a terribly bold one.

This quatrain was one of several that the Nazis used for propaganda during World War II. The pro-Axis volume *What Will Happen in the Near Future?,* written by the pseudonymous Norab, claims that the 290 years are to be counted from the beheading of Charles I in 1649 (allegedly the first of these changes), which would bring us to 1939, "a critical year for England."[44] For Norab's quite predictable—but quite incorrect—forecast of the outcome, we shall look at the next quatrain.

58.

Aupres du Rin des montaignes Noriques
Nastra un grand de gents trop tard venu,

Qui defendra saurome & Pannoniques,
Qu'on ne saura qu'il sera devenu.

Near the Rhine of the mountains of Noricum,
Will be born a great one of a race come too late,
Who will defend SAUROMES and Pannonia;
Such that one will not know what will become of him.

Nostradamus often uses antique names for nations and regions. Noricum was a province of the Roman Empire that roughly coincides with today's Austria: Pannonia, a neighboring province, occupied parts of what is today Hungary, Slovenia, and Croatia (cf. V.13, IX.28, 90). SAUROMES (capitalized in the original) is not as clear; usually it is taken to refer to Sarmatia, an ancient region in what is now the Ukraine. In Nostradamus's time it was part of the Polish-Lithuanian commonwealth.

Presumably, then, this great man is to be born in the Alps, near the headlands of the Rhine. He will defend Hungary and Poland from the onslaughts, most likely, of the Turks. Nostradamus is thinking of a hero who will come out of the Hapsburg domains and will save the region from the Turks.

What is peculiar about this quatrain is that it is sometimes read as a prophecy of Hitler, who was born in the Austrian Alps. But his fate is clearly known (despite speculations about his survival and attempts to locate him in South America and elsewhere), and to say that he "defended" Poland and Hungary is a grotesque misreading of history, unless one takes the French *défendre* in its meaning of "prohibit," in which case the reading becomes more plausible—but only barely.

The pro-Nazi propagandist Norab takes the last line as predicting "the Führer's amazing rise to power which even the German people hardly thought possible before 1939."[45] Norab then refers to X.31, which says that "the holy scepter will come to Germany," to predict an Axis victory. If this is what Nostradamus foresaw, it is just as well that he was wrong.

61.

La grand band & secte crucigère
Se dressera en Mesopotamie:
Du proche fleuve compagnie legiere,
Que telle loy tiendra pour ennemie.

The great band and sect bearing the cross
Will rise up in Mesopotamia:
From the near river, light company,
Which will hold such a law as an enemy.

Nostradamus himself was probably foreseeing a new crusade that
would take Mesopotamia from the Turks, which did not happen.
Nevertheless, it is interesting to contemplate this quatrain in the
light of current events. The "great band and sect wearing the cross"
could be construed as the U.S. Army, sent to liberate Iraq at the
behest of the militantly Christian George W. Bush. Given this
reading, the third line is not particularly clear, but the fourth line
would suggest that the Iraqi people would regard the American-
imposed order as inimical—a plausible interpretation as of this
writing in the summer of 2005.

65.

Quand le sepulcre du grand Romain trouvé,
Le jour apres sera esleu pontife:
Du senat gueres il ne sera prouvé:
Empoisonnné son sang au sacré scyphe.

When the great Roman's sepulchre is found,
The next day he will be elected pontiff.
By the Senate he will hardly be approved,
His blood poisoned in the sacred chalice.

The most plausible suggestion for this quatrain is Peter Lemesurier's. He suggests that it echoes the year 1521, in which it was believed

that the tomb of Caesar Augustus had been discovered in Rome. Pope Leo X died the same year, allegedly poisoned, having been bled into the chalice used for collecting votes for new popes. Like many of Lemesurier's suggestions, this is quite persuasive as a likely source, but does not suggest what Nostradamus would have had in mind for the future.

John Hogue sees in this a prophecy of the year 1978, in which, he says, some Italian archaeologists claimed to have found the tomb of St. Peter. In that year, Pope John Paul I was elected and served as pope for only a month. Some have speculated that he was poisoned for being insufficiently faithful to the interests of the Vatican power structure.

I personally suspect that this quatrain is intended to echo the prophecies of St. Malachy, a twelfth-century Irish bishop who created (or allegedly created) a prophetic list of popes from his own time to our own. (Benedict XVI is the next to last by the numbering of this list.) Of the last pope, Malachy writes: "In extreme persecution, the seat of the Holy Roman Church will be held by Peter the Roman, who will feed his sheep through many tribulations. When this has been done, the city of seven hills will be destroyed, and the terrible Judge will judge his people."

By this interpretation, Nostradamus would be saying that when the tomb of Peter (arguably the "great Roman") is found, another Pope Peter will be elected, without the approbation of the College of Cardinals. He will be poisoned soon afterward.

66.

Le grand baillif d'Orléans mis à mort
Sera par un de sang vindicatif:
De mort merite ne mourra, ne par sort:
Des pieds & mains mal le faisoit captif.

The great bailiff of Orléans sent to death
Shall be by one of vengeful blood.

He will die a death neither merited nor by chance:
Hands and feet badly made him captive.

Edgar Leoni suggests that this refers to one Jérôme Groslot, bailiff of Orléans, who would be condemned for opening the gates of the city to the Protestants in 1562, during the civil wars of religion that were tearing France apart. Groslot would be condemned by the Inquisition in 1569, but would manage to escape.

A more intriguing possibility is suggested by John Hogue. He refers it to the Duc d'Orléans, cousin to King Louis XVI, who took the side of the people during the French Revolution, even going so far as to style himself "Philippe Égalité"—"Philip Equality." Sitting on the revolutionary tribunal, he cast a vote for his kinsman's execution, only to perish himself later in the Reign of Terror. Thomas Carlyle's *French Revolution* draws a memorable portrait of Philippe Égalité as he faced death: eating a meal of "oysters, two cutlets, and the best part of an excellent bottle of claret" and dressing himself elegantly in a green frock coat. But this would seem to give the lie to the harsh captivity suggested by the last line.

67.

Une nouvele secte de Philosophes
Méprisant mort, or, honneurs & richesses,
Des monts Germains ne seront limitrophes:
À les ensuivre auront apui & presses.

A new sect of philosophers,
Despising death, gold, honors, riches,
They will not be limited to the German mountains:
To follow them they will have support and crowds.

This quatrain is usually understood as referring to the Anabaptists, a radical Protestant sect that arose in sixteenth-century Germany, but this is hardly plausible. Nostradamus would not refer to the Anabaptists as "philosophers"—a term that indicated the highest amount of respect, not only for learning, but for spiritual advancement. The Anabaptists were freewheeling, quasi-anarchic upstarts who were unlikely candidates for the admiration of a Nostradamus. Quatrain III.76 immediately below suggests how he would describe the Anabaptists.

More likely Nostradamus had in mind a sect of mystical adepts of the sort described by the Rosicrucian manifestos that were published around 1615, and whom he may already have mentioned in I.25. According to one of these tracts, the *Fama fraternitatis,* or "Rumor of the Brotherhood," the Rosicrucians had no other profession "than to cure the sick, gratis." This certainly jibes with the contempt for gold that Nostradamus mentions here. Moreover, the manifestos speak of the Rosicrucians as forming in Germany. Once their existence was publicized, a large number of savants tried to make contact with them—to no avail, as far as anyone knows.

Whether or not Nostradamus had any connection with the movement that later developed into Rosicrucianism, he probably had in mind here the ideal of the philosophic sage that was held in such high esteem in the Renaissance. Arguably he was predicting that a sect of such philosophers would make itself known in Germany and would attract a wide number of followers—as indeed happened in the next century.

76.

En Germanie naistront diverses sectes,
S'approchans fort de l'heureux paganisme.
Le cueur captifs & petits receptes,
Feront retour à payer le vray disme.

In Germany will be born diverse sects,
Closely approaching happy paganism.
Captive hearts and small income,
They will return to paying the true tithe.

This quatrain comes closer than does III.67 to a description of the Anabaptists and other radical Protestant sects of the Reformation. The religious upheavals of the day produced all sorts of groups, including some that were genuinely antinomian—dispensing with moral rules and codes, especially those pertaining to sexuality. This would, then, be the likely meaning of a return to "happy paganism." The third line suggests that these sectarians will come from the lower orders of society; the fourth, that eventually they will make their way back to paying the "true tithe"—that is, submitting to the Catholic Church.

89.

En ce temps là sera frustré Cypres
De son secours, de ceux de mer Égée:
Vieux trucidés: mais par masles & lyphres
Seduict leur roy, royne plus outragée.

In that time Cyprus shall be deprived
Of her aid by those of the Aegean Sea:
Old ones slaughtered; but by males and debauchees
Seduced their king, queen more outraged.

The first two lines are reasonably clear, and reasonably prophetic: in 1570 the Turks would invade Cyprus, then controlled by the Venetian Republic. The Venetians sent a fleet to rescue the defenders, but when it arrived in September of that year, the Turks already held the whole island, and the Venetian fleet sailed home without offering combat. "Those of the Aegean Sea" would in this case be the Turkish fleet.

The last two lines are much murkier; as often happens in Nostradamus, a small fragment of a prophecy appears meaningful and prescient, while the rest of it remains garbled and unclear. The "king" and "queen" would presumably refer to Cyprus—but Cyprus did not have a king at that point, being ruled by the Venetians. The translation of *lyphres* is totally speculative: *lyphre* is not a word in either French, Latin, or Greek. It has been translated as "debauchees," which would make most sense in the context, and as "lamentations." The most ingenious suggestion is Edgar Leoni's: he says it might come from *Lifrelofre*, a derogatory name applied to Germans by the satirist François Rabelais on the grounds that all the words in their language sounded like that.

94.

De cinq cents ans plus compte lon tiendra
Celuy qu'estoit l'ornement de son temps:
Puis à un coup grande clarté donrra
Que par ce siècle les rendra trescontents.

Five hundred years later one will take more account
Of him who was the ornament of his time.
Then in one blow he will give great light,
Which will make those of that age very happy.

This could refer to anyone who has been more appreciated five hundred years after his lifetime than he was in his own day. Most commentators think Nostradamus is speaking of himself.

97.

Nouvelle loy terre neufve occuper
Vers la Syrie, Judée, & Palestine:
Le grand empire barbara corruer,
Avant que Phebès son siècle determine.

New law to occupy new land
Near Syria, Judea, and Palestine.
The great barbaric empire to crumble,
Before Phoebus completes his age.

As I have suggested in the introduction, this quatrain presages the end of the Ottoman Empire, the "barbaric empire" that ruled

Syria and Palestine in Nostradamus's day—although the empire would not crumble until after World War I. In this case, the "new law" would be the British and French mandates granted over Syria and Palestine by the League of Nations, which would eventually lead to the "new land," the states of the Middle East as we know them today.

"Phoebus completes his age" probably refers to the planetary rulerships of different eras. In this case, Phoebus is the sun, and it is thought that his "age" commenced in 1887 and will extend to 2242. This prediction thus holds up well, as the "new law" did come into effect in the "age of Phoebus" by this reckoning.

Century IV

5.

Croix, paix, sous un accompli divin verbe,
L'Hespaigne & Gaule seront unis ensemble.
Grand clade proche, & combat très acerbe:
Cueur si hardi ne sera qui ne tremble.

Cross, peace, under one the divine Word accomplished,
Spain and Gaul will be united together.
Great slaughter near, and combat most bitter:
There will be no heart too bold to tremble.

The union of Spain and France, predicted here, has to this day
never come about. The closest it came, perhaps, was under Napoleon I, who installed his brother Joseph on the throne of Spain in
1808. Joseph ruled until 1813, when he was deposed in the wake of
Napoleon's fall from power. But this was hardly a peaceful time, as
the first line would suggest: the third and fourth lines more closely
match the era of the Napoleonic Wars, which were on a larger scale
than Europe had ever seen before.

Erika Cheetham ascribes this prophecy to the War of the Spanish Succession (1701–14), which began when Philip V, grandson of the French King Louis XIV, ascended to the Spanish throne, thus triggering war with most of the rest of Europe, which feared the power of a combined France and Spain. But the war ended with the Treaty of Utrecht, in which France and Spain agreed that they would never unite.

Or does this verse presage some era to come, when Spain and France will be united under some future European constitution? If so, Nostradamus is not predicting a peaceful fate for this united Europe.

8.

La grande cité d'assaut prompt repentin
Surprins de nuict, gardes interrompus:
Les excubies & veilles sainct Quintin,
Trucidés gardes & les pourtails rompus.

The great city, by sudden, prompt assault,
Surprised at night, the guards overtaken.
On the night of St. Quentin's Eve and vigil,
Slaughtered guards and portals broken.

It is tempting to read into this a prophecy of the battle of St. Quentin in 1557. But the battle took place on St. Lawrence's Day, August 10, not on the eve of St. Quentin's Day, October 31. The only similar event I have been able to detect that took place on October 30 (that is, St. Quentin's Eve) occurred during the Vietnam War in 1965. Near Da Nang, U.S. marines repelled an intense attack by Vietcong forces, killing fifty-six guerrillas. Among the dead, a sketch of marine positions was found on the body of a thirteen-year-old Vietnamese boy who sold drinks to the marines the day before. There is not a terribly close connection between this event and the prophecy, and it is hardly significant enough to have merited the attention of a prophet four centuries earlier.

At the actual Battle of St. Quentin, French forces under the

Duc de Montmorency were smashed by the armies of Philip II of Spain, with help from the English, on August 10, 1557. Montmorency himself was taken prisoner. The victory was such a major one that Philip built his great palace, the Escorial in Madrid, to commemorate it. Nevertheless, the battle was won not by surprise, but after a vicious seventeen-day siege.

This quatrain illustrates a common problem that faces the commentator on Nostradamus: one or two details in a quatrain (in this case, the name "St. Quentin") seem to point toward an actual prophecy of some great occurrence in the future, but then very few of the other facts end up bearing any connection to it.

12.

Le camp plus grand du route mis en fuite,
Guaires plus outre ne sera pourchassé;
Ost recampé, & legion reduicte,
Puis hors des Gaules du tout sera chassé.

The greatest army of the road put to flight,
Hardly any further will it be pursued;
Army reassembled, and legion reduced,
Then out of Gaul will it be completely chased.

At first, this quatrain appears to foretell the disaster experienced by Napoleon's Grand Army in Russia in 1812 (cf. I.60, V.26, IX.99). Numbering some 442,000 men at the outset, it could well be called the "greatest army of the road." Moreover, by the time the retreating French left Russia, their numbers were so decimated (reduced to 10,000) that the Russians did not feel the need to pursue them beyond their own borders. In 1815, the Grand Army reassembled when Napoleon returned from exile in Elba, but was decisively defeated at Waterloo.

The chief objection to this reading is that the quatrain sounds as if it is speaking of invaders of France rather than the French themselves. Hence some have taken it as referring to the retreat of

Hitler's army 1944–1945. But one could not say that the German army was pursued "hardly any further," since the Allies fought their way into Germany itself.

A less speculative interpretation would see this as a reference to a Spanish invasion of France in Nostradamus's day. But the details of the prophecy do not match those of the Spanish incursion into France in 1557, climaxing with the battle of St. Quentin (see the verse immediately above). The Spanish won this battle, and all in all the war seems to have been a draw. It ended in 1559 with the Treaty of Cateau-Cambrésis, in which both France and Spain made concessions. The rout of an invading force that Nostradamus envisages here did not take place.

18.

Des plus letrés dessus les faits celestes
Seront par princes ignorans reprouvés:
Punis d'Edit, chassés comme scelestes,
Et mis à mort là où seront trouvés.

Some of the most learned on celestial things
Will by ignorant princes be reproved,
Punished by edict, chased like criminals,
And put to death wherever they are found.

This verse reveals the equivocal position that astrologers and others with reputation for occult knowledge had in the early modern era. The doctrinal certainties of the Middle Ages were fading, and the scientific worldview that now forms the intellectual background of our own time had not yet been born. Consequently, the era in between was the Golden Age of the occult philosopher, who formed a bridge between the theological orientation of the past and the dawning scientific enterprise. It was this atmosphere that partly accounts for Nostradamus's own reputation.

But if the occult savant was respected for his knowledge, he was also often feared as a sorcerer in league with the Devil. Nostradamus's prophecy here is not an indication of any specific event, either in his time or later, but rather a reminder of the dangers that hung over the heads of any who sought out hidden knowledge.

24.

Ouy sous terre saincte d'ame voix fainte,
Humaine flamme pour divine voyr luire,
Fera des seuls de leur sang terre tainte
Et les saints temples pour les impurs destruire.

Heard underground, the soul's faint but holy voice,
Human flame to glow in place of the divine—
Will make the earth stained with solitaries' blood,
And destroy holy temples on behalf of the impure.

Two themes are at play here. One is the conventional—not to say clichéd—apocalyptic idea that in the last days religion will decline and people will fall away from God: monks will be persecuted and churches sacked. As we have seen, the religious tumults of the sixteenth century were giving rise to such occurrences. Moreover, various prophets, such as St. Malachy, had predicted persecution for the Church in the last days (see the commentary on III.65).

The other theme involves the observation that knowledge of things human is supplanting theology in the minds of the learned. This, too, was happening in Nostradamus's time. During the previous century, the savants of the Renaissance had been promoting the humanities—the learning of pagan antiquity—in place of the Scholastic theology that underlay the central teachings of the medieval Catholic Church.

What is particularly poignant in this verse is the first line, which is telling us that amid the din of this new human knowledge, the voice of the soul becomes harder to hear. Nostradamus no doubt felt this to be true of his era; the sense of alienation and isolation that is so prevalent now suggests it is true of our own time as well.

25.

Corps sublimes sans fin à l'oeil visibles
Obnubiler viendront par ses raisons:
Corps, front comprins, sens, chief & invisibles,
Diminuant les sacrées oraisons.

Infinite sublime bodies visible to the eye
They shall come to cloud over with reason:
Body, forehead, sense, head, and things invisible,
Diminishing the sacred orisons.

This quatrain raises a question that is often neglected in discussions of mysticism and esotericism. On the one hand, we have numerous accounts, often from the past, of people seeing ghosts, spirits, and subtle forms of the sort Nostradamus mentions in the first line. On the other hand, these forms are rarely if ever visible to us today. Nostradamus seems to be suggesting that the ascent of reason in the human mind has made these forms of extrasensory perception increasingly difficult or impossible. In the third and fourth lines he is arguably saying that the forms of subtle bodies are becoming invisible to the naked eye, and are consequently reducing religious devotion.

This raises an enormous issue—whether, in an age before reason came to the fore in human cognition, people literally perceived things that we do not see, or that we see far more rarely. If this is so, then accounts of supernatural occurrences, particularly in preindustrial cultures, take on a far different status. I do not myself know whether this is the case. The only thinker who addresses this issue in any detail is the Austrian esotericist Rudolf Steiner, who claimed that human perception was quite different in ancient times, before the conscious ego was fully developed. But

I do not see how such a claim could be verified in any definitive way.

26.

Lou grand eyssame se levera d'abelhos,
Que non sauran don te siegen venguddos.
De nuech l'embousq: lou gach dessous las treilhos,
Cieutad trahido per cinq lengos non nudos.

The great swarm of bees shall rise,
And no one will know where they came from.
An ambush at night: the guard under the trellis,
A city betrayed by five tongues not naked.

In antiquity, a swarm of bees was regarded as an ill omen. Here it points to the betrayal of a city by five deceitful individuals, taken through an ambush at night. This verse (incidentally, the only one written in Provençal rather than French) is frequently taken as a prediction of Napoleon's coup d'état in 1799, where he deposed the French Directory and set himself up as First Consul. This interpretation is based upon the fact that Napoleon's coat of arms included a swarm of bees, and that he came from an obscure background, as the second line seems to hint. Moreover, the word *treilhos* is sometimes read as a veiled reference to the Palace of the Tuileries in Paris, which was Napoleon's headquarters.

This interpretation, if nothing else, gives a hint of the ingenuity that Nostradamus's commentators have often been forced to exercise on his puzzling texts. It is, of course, part of his genius to have left so much room for speculation and imagination in the unraveling of his verses; probably they would not have proven so consistently fascinating had he done it otherwise.

32.

Es lieux & temps chair au poisson donra lieu,
La loi commune sera faicte au contraire:

Vieux tiendra fort, plus osté du millieu,
Le panta koina filvn mis fort arrière.

In places and times flesh will give way to fish,
The common law will be turned to its opposite:
Old will cling hard, then will be removed from the middle,
The *panta koina philon* placed far behind.

Panta koina philon in the fourth line is Greek for "all things in common among friends." It is based on an adage of the great humanist Desiderius Erasmus: *amicorum communia omnia,* as Lemesurier indicates. The phrase also echoes a detail about the early Christian community in Acts 2:44: "And all that believed were together, and had all things in common."

Many commentators have seen in this a prediction of the fall of communism. Both Edgar Leoni and Erika Cheetham make this equation, and they were writing in the 1960s and 1970s, when this was regarded as an extremely remote possibility.

In fact the quatrain serves as a reasonably good description of the collapse of the Soviet Union. The Communist old guard did cling hard, only to be cast aside. And the "common law" was in fact "turned to its opposite"—a particularly rapacious form of capitalism. (Of course, the ideal of "all things in common" had long since been turned into a travesty by the Communists themselves.)

In the first line, "returning to fish" may be taken as a reference to a revival of Christianity in Russia. Not only is the fish an ancient symbol of Christ, but fasts as practiced by both Catholics and Orthodox Christians often involve abstinence from meat on certain days. Fish, however, is generally allowed. Another common interpretation says this line speaks of a time of increasing austerity, fish being a humbler food than meat.

39.
Les Rodiens demanderont secours
Par le neglect de ses hoyrs delaissée.

L'empire Arabe revalera son cours
Par Hesperies la cause redressée.

The Rhodians will ask for help
Abandoned by the neglect of its heirs.
The Arab empire will retrace its steps,
By Westerners the cause set right.

Nostradamus is addressing the fate of the island of Rhodes off the coast of Asia Minor. Again the Turks (figuratively called "the Arab empire") are a major concern: the Knights Hospitallers, a Christian military order that had ruled the island since the fourteenth century, held out against them until 1522, almost seventy years after the Byzantine Empire fell in 1453. At that point the Knights, under pressure from the island's Greek inhabitants, capitulated to the Turks and evacuated, eventually reestablishing their headquarters on Malta.

Here Nostradamus is predicting that Rhodes will be retaken from the Turks by Christians from the West, presumably including the Knights Hospitallers with assistance from the Christian monarchs (cf. V.16). This did not happen in his own day, nor did it even come close. Only in 1912 would the islands be occupied by the Italians, who held it until the end of World War II. In 1948, Rhodes was united with Greece (cf. VI.21). The prophecy was fulfilled only in the most general sense: Rhodes eventually did return to Western hands after the Ottoman Empire fell apart.

43.

Seront ouys au ciel les armes battre:
Celuy an mesme les divins ennemis
Voudront loix sainctes injustement debatre:
Par foudre & guerre bien croyans à mort mis.

Arms will be heard to clash in heaven:
In the same year the divine enemies

Will wish to fight the holy laws unjustly.
By thunder and war good believers put to death.

Another ostensible prophecy of war in heaven (cf. I.64). Here it is connected to religious strife and persecution, as the last three lines suggest. The simplest explanation is that Nostradamus is predicting not the aerial battles of the future but a spiritual "war in heaven" that parallels—and may stimulate—religious conflict on earth. Religious persecution was so persistent and so acute in Nostradamus's time that it would be hard to relate this prophecy to any specific incident.

45.

Par conflit Roy regne abandonera,
Le plus grand chef faillira au besoing:
Mors profligés peu en rechapera,
Tous destranchés un en sera tesmoing.

By conflict king kingdom will abandon:
The greatest chief will fail when needed:
Dead, wasted, few will escape it,
All of them cut up; one of them will witness it.

John Hogue suggests that this prophecy foreshadows the expedition of Portugal's naive twenty-five-year-old King Sebastian I to conquer Morocco in August 1578, which was to end in the disastrous Battle of Alcázarquivir, near Tangier, in which many of the Portuguese were killed or captured; Sebastian himself lost his life.

The French historian Fernand Braudel describes the battle's aftermath: "A large section of the country's nobility . . . remained in enemy hands. In order to provide ransoms so huge that they could not be paid in cash, the country had to send all its available coinage as well as jewels and precious stones to Morocco and Algiers. And without those imprisoned, the Kingdom was bereft of its administrative and military elite. The combination of

blows left Portugal more defenseless than at any other time in her
history."[46]

The last line of this quatrain echoes Job 1:16: "And I only am
escaped to tell thee."

47.

Le noir farouche quand aura essayé
Sa main sanguine par feu, fer, arcs tendus:
Trestout le peuple sera tant effrayé,
Voyr les plus grans par col & pieds pendus.

When the savage black has tried
His bloody hand with fire, irons, stretched bows:
All the people will be so terrified
To see the greatest hung by neck and feet.

The reference to the "savage black" would seem to point to
the Moors, and like II.45, this could be taken as a prophecy of
Alcázarquivir.

John Hogue sees in it a reference to the St. Bartholomew's Day
Massacre of August 24, 1572, in which Admiral de Coligny and the
leaders of the French Huguenots were murdered in Paris, triggering a mass assault against the Protestant minority across the nation
(cf. IV.62, IX.79). But this interpretation would require taking "the
savage black" as King Charles IX of France, which does not seem
apt (although Nostradamus commentators are fond of reading
noir, "black," as a sort of anagram for *roi,* "king"). And while the
people may have been "terrified" by this sight, they almost immediately exceeded the initial, royally sponsored purge with their
own outrages against the Huguenots.

50.

Libra verra regner les Hesperies
De ciel & terre tenir la monarchie:

D'Asie forces nul ne verra peries
Que sept ne tiennet par rang la hierarchie.

Libra will see the West rule,
Of heaven and earth to hold the monarchy:
Asia's forces no one will see perish
Until seven hold the rank of hierarchy.

The first two lines of this quatrain allude to the *Astronomica,* a didactic poem on astrology by Manilius, a Roman poet of the first century A.D.: "*Hesperiam sua Libra tenet, qua condita Roma / orbis et imperium retinet discrimina rerum*"; "Hesperia is held by Libra, under which sign Rome was founded and its empire makes the decisions in the world's affairs."[47] Libra is the astrological sign that governs justice and rule.

Manilius is speaking of Rome; Nostradamus probably is not. Nostradamus associates Libra with Austria, that is, the Hapsburg power (cf. II.81, IV.96). As for "Hesperia," it could refer to any Western nation, although Britain is a good choice, since Nostradamus links it closely with the West (cf. III.35, V.34). If so, it is a striking prophecy, given that Nostradamus was, as a Frenchman, not likely to be sympathetic to Britain, which at this time was dynastically connected with France's archenemy, Spain.

Alternately, this verse could be taken as a prophecy of America as superpower, given that America's military might is predicated on superiority in the air (as the second line hints). Britain's superpower status was based not on superiority in the air but on the sea.

"Until seven hold the rank of hierarchy" is usually taken to allude to the papacy. The last two lines would then suggest that Turkish power would not be broken until "seven hold the papacy." If that were to mean seven popes from Nostradamus's time, it would not go very far into the future—only to the late sixteenth century, depending upon which pope one started with. (The year

1555, when these verses appeared, had two popes.) By 1600, Turkey was no longer much of a menace on the Mediterranean, but it was still a power to be reckoned with in the Balkans and in Eastern Europe.

54.
Du nom qui onques ne fut au Roy gaulois,
Jamais ne fut en fouldre si craintif:
Tremblant l'Italie, l'Espagne, & les Anglois,
De femmes estrangiers grandement attentif.

Of a name that never belonged to Gallic kings,
Never was there thunder so frightful:
Italy, Spain, and the English trembling,
To foreign women greatly attentive.

This verse fits Napoleon extremely well, as commentators have suggested since the emperor's own time. He had a name that had never been previously possessed by a French king; he caused an enormous amount of war and terror, fighting in Italy and Spain and combatting the English. He was certainly "greatly attentive" to foreign women: his first wife, Joséphine de Beauharnais, was born in Martinique; his second wife, Marie-Louise, was the daughter of the Austrian emperor Francis I.

57.
Ignare envie au grand Roi supportée,
Tiendra propos deffendre les escriptz:
Sa femme non femme par un autre tentée,
Plus double deux ne fort ne crys.

Ignorant envy, before the great king upheld,
Will propose forbidding the writings:
His wife not his wife tempted by another,
No more will the double two make their cries.

The "great king" would appear to be Henri II, who ruled France when this verse was written. Commentators generally take the first two lines to refer to Nostradamus's concern that his own writings will be banned, which did not happen, although he did receive his share of criticism from the skeptics of his day. The queen, Catherine de' Medici, with her enormous fascination with the occult, would in fact become a great supporter of Nostradamus.

"His wife not his wife" would then refer to Henri's mistress Diane de Poitiers, who, Nostradamus hints, will be tempted to be unfaithful to him. In this case, the last line, "no more will the double two make their cries," could mean that Henri would no longer be coupling with both his queen and his mistress. The translation I give of this cryptic and broken line depends on reading *ne fort ne cris*—which literally translates into the incomprehensible "neither strong nor cries"—as *ne feront cris,* as Lemesurier suggests.

62.
Un coronnel machine ambition,
Se saisira de la plus grande armée:
Contre son prince faincte invention,
Et descouvert sera soubz la ramée.

A colonel schemes ambition,
Will seize hold of the greatest army:
Against his prince, false invention,
And will be discovered under the branch.

Numerous candidates have suggested themselves for this quatrain: Admiral de Coligny, the Huguenot leader whom Nostradamus would then be accusing of a plot against Henri II; Oliver Cromwell, who built his New Model Army to overcome the forces of King Charles I in the English Civil War of the 1640s; even Colonel Moammar Qaddafi, who took power in a 1969 coup against the king of Libya. The quatrain is general enough to accommodate all these, although none of them is borne out by the last line, which seems to indicate that the plot will be uncovered in time.

The core situation foreseen here—a military leader plotting against a monarch—happens so often in history that this prophecy will no doubt fulfill itself again and again.

65.

Au deserteur de la grand forteresse,
Après qu'on aura son lieu abandonée:
Son adversaire fera si grand prouesse,
L'Empereur tost mort sera condemné.

To the deserter of the great fortress,
After his place has been abandoned,
His adversary will display such great prowess.
The Emperor will soon be condemned to death.

This quatrain is usually applied to Napoleon III, the ill-fated nephew of Napoleon I who ruled France from 1852 to 1870. Napoleon III, originally called Louis Napoleon, had been imprisoned in the fortress of Ham until he escaped from it in 1846. In 1870 he provoked a war with Bismarck's Prussia, "his adversary," which did indeed show "such great prowess" that the war rapidly ended in a debacle for France and cost the emperor his throne. He was not condemned to death, but died in exile in England in 1873, two years after he was deposed.

68.

En l'an bien proche non esloigné de Venus,
Les deux plus grans de l'Asie & d'Affrique
Du Ryn & Hister qu'on dira sont venus.
Crys, pleurs à Malte & coste ligustique.

In a year very near, not far from Venus,
The two greatest of Asia and Africa,

Of Rhine and Hister will be said to arrive.
Cries, tears in Malta and on the Ligurian coast.

The word "Hister" in the third line has led the more imaginative commentators to connect this verse with Hitler and World War II (cf. II.24, V.29, VI.49). But it is hard to see what in the events of that era would bear this prophecy out. Malta and the Ligurian coast of Italy were far from the most devastated sites in this struggle—and then who are "the two greatest of Asia and Africa"? Some say the Japanese and Mussolini, but this is far-fetched. Mussolini's African empire, consisting of Libya and Ethiopia, hardly made him the greatest power on that continent. And Japan, even at the height of its power, could have hardly been called the greatest in Asia, where Britain, ruler of India, Burma, and Malaysia; the U.S.S.R.; and even war-ravaged China were at least as "great."

As is often true, the prophecy makes more sense if brought closer to Nostradamus's time. The verse speaks of "two greatest": one of Asia and Africa, the other of "Rhine and Hister." These would be the Turks and the Hapsburgs, respectively ("Hister" means the Danube, as we have already seen). Nostradamus would then be forecasting that these two powers will clash in a place "not far from Venus"—which is often taken as a punning allusion to Venice. This clash, he is suggesting, will bring grief to Malta (then held by the Knights Hospitallers after they had quitted Rhodes; see IV.39 above) and to the Republic of Genoa, at the time a minor but still significant maritime power. In this form, this is a perfectly sensible prophecy and fits in with the geopolitical situation of Nostradamus's day.

In fact the Turkish fleet did strike at Malta in May 1565. The island was bravely defended by the Knights Hospitallers, and eventually the Spaniards came to their relief, driving the Turks away. Even so, the prophecy is probably better understood as a general warning that the clash between Spain and Turkey would bring harm to Genoa and Malta, which lay between them—as was true enough in that era.

70.

Bien contingue des grans monts Pyrenées
Un contre l'aigle grand copie adresser:
Ouvertes veines, forces exterminées,
Que jusque à Pau le chef viendra chasser.

Very close to the great Pyrenees mountains,
One against the eagle to raise a great army:
Opened veins, forces exterminated,
Which as far as Pau the chief will come to chase.

The gist of this quatrain is relatively clear. A great army will be raised to cross the Pyrenees. There will be a great clash, and the leader will chase the broken forces as far as Pau, which is in Navarre (that is, in France), a short distance from the mountains.

A common interpretation relates this quatrain to the Duke of Wellington, who led the British forces during the Peninsular War against Napoleonic France from 1808 to 1814. After driving the French out of Spain, on April 10, 1814, Wellington defeated the French commander, Marshal Soult, at Toulouse, which is actually farther into French territory than Pau. (The battle was unnecessary, as Napoleon had abdicated four days earlier, but the news had not yet reached the field.) This interpretation entails reading the "eagle" as Napoleon.

This is one instance where Nostradamus's prophecy fits a more remote situation better than one of his own era, where it would mean that the French would invade Spain (ruled by the Hapsburg "eagle") through the Pyrenees but would be driven back to Pau.

77.

SELIN monarque l'Italie pacifique,
Regnes unis Roy chrestien du monde:
Mourant voudra coucher en terre blesique
Apres pyrates avoir chassé de l'onde.

SELIN monarch, Italy at peace,
Kingdoms united, Christian king of the world:
Dying he will want to lie in the soil of Blois
After having chased pirates from the waves.

We have already encountered the word SELIN (capitalized in the original) in reference to the Turks: "Port Selyn" in II.1 means the Sublime Porte of the Ottoman Sultan; "Seline's banner" in II.79 also refers to the Ottomans. In this case, however, it is alluding to Henri II of France, *le grand CHYREN*, an identification made more explicitly in VI.27. Here the allusion to *selene*, Greek for "moon," has a double significance: Henri II had the moon on his banner, and his mistress was Diane de Poitiers, Diana being the goddess of the moon.

If this interpretation is correct, the prophecy is totally wrong. Henri II did not unify the nations of the world and rule them as a universal monarch; he did not chase the pirates out of the Mediterranean; and he was not buried at the Château de Blois, the seat of Louis XII in the fifteenth century—he was buried at Saint-Denis, outside Paris.

The prophecy, although incorrect, was not entirely misguided. In that age it was far more politic to flatter a monarch by hinting at great triumphs for him than to predict the opposite. The quatrain I.35, famous for predicting Henri's bizarre death, is phrased much more obscurely.

82.

Amas s'approche venant d'Esclavonie,
L'Olestant vieulx cité ruinera:
Fort désolée verra la Romanie,
Puis la grand flamme estaindre ne scaura.

A mass approaches coming from Slavonia,
The old Destroyer will ruin a city:
Quite desolate will he see Romania,
Then the great flame he will be unable to quench.

This is often taken as a prophecy of Napoleon's doomed retreat from Moscow. "Slavonia" would be a metonymy for "Russia," and Napoleon himself would be "the old Destroyer." The translation of *l'Olestant* as "Destroyer" is conjectural, but it makes sense as a kind of portmanteau word deriving from the Greek *ollunai*, "to destroy," combined with the French *molester*, "molest." *Romanie* would then have to mean "the Roman Empire" rather than Romania as we know it today (and as a matter of fact it did not have that name in Nostradamus's time, when it was called Wallachia). Metaphorically, *Romanie* would refer to the French Empire.

Personally, however, I cannot read these verses without thinking of the end of World War II—with the Soviet armies marching on Berlin, Hitler contemplating the ruin of his Thousand-Year Reich, and the scorched-earth policy he ordered his underlings to inflict upon Germany. Even the last line fits, "the old Destroyer" being unable to put out the flames that immolated his body after he had shot himself.

89.

Trente de Londres secret conjureront,
Contre leur roy sur le pont l'entreprise:
Luy, satelites la mort degousteront,
Un Roy esleu blonde, natif de Frize.

Thirty of London will conspire in secret,
The enterprise against their king over the sea:
He, his satellites will find death distasteful,
A blond chosen king, native of Friesland.

A verse generally applied to the Glorious Revolution in Britain in 1688. Parliament, exasperated with James II, who sought to make the nation Catholic again, begged the Dutch William of Orange to take the throne. William agreed and landed with his army in November 1688. James II, finding "death distasteful," abdicated and fled to France. William was not blond—his portraits show him wearing a dark wig—and he was born in The Hague, but "Friesland" can be taken as a synecdoche for the Netherlands as a whole.

96.

La soeur aisnee de l'isle Britannique,
Quinze ans devant le frere aura naissance:
Par son promis moyennant verrifique,
Succedera au regne de balance.

The older sister of the British Isle,
Fifteen years before her brother will have her birth.
By her fiancé, if proven true,
Will succeed to the kingdom of the Balance.

The "older sister of the British Isle" is most likely Mary I, who was queen of England at the time this verse was written. As a matter of fact, she was born twenty-one years before her brother, who preceded her as King Edward VI and whom she succeeded to the throne after his death in 1553. "Her fiancé" no doubt refers to Philip II of Spain, who was her husband by the time this quatrain was written; she had married him in 1554. Nostradamus indicates that Mary will inherit the Hapsburg throne of Austria through Philip, since he was heir to this empire through his father, Emperor Charles V. (As we have seen in II.81 and IV.50, Libra, "the Balance," sometimes refers to Austria.) But this did not happen, as she was to die in 1558. In any event, Charles V divided his inheritance, giving his brother, Ferdinand I, the throne of Austria. Philip would rule Spain only.

Century V

3.

Le successeur de la duché viendra,
Beaucoup plus outre que la mer de Toscane:
Gauloise branche la Florence tiendra,
Dans son giron d'accord nautique Rane.

The successor of the Duchy shall come
Far beyond the Tuscan sea:
Gallic branch Florence shall hold,
In its gyron according with the sea-fish.

The first three lines of this verse suggest that the rule of Florence will pass to a French line. As Edgar Leoni notes, this in fact happened in 1737. The Medici, for centuries the Florentine ruling family, died out and were replaced by Duke Francis of Lorraine, a member of the French royal line, as Grand Duke of Tuscany.

The last line is not as clear. *Giron* can mean either "gyron," a term meaning a triangular shape in heraldry, or "lap." *Rane* is presumably derived from the Latin *rana,* or "frog," and may mean either an actual frog or a type of fish called the "sea-frog" or "sea-fish" (*rana maritima* in Latin). The line seems to indicate that this future heir to the Grand Duchy of Tuscany will have a frog on his coat of arms—another way of saying that the heir will come from the French royal line, since Clovis, the first Christian king of the Franks, had (or was believed to have had) three frogs or toads on his heraldic device. Some heraldic experts even claim that the fleur-de-lys, the lily that appears on the coat of arms of the French royal family, was originally a frog. This, incidentally, is why Frenchmen are derogatorily known as "frogs."

5.

Soubz umbre faincte d'oster de servitude,
Peuple & cité, l'usupera luy mesmes:
Pire fera par fraulx de jeune pute,
Livré au champ lisant le faulx proëme.

Under the feigned shadow of lifting servitude,
People and city, he will usurp it himself:
He will do worse by the young whore's deception,
Delivered to the field reading the false proem.

This is another quatrain sometimes ascribed to Hitler, who pretended to deliver France from the Jews and international bankers by invading it. In this case, "the young whore" would be the corrupt French Third Republic (or perhaps the puppet Vichy government), and "the false proem" would be deceitful propaganda, or even Hitler's manifesto *Mein Kampf.*

The situation described is so general, however, that it could be applied to almost any case of usurpation. Tyrants rarely grace their tyranny with the name it deserves, and they are frequently surrounded with accomplices and quislings who merit the appellation "young whore."

6.

Au roy l'Augur sus le chef la main mettre,
Viendra prier pour la paix Italique:

À la main gauche viendra changer le sceptre
De Roy viendra l'Empereur pacifique.

On the king's head the augur to place his hand,
Will come to pray for the Italian peace:
To his left hand will he come to change the scepter,
From a king he will become a pacific emperor.

Another quatrain prophesying the coming of a universal ruler who
will bring peace to the world (cf. I.4). Although many commentators apply it to Henri II (cf. IV.77), there are no details in this verse
that connect it specifically to him. The left hand is traditionally
regarded as passive, the right hand as active, so this line is explained
by the line that follows: from pursuing war with a strong right
hand, the king will reign peacefully with his left.

7.

De Triumvir seront trouvez les os,
Cherchant profond tresor aenigmatique.
Ceulx d'alentour ne seront en repos,
De concaver mabre & plomb metalique.

Of the Triumvir the bones will be found,
Seeking deep, enigmatic treasure.
Those around will not remain at rest,
From hollowing out marble and metallic lead.

An echo of III.65, where Nostradamus predicts that the body of
some great Roman will be discovered. "Triumvir" refers to the two
triumvirates that dominated Rome in the last days of the republic in the first century B.C.: the First Triumvirate consisted of Julius Caesar, Pompey, and Crassus; the second of Octavius (later
Augustus), Mark Antony, and Lepidus. Consequently, this verse,
like III.65, could be predicting the discovery of Augustus's tomb.

The third and fourth lines have a macabre quality, hinting that this archaeological excavation may disturb the dead, but as frequently happens with Nostradamus, the broken grammar does not leave it entirely clear who is doing the hollowing.

13.

Par grande fureur le Roy Romain Belgique
Vexer voudra par phalange barbare:
Fureur grinsseant, chassera gent libyque,
Despuis Pannons jusques Hercules la hare.

With great fury the Belgian Roman king
Will want to vex the barbarian with his phalanx:
Fury gnashing, he will chase the Libyan people
From Pannonia to the Pillars of Hercules.

"The Belgian Roman king" seems to refer to the Holy Roman emperor Charles V, who ruled the Netherlands as well. This quatrain predicts that Charles, or one of his successors, will drive "the barbarian"—that is, the Turks—out of Pannonia, roughly equivalent to modern Hungary (cf. III.58, IX.28, 90). He will also chase the North African corsairs ("the Libyan people") out of the Strait of Gibraltar (known in classical antiquity as "the Pillars of Hercules"). Charles himself did not fulfill this prediction. The Austrian Hapsburgs did drive the Turks out of Hungary, but not until the end of the seventeenth century (cf. I.49). While the power of the North African corsairs was broken (cf. II.4, III.1), they remained a problem in the Mediterranean into the nineteenth century.

15.

En navigant captif pris grand pontife,
Grans apretz faillir les clercz tumultuez:
Second esleu absent son bien debiffe,
Son favory bastard à mort tue.

While sailing, the great pontiff taken captive,
Afterward the great one to fail the riotous clergy.
Second elected, his welfare declines,
His favorite bastard put to death.

A prediction of the captivity of some future pope. "Sailing" probably refers metaphorically to the pontiff's steering the bark of Peter (cf. I.4). The French held both Pius VI and Pius VII captive in 1799 and 1809–14, respectively, but one could also apply this verse to the period after 1870, when the Papal States were appropriated by the unified Kingdom of Italy. To protest this act, the popes of the era refused to leave the Vatican. As a result, the pope was known as the "prisoner of the Vatican" until Pius XI signed the Lateran treaties with Benito Mussolini in 1929, which granted the papacy sovereignty over Vatican City. But Nostradamus more likely has in mind the corrupt church of his day, with its riotous clergy and papal bastards.

16.

A son hault pris plus la lerme sabee,
D'humaine chair par mort en cendre mettre,
A l'isle Pharos par croisars perturbee,
Alors qu'a Rhodes paroistra dur espectre.

The Sabaean tear at its high price no more,
To turn human flesh to ash by death
At the isle of Pharos disturbed by Crusaders,
While at Rhodes appears a harsh specter.

"The Sabaean tear"—*la lerme sabee*—is commonly understood as meaning frankincense, which was used for embalming. Sabaea, on the southern coast of the Arabian peninsula, was famed for its frankincense; it was probably the biblical Sheba. Because of an ambiguity in the French, this line is, curiously, translated in two ways; the other version would go, "The Sabaean tear at its highest price." I have chosen the version above for the simple reason that the second line seems to me to refer to cremation, which of course requires no embalming; consequently, frankincense would have no value. The reference, then, would be to the plague, which often required the burning of bodies, partly as a sanitary measure, partly to deal with the sheer excess of corpses. This is an extreme measure, since the Catholic Church generally forbade cremation so that the body would be to some degree intact for resurrection at the Last Judgment. (The Church lifted its ban on cremation in 1963.)

Pharos, off the coast of Egypt, was at the time in the hands of the Turks, as was Rhodes, so Nostradamus seems to be predicting a Christian counterinvasion of lands lost to the Ottomans, with the consequence of plague or starvation among the nations invaded. *Croisars* literally means "ones with crosses," hence "Crusaders," but Nostradamus probably has in mind the Knights Hospitallers, who were driven from Rhodes in 1522 (cf. IV.39). But the Hospitallers never returned to Rhodes. They kept their headquarters on Malta until the eighteenth century.

23.

Les deux contens seront unis ensemble,
Quant la pluspart à Mars seront conjoinct:
Le grand d'Affrique en effrayeur & tremble,
DUUMVIRAT *par la classe desjoinct.*

The two contenders will be united together,
When the majority are with Mars conjunct:
The great one of Africa in fright and trembles,
Duumvirate separated by the fleet.

As in the previous quatrain, the first line could be translated in the opposite way, as "The two happy ones will be united together": *contens* in the French of the era could mean either "happy" (as in the modern language) or "contender." The verse is speaking of a stellium—that is, a bunching of planets together in the sign of Mars—combined with an assault against the Muslim states of North Africa. "Duumvirate" means an alliance of two men: we have already seen a reference to the triumvirate in V.7. In this case, it would seem to refer to a separation of North Africans from their Turkish allies by the Spanish fleet. One could see a fulfillment of this prophecy in the aftermath of Lepanto in 1571.

26.

La gent esclave par un heur martial,
Viendra en hault degré tant eslevee:
Changeront prince, naistre un provincial,
Passer la mer copie aux monts levee.

The Slavic people by a martial hour
Will become so elevated to a high degree:
They will change princes, a provincial to be born,
A force raised in the mountains to cross the sea.

Esclave in the first line has a double meaning: "Slav" and "slave" (the two words come from the same root, the Byzantines believing that the Slavic peoples made excellent slaves). It is hard to say which Slavic nation Nostradamus is referring to, but in all likelihood he means the Slavs of the Balkans or Carpathians, since he speaks of a "force raised in the mountains." He is probably trying to say that a Slavic army will reverse the Turkish invasion of the Balkans and eventually cross the Dardanelles to retake Asia Minor for Christendom. This did not happen.

A more modern interpretation could point toward Russia, which was "elevated to a high degree" after its triumph over Napoleon in 1812 (cf. I.60, IV.12, IX.99) and over Hitler in 1945. In the latter case, the victory was accomplished after the Revolution, which was indeed "a change in leadership." Stalin, moreover, was from the remote province of Georgia in the Caucasus. On the other hand, the Russian army did not cross the sea in either of these exploits.

29.

La liberté ne sera recouvree,
L'occupera noir fier vilain inique:
Quant la matiere du pont sera ousvree,
D'Hister, Venise faschée la republique.

Liberty will not be regained,
One black, proud, villainous, unjust will take it:
When the matter of the bridge is opened,
By Hister will the Venetian republic be angered.

"Hister" reappears in the fourth line here, prompting many commentators to situate this quatrain in the time of the Second World War (cf. II.24, IV.68, VI.49). The dark and ominous tone of the verse would seem to confirm it. Unfortunately, there is little in the history of the Second World War that fits the situation described here, although some read *pont*—"bridge"—in the third line as a cryptic reference to the pontiff and the Vatican's ambiguous relationship with the Axis powers.

More plausibly, Nostradamus is predicting that the nations in southeastern Europe occupied by the Turks will not see their liberty again, and that Austria ("Hister") will not support the Venetians when they need it. The position of Venice in Nostradamus's time was a difficult one. In many ways it was like Finland during the Cold War. Although it was Christendom's first line of defense against the Ottomans, its proximity and vulnerability to a far larger enemy made it steer a course away from direct confrontation whenever possible. When it did fight, support from larger powers such as the Hapsburg states was vital.

Curiously, the apparent gist of this quatrain is very much the opposite of the one immediately preceding. Nostradamus seems to have hedged his bets. If the Ottomans were driven from southeastern Europe, he could claim to be right; if they were not, he could also claim to be right. The predictions are moreover so vague that their mutual contradictions can be explained away, as Nostradamus aficionados often do.

32.

Ou tout bon est, tout bien Soleil & lune
Est abondant, sa ruyne s'approche:
Du ciel s'advance vaner ta fortune,
En mesme estat que la septiesme roche.

Where all is good, all is well, sun and moon
Abundant, its ruin approaches.
From the sky proceeds the winnowing of your fortune,
In the same state as the seventh rock.

A generalized quatrain on the vanity of human fortune, with an alchemical touch. "Sun and moon" probably refers to the metals that traditionally correspond to them: gold and silver, respectively, hence indicating prosperity. Ruination comes from the stars, which have long been seen to govern destiny. "The seventh rock," as Peter Lemesurier indicates, probably refers to Saturn, the seventh planet according to the astronomy of Nostradamus's day. Its corresponding metal is lead, and it is traditionally considered the most maleficent of all the planets. The quatrain is thus a version of standard warnings from the Bible and other traditional sources—for example, "Pride goeth before destruction, and a haughty spirit before a fall" (Prov. 16:18). For a quatrain with a similar though more specific theme, see I.32.

34.

Du plus profond de l'occident Anglois,
Ou est le chef de l'isle britannique,

Entrera classe dans Gironde par Blois,
Par vin & sel, feuz cachés aux barriques.

From the depths of the English West,
Where the head of the Britannic isle is,
A fleet will enter Gironde through Blois,
By wine and salt, fire hidden in the barrels.

This quatrain evokes the D-day invasion of World War II, when a fleet "from the depths of the English West" invaded occupied France. The first two lines would then refer to a combined British-American force; the second line could be read as a veiled indication that America is the leading partner in this coalition. To speak of a fleet entering Gironde—or indeed anywhere else—by Blois is peculiar, since Blois is very far inland. Taken as an allusion to an amphibious force, it is somewhat clearer. The "fire hidden in the barrels" would refer to firearms, which were in widespread use in Nostradamus's day. "Wine and salt," however, remains obscure.

35.
Par cité franche de la grand mer Seline,
Qui porte encore à l'estomach la pierre:
Angloise classe viendra soubz la bruine
Un rameau prendre: du grand ouverte guerre.

By a free city of the great Seline sea,
Which still carries the stone in its stomach,
English fleet shall come under the drizzle
To take a branch; war opened by the great one.

We have already seen the puzzling word "Selin" and its variant "Selyn" (II.1, II.79, IV.77) used in reference both to the Turks and to Henri II. Here most commentators see it as meaning "crescent," by analogy to *selene,* or "moon." And yet "great sea" in itself points toward the Mediterranean, and "Seline" suggests the Turks; thus it would mean the eastern Mediterranean. The most likely reference is Venice, which was still a republic—a "free city"—in Nostradamus's time. If so, then Nostradamus is predicting operations for the English fleet in this theater, probably at the invitation of the Venetians. England would become a major force on the Mediterranean only in the nineteenth century, so this quatrain shows genuine prescience, even though by that time Venice had long gone into eclipse as a maritime power.

38.

Ce grand monarque qu'au mort succedera
Donnera vie illicite & lubrique:
Par nonchalance à tous concedera,
Qu'à la fin fauldra la loy Salique.

That grand monarch who succeeds the dead
Will lead a life illicit and lubricious.
By indifference he will concede to all,
So that in the end the Salic law shall fail.

The general thrust of this quatrain is plain: there will be a decadent monarch who will in the end cause the Salic law to fail. The Salic law stipulates that the crown can only pass to male heirs; hence Nostradamus appears to be saying that women will be ruling the nation (which was not regarded as desirable in Nostradamus's time). Many commentators link this verse to Louis XV of France, who did lead a licentious life and whose mistresses, Mmes. du Pompadour and du Barry, held great power over him. Partly thanks to his neglect of state, which led to the overthrow of the monarchy under his successor, Louis XVI, the royal inheritance did fail.

Looking closer to Nostradamus's time, one might settle upon Henri III—the son of Henri II—who ruled France from 1574 to 1589. Although he was not as susceptible to the influence of his mother, Catherine de' Medici, as was his brother and predecessor,

Charles IX, Catherine remained a formidable influence throughout his reign, and died only a few months before Henri III himself
was assassinated.

As for licentiousness, Henri was a transvestite who surrounded
himself with young men whom he called his *mignons* ("darlings").
Consequently he did not produce an heir. The Valois dynasty of
France came to an end, and Henri III was succeeded by Henri of
Navarre, bringing the Bourbon dynasty to the throne.

41.

Nay soubz les umbres & jornee nocturne,
Sera en regne & bonté souveraine:
Fera renaistre son sang de l'antique urne,
Renouvelant siecle d'or pour l'aerain.

Born under the shadows and the nocturnal day,
He will be in kingdom and sovereign happiness:
Will resurrect his blood from the ancient urn,
Renewing the Golden Age for the Bronze.

Another quatrain that portends the coming of a universal monarch.
We have already seen the theme of the "nocturnal day" in I.64.
The idea of the Golden Age is an ancient one. In the West it goes
back to the Greek poet Hesiod in the eighth century B.C., who in
his *Works and Days* (106–201) tells of the Five Ages of Man: the
Gold, Silver, and Bronze ages; the Age of Heroes; then finally our
own Iron Age, when "men never rest from labor and sorrow by day,
or from perishing at night." Hesiod predicts that this race will die
out when newborn children have gray on their temples. He does
not mention the possibility that these ages go in cycles, but Virgil's
famous Fourth Eclogue, written in the first century B.C. (cf. II.46),
speaks of an imminent time when "the iron race ceases and the
golden race arises throughout the world," and no doubt Nostradamus has this verse in mind.

The third line could be alluding to the Age of Aquarius, since the urn is a metaphor for this sign of the zodiac, as we saw in II.81. In this case, Nostradamus could be saying that with the coming of the Age of Aquarius, the Golden Age will recommence.

42.
Mars eslevé en son plus haut beffroy,
Fera retraire les Allobrox de France:
La gent Lombarde fera si grand effroy,
A ceux de l'Aigle comprins soubz le balance.

Mars raised to his highest belfry
Will make the Allobroges retreat from France:
The Lombard race will cause such great affright
To those of the Eagle included under Libra.

"Mars raised to his highest belfry," taken astrologically, would refer to a time when Mars is in Capricorn, in which sign it is exalted, astrologically speaking. The circuit of Mars through the zodiac takes about two years, during which time the planet spends about two months in Capricorn, so this is not a terribly infrequent occurrence.

The meaning of this verse is ambiguous. "Allobroges" is the classical name for the Savoyards. As we have already seen, "Libra" (*la Balance* in French) is viewed as ruling Austria; "the Eagle" is, as often, the Hapsburg dynasty. Nostradamus could be predicting that Savoy, which at the time was in the possession of France, will return to the rule of the Hapsburgs (the "Eagle"). This did occur in 1559, about two years after this prophecy first appeared. Having lost its war with the Hapsburgs, France was forced to concede Savoy to them.

On the other hand, "Allobroges" could be a pretentious classical epithet for "foreigners," the probable original meaning of the name in antiquity. In this case Nostradamus would be predicting that the French will repel a foreign invasion—again presumably the Hapsburg power—with the assistance of the Lombards in Tuscany.

This did not happen. As a matter of fact, France, invaded by the Hapsburg-ruled Spaniards in 1557, did not drive them out with the help of the Lombards or of anyone else. France lost the war. The war ended in the negotiated peace of the Treaty of Cateau-Cambrésis of 1559—mostly because Spain, although victorious in the field, had run out of money.

53.
La loi du Sol & Venus contendens
Appropriant l'esprit de propheties.
Ne lun ne lautre ne seront entendens,
Par Sol tiendra la loy du grand Messie.

The law of the Sun and Venus contending,
Claiming the spirit of prophecy.
The one will not be understood by the other;
By the Sun the law of the great Messiah will prevail.

Most commentators take this to reflect the dispute between Christianity and Islam, making Nostradamus say that the two will always be at variance, and that Christ, the Messiah, will eventually vindicate Christianity, represented by "the Sun." Islam would then be equated with Venus.

It is reasonable to represent Christianity by the sun. Christ is called the "Sun of Righteousness," and—whether Nostradamus knew it or not—Christianity in the fourth century took over some characteristics of the cult of Sol Invictus, the "Invincible Sun," which was popular at the time. The choice of December 25, for example, as Christ's birthday is probably a borrowing from the Sol Invictus cult, which celebrated the "birthday of the sun" on that day.

The connection between Venus and Islam is harder to see, but partly lies in the fact that Friday, the Muslim Sabbath, is the day of Venus (*dies Veneris* in Latin, *vendredi* in French). Venus is also said to be the star in the Muslim symbol combining the crescent and the star.

It is interesting to note that in a verse that supposedly originally appeared in the Qur'an (in place of the present verse 53:21), Muslims were enjoined to seek intercession from the goddesses of the moon and Venus. By Allah's command, the story goes, Muhammad himself later struck the verse—one of the "Satanic verses" made famous by Salman Rushdie's novel—from the Qur'an. This story is controversial among Muslims, many of whom say it is a slander concocted by infidels, but its existence helps account for the connection between Islam and the morning star.

54.

Du pont Euxine & la grand Tartarie,
Un roy sera qui viendra voir la Gaule:
Transpercera Alane & l'Armenie,
Et dans Bisance lairra sanglante Gaule.

From the Black Sea and Great Tartary,
There will be a king who will come to see Gaul.
He will pierce through Alania and Armenia,
And in Byzantium will leave his bloody rod.

Nostradamus almost certainly has in mind the Mongol invaders under Genghis Khan, whose reappearance he indicates in these lines. This time the invasion from the steppes of Central Asia, or "Great Tartary," will reach France after "piercing" the Ukraine (once home to the tribe of the Alans) and Armenia and causing much slaughter in "Byzantium," or Constantinople.

The prophecy is clear enough, but so far it has not been fulfilled. The man who came the closest was Tsar Alexander I, who ruled Russia from 1801 to 1825. His domains included both "the Black Sea" and "Great Tartary." Alexander marched triumphantly through Paris in 1814 after the defeat of Napoleon. It was the great dream both of Alexander and the other tsars to recapture Constantinople from the Turks and return it to Orthodox sovereignty, but, despite many attempts, Russia has never managed to take control of this city.

55.

De la felice Arabie contrade,
Naistra puissant de loy Mahometique:
Vexer l'Espaigne conquester la Grenade,
Et plus par mer à la gent lygustique.

From the country of Arabia Felix
Will be born a strong one of the Mohammedan law,
To vex Spain, conquer Grenada,
And farther by sea to the Ligurian people.

By now we have seen a number of predictions of invasions of Europe by the Turks and by the North Africans. This quatrain differs in one key respect: the Muslim conqueror will not come from these nations (whom Christian Europe fought almost perpetually) but will come from the more remote area of Arabia Felix, a name given by ancient geographers to the south coast of the Arabian peninsula (roughly equivalent to today's Yemen), probably because it was the source of frankincense and other aromatics. It was also known as Sabaea (cf. V.16).

The man described in this quatrain will come from this distant part of the world to reconquer Grenada in southern Spain, which was the last Moorish enclave to hold out against the Catholic Spaniards. This conqueror will then proceed to harass the Genoese (Ligurians) by sea. The prophecy has not been fulfilled by anyone to this date. Like many of Nostradamus's verses, it chiefly serves to express an underlying fear that Western Europe will fall again to "barbarians"—this time from the Islamic world.

56.

Par le trespas de tresviellart pontife,
Sera esleu Romain de bon aage:
Qu'il sera dict que le siège debiffe,
Et long tiendra & de picquant ouvrage.

> On the passing of the very aged pontiff
> Will be elected a Roman of good age.
> It will be said that he wears out the throne,
> And will hold it long and with sharp effect.

A very old pope will die and will be succeeded by an aged Roman who nonetheless holds the papal seat for a long time, and with pronounced consequences for the Church as a whole. The late John Paul II, who reigned from 1978 to 2005, held the papal seat longer than all but two popes in the history of the Catholic Church. But he was not a Roman, and the pope he succeeded, John Paul I, was, at age sixty-five, not particularly old when he died. Nor can Benedict XVI, a German by birth, be called a "Roman."

A better candidate for this quatrain is Leo XIII, who was pope from 1878 to 1903—twenty-five years. He succeeded Pius IX, who died at the age of eighty-five, and was himself just under sixty-eight when he took the papal seat. As a native of the town of Carpineto Romano, Leo could be called a "Roman"; Leo also studied at the Collegio Romano. His tenure was marked by "sharp effects." He continued the Vatican's policy of protesting the acquisition of the Papal States by the unified Kingdom of Italy; he was highly involved in political rapprochements with the major powers of the day; and he is perhaps best remembered for taking a sharp anti-Socialist position in his 1891 encyclical *Rerum Novarum* ("On Revolution"). Another of Leo's encyclicals, *Humanum Genus* ("The Human Race," 1884), urges the faithful to expose alleged Masonic subversions.

Of course, Nostradamus's prediction is extremely general. Popes tend to be Italians (if not always Romans), and they tend to be elected when they are old. Furthermore, the prophecy is open-ended, so it could have been fulfilled at any point after it was written. Thus the situation described here was entirely likely to manifest at one time or another. Whether we credit Nostradamus for his prescience or write this prediction off as something cannily vague will, no doubt, depend on individual tastes.

57.
Istra du mont Gaulsier & Aventin,
Qui par le trou advertira l'armee:
Entre deux rocs sera prins le butin,
De SEXT. *mansol faillir la renommee.*

He will come from Mont Gaussier and Aventine,
Who will warn the army through the hole:
Between two rocks the booty will be taken,
The fame of Sextus's mausoleum to fail.

Peter Lemesurier connects this obscure quatrain with Mont Gaussier, a promontory in Provence that contained holes through which
scouts could look out—a plausible reading. (Mont Gaussier was
also the subject of an 1889 painting by Vincent van Gogh.) Other
commentators, however, read *mont Gaulsier* as "Montgolfier," since
early editions of Nostradamus use the old form of "s," which looks
like an "f" with a truncated crossbar. The verse then would allude
to the Montgolfier brothers, who invented the hot-air balloon in
1783, launching the age of aerial reconnaissance. This is quite far-
fetched, but it is useful as an illustration of how the extremely fluid
spelling of the sixteenth century can be used to extract all sorts of
predictions out of Nostradamus.

72.
Pour le plaisir d'edict voluptueux,
On meslera la poyson dans l'aloy:
Venus sera en cours si vertueux,
Qu'obfusquera du Soleil tout aloy.

For the pleasure of a voluptuous edict,
Poison is mixed into the alloy.
Venus will be so strong in her course
That she will outshine all the alloy of the Sun.

Many commentators apply this prophecy to the Edict of Poitiers of 1577, in which King Henri III granted legitimacy to the Protestants and allowed clergymen to marry. Peter Lemesurier sees in the references to Venus and the sun a meaning akin to the one in V.53, where the sun supposedly stands for Christianity and Venus for Islam. By this reading, Nostradamus would be saying that because of this concession to human carnality, Islam will become stronger than Christianity.

In this context, the equation of the planets with the two religions seems overcomplicated. Nostradamus is more likely alluding to the esoteric principles in the human character that are associated with these two planets. The sun corresponds to one's essence, that in oneself which is (or should be) the master. It is equated, among other things, with gold and kingship. Venus, on the other hand, is equated with pleasure and passion. If the concupiscent aspect of human nature is allowed to get the upper hand, Nostradamus is saying, then "poison is mixed into the alloy"—an idea that is extremely common in the religious thought of all eras.

The use of the word "edict" suggests that Nostradamus is not merely making a moral observation but has some piece of legislation in mind. Whether this is to be equated with the Edict of Poitiers is not clear; no doubt one could make a case for connecting it with any law that grants greater sexual freedom. (We cannot expect to find modern ideas about sexual liberation in a sixteenth-century seer.)

In the last line, *tout aloy*—"alloy"—looks like a typographical error. It makes more sense to read *toute loy,* making the line read, "That she will outshine every law of the Sun."

73.
Persecutee sera de Dieu l'Eglise,
Et les sainctz temples seront expoliez:
L'enfant la mere mettra nud en chemise,
Seront Arabes aux Polons raliez.

The church of God shall be persecuted,
And the holy temples shall be despoiled:
The mother will put out the child naked in a shirt;
Arabs shall be allied with Poles.

A generalized prediction of the degeneracy of the Last Days. The first line is ambiguous. It could also be translated, "The church shall be persecuted *by* God," which would point up alleged Protestant sympathies in Nostradamus. The second line would then mean that God has ordained the spoliation of the churches by the Protestants. But this is the less likely reading, given the context of the rest of the quatrain.

The third line is equally ambiguous. Some translate it, "The child will put out the naked mother in a shirt," which would point to a prediction of filial ingratitude in a degenerate age. But *nud*, "naked," is masculine in form here. French adjectives change their endings to agree with the gender of the noun they modify. Consequently, *nud* agrees with the masculine *enfant* rather than the feminine *mère*. Thus I have chosen to render it as above. In this case, the situation Nostradamus foresees is even worse: it is so bad that it overrides even the powerful maternal instinct.

The last line of the quatrain seems to be saying that depravity will reach such an extent that Christians (Poles) will ally with Muslims (Arabs), presumably against the Hapsburgs. Since France itself had no scruples about allying with the Ottomans in Nostradamus's time, it is not easy to see why he found this idea so shocking.

79.

La sacree pompe viendra baisser les aesles,
Par la vertue du grand legislateur:
Humble haulsera, vexera les rebelles,
Naistra sur terre aucun aemulateur.

Sacred pomp will come to lower its wings
By the strength of the great legislator.

He will raise the humble, vex the rebellious,
His equal shall never be born on earth.

Another general quatrain speaking about a universal monarch who
will bring justice and reduce the arrogance of the clergy. This may
not have been as subversive as it may seem: there was a long tradition in medieval literature of God humbling the mighty—including
ecclesiastics—and exalting the poor, citing of course the teachings
of Christ himself.

Edgar Leoni points out that this verse could well apply to Napoleon, who inflicted numerous humiliations upon the popes,
even, as we have seen, taking away their territories. Moreover, most
of Bonaparte's contingent of generals and dignitaries were people of
common rank—no small thing when only a few years before, such
honors were limited to the nobility. He also promulgated the Code
Napoléon, which granted sweeping civil rights, including equality
of all in the eyes of the law, abolition of titles of nobility, freedom
of religion, and freedom to work in an occupation of one's choice.
In this respect he was indeed a "great legislator."

85.

Par les Sueves & lieux circonvoisins,
Seront en guerre pour cause des nuees:
Camps marins, locustes & cousins,
De Leman faults seront bien desnuees.

By the Suevi and the neighboring places,
They will be at war because of clouds:
Maritime armies, locusts, and cousins;
Geneva's faults will be well disclosed.

The Suevi were an ancient tribe who inhabited what is now Switzerland; that, plus the reference to Lake Geneva (*Leman*) in the
fourth line, make the geographic reference clear. Given that Geneva
in Nostradamus's time was a theocratic state ruled by the French

Reformer John Calvin (cf. I.47), the import is also clear: there will be war over religious ideas (presumably what is intended by "clouds"), and in the end Calvinism will fail: "Geneva's faults will be well disclosed."

Taken as a prediction of the future of France, the prophecy is reasonably accurate. The last forty years of the sixteenth century were marked by bitter religious warfare between Catholics and Protestants, as we have already found. It ended only when the Protestant Henri of Navarre took the throne in 1598 and issued the Edict of Nantes, permitting limited freedom of religion to members of both faiths. At that point Henri converted to Catholicism, uttering the famous quip, "Paris is worth a mass."

The Edict of Nantes was revoked by Louis XIV in 1685, "in order wholly to obliterate the memory of the troubles, the confusion, and the evils which the progress of this false religion [Calvinism] has caused in this kingdom," as Louis's decree put it. The Huguenots who did not convert to Catholicism had to flee abroad. Nostradamus was right in predicting that the Protestants would lose out in France.

93.
Soubz le terroir du rond globe lunayre,
Lors que sera dominateur Mercure:
L'isle d'Escosse fera un luminaire,
Qui les Anglais mettra à desconfiture.

Under the terrain of the great lunar globe,
While Mercury is dominant,
The isle of Scotland will bring a luminary
Who will put the English through discomfiture.

The first two lines of this quatrain are thick with astrological jargon. The first line, "Under the terrain of the great lunar globe," is simply a high-blown way of describing the earth in general. According to the geocentric worldview that was still dominant at the time, the earth sits at the center of the seven concentric spheres of the planets. In Renaissance esotericism, this "sublunary world" was considered to be the place governed by the planets; if one were to ascend through the spheres of the planets—as Dante does in the *Paradiso*—one would become progressively free of their influence.

In regard to the second line, it is not always obvious what Nostradamus means when he says a planet is dominant. Richard Roussat, who wrote a treatise on esoteric astrology entitled *De l'estat et mutation des temps* ("On the State and Mutation of Time"), published in Lyon in 1550 and very likely used by Nostradamus as a source, speaks of different ages when different planets were dominant. But he says Mercury was dominant from 824 to 1179, which makes the period irrelevant to a prophecy written in the mid-1550s. Another interpretation might see this as a time when Mercury is (in astrological terms) exalted, that is, when its influence is particularly pronounced. Mercury is exalted in Virgo, but this happens for about a month each year.

Since the first couplet is so vague, one might seize upon almost any candidate as a fulfillment of this prophecy. One possibility is King Charles I of England, who was born in Fife, Scotland, in 1600. He ascended the English throne in 1625, and caused the people enough "discomfiture" that they deposed and beheaded him in 1649.

96.

Sur le millieu du grand monde la rose,
Pour nouveaux faictz sang public espandu:
A dire vray on aura bouche close,
Lors au besoing viendra tard l'attendu.

In the midst of the great rose of the world,
For new things, public bloodshed;
To speak the truth, one will keep one's mouth shut,
Until the long-awaited one comes to fill the need.

The quatrain speaks of revolution (which in Latin is *res novae,* literally "new things"). The customary interpretation for the "rose of the world" is Rome, but I am not so sure. As we learn from Dante, Jerusalem was traditionally regarded as the center of the world, so Nostradamus, like many prophets before and since, may be forecasting mayhem in the Holy Land before the Second Coming.

I also find it intriguing that the twentieth-century Russian visionary Daniel Andreev entitled his magnum opus *The Rose of the World.* Andreev, who had many of his haunting and profound visions while incarcerated in the Soviet gulag, saw the "rose of the world" not as any one city or place but as a cosmic entity composed of all the world's religions, each of which would form one petal of this rose.[48] Andreev's vision is a beautiful one and is worthy of some study, although I doubt Andreev had Nostradamus in mind when he wrote his book.

The third line of this quatrain is also curious. As John Hogue notes, what it actually says is that in order to speak the truth, it is necessary to remain silent. Nostradamus may be reminding us in a veiled fashion that silence has always been a hallmark of mystical teachings. In fact, the word "mysticism" comes from the Greek *myein,* "to keep silent."

99.
Milan, Ferrare, Turin, & Aquilleye,
Capne, Brundis vexés par gent Celtique:
Par le Lyon & phalange aquilée,
Quand Rome aura le chef vieulx Britannique.

Milan, Ferrara, Turin, and Aquileia,
Capua, Brindisi vexed by the Celtic people:
By the lion and the eagle's phalanx,
When the old Britannic chief shall have Rome.

In Nostradamus, the identity of "the Celtic people" is not always obvious. Frequently he uses it to speak of the French, whose ancestors, the Gauls, were Celts. Here, however, the fourth line indicates that the phrase is more likely to refer to the denizens of the British Isles.

The situation that best fits this quatrain, as John Hogue indicates, is the Allied invasion of Italy during World War II. The peninsula as a whole was "vexed" by the British "lion" and the "phalanx" of the American "eagle," and "the old Britannic chief"— whether one wants to think of him as Churchill or Roosevelt or as a personification of the Anglo-American leadership as a whole— did indeed take possession of Rome.

Century VI

2.

En l'an cinq cens octante plus & moins,
On attendra le siecle bien estrange:
En l'an sept cens & trois cieulx en tesmoigns,
Que plusieurs regnes un à cinq feront change.

In the year 580, more and less,
One will expect an extremely strange era:
In the year 703, with the heavens as a witness,
Many kingdoms—one to five—will change.

The years in this quatrain are generally understood to mean 1580 and 1703. Commentators have—incomprehensibly—seen this verse as a vindication of Nostradamus's predictive powers. Certainly one can find historical events to fill those years: for 1580, the annexation of Portugal by the Spain of Philip II; yet another in the interminable wars of religion in France; and a consequent deterioration of the social order in Nostradamus's native Provence. But none of these, alone or combined, add up to a date that marks a watershed in history. The seer, perhaps suspecting as much, gave himself an out with the addition of "more and less."

The year 1703 can similarly invoke historical events on behalf of its importance: a change in Ottoman sultans; the founding of the city of St. Petersburg by Peter the Great of Russia; even the signing of the Methuen Treaty between Portugal and Britain, giving preferential rates to Portuguese wine imports and thus inaugurating a long era of port drinking in the British Isles. Some commentators mention the War of the Spanish Succession, even claiming that this is cryptically suggested in the term "one to five": Louis XIV of France tried to engineer the Spanish succession in favor of his grandson, who became Philip V of Spain. But the war actually started in 1701.

All in all, however, neither 1580 nor 1703 stands out as a particularly important date in history. One commentator has tried to fudge the issue by saying that Nostradamus began his dating with the Council of Nicaea in 325 A.D., but I can see no reason to believe this.

5.

Si grand famine par unde pestifere,
Par pluye longue le long du polle arctique:
Samarobryn cent lieux de l'hemisphere,
Vivront sans loy, exempt de politique.

So great a famine by a pestiferous flood,
By long rains along the Arctic pole:
Samarobryn a hundred leagues from the hemisphere;
They will live without law, exempt from politics.

The first two lines of this quatrain reflect a common theme in Nostradamus's prophecies: the bad weather that was a feature of the Little Ice Age of the sixteenth century. On the other hand, to speak of "long rains along the Arctic pole" may sound peculiar. Someone looking for a more up-to-date interpretation may want to see in it a premonition of global warming, with widespread flooding and rain rather than snow in the circumpolar areas (cf. II.3, VIII.16).

"Samarobryn" has long exercised the ingenuity of Nostradamus's interpreters. For Peter Lemesurier, it refers to the ancient name for Amiens—Samarobriva—and indicates that this city in Picardy will form a boundary between the "hemispheres" of East and West, that is, between the Holy Roman Empire and France. For Edgar Leoni, to be a hundred leagues from the "hemisphere" means to be in space. (A French "league" was a somewhat plastic unit of measure ranging from 2.5 to 4.5 miles.) Leoni even suggests that "Samarobryn" may be Nostradamus's garbled intuition of a future astronaut named Sam R. O'Brian. By this account, the fourth line would be saying that space stations are not encompassed within any specific political boundaries.

The only suggestion I can add to this farrago is that Amiens, at 2 degrees east longitude, is a comparatively short distance from the 0 degree longitude, which does mark the boundary between hemispheres. But this is more an indication of the kind of intellectual gymnastics Nostradamus inspires in people than any likely reflection of what he had in mind. The precise specification of 0 degrees longitude, passing through the Greenwich Observatory near London, as accepted today was not introduced until 1884. In the end it is hard to assemble this quatrain into a coherent prediction of anything.

8.

Ceulx qui estoient en regne pour scavoir
Au royal change deviendront apouvris:
Uns exilés san appuy, or n'avoir,
Lettrés & lettres ne seront à grans pris.

Those who were in esteem for knowledge
Upon the royal change will become deprived.

Some exiled without support, to have no gold;
Letters and literate ones will not be greatly valued.

This quatrain reflects an almost universal complaint among the educated: learning and knowledge are not esteemed; those who have knowledge do not have money or power.

The second line, with its mention of "the royal change," is usually understood as meaning that the status of the learned will fall when one king replaces another, but I wonder if the French word *change* is being used in the sense of monetary exchange—that is to say, in the currency of a royal court, learning does not count for much. In any event, numerous instances in practically every place and time can be cited as fulfillments of this prophecy.

10.

Un peu de temps les temples des couleurs
De blanc & noir des deux entremeslee:
Roges & jaunes leur embleront les leurs;
Sang, terre, peste, faim, feu, d'eau affollee.

In a little while, the temples of the colors
Of white and black intermixed by the two:
Reds and yellows will carry off their things;
Blood, land, plague, hunger, fire, by water maddened.

Generally taken as a prophecy of a time of religious hypocrisy. "White" and "black" probably refer to polar opposites whose lines, as the quatrain suggests, are beginning to blur. "Reds" in Nostradamus sometimes stand for cardinals or ecclesiastics. The last line is a rather general prophecy of doom. One has the impression that Nostradamus occasionally uses such admonishments simply to fill out a quatrain.

To take the prediction in another direction, the four colors here are those of the four races of humankind. One might then take the verse as a premonition of the present age, with its increasing admixture of the races.

17.

Apres les limes bruslez les asiniers,
Constrainctz seront changer habitz divers:
Les Saturnins bruslez par les meusniers,
Hors la pluspart qui ne sera couverts.

After the files, the ass-drivers are burned;
They will be forced to change their varied attire;
The Saturnians burned by the millers,
Except for the majority, who will not be covered.

Interpreters tend to despair at the obscurity of this quatrain. In the first line, *limes* means "files" in the sense of tools used for filing; in Middle French it sometimes has the meaning of "hypocrites."

To me, the most likely interpretation is in reference to the persecution of the Jews and Moriscos, Moors who had at least nominally converted to Christianity. In Nostradamus's time, the Christian majority in Spain was pressuring the Moriscos to abandon their native attire, which would provoke them to revolt in 1568 (cf. III.20). The second line could be alluding to this eventuality.

The term "Saturnians" is generally understood as referring to the Jews, whom the astrologers of the era placed under the governance of the planet Saturn (after all, Saturday, the day of Saturn, is the Jewish Sabbath). The "millers" are sometimes seen as a veiled reference to monks. *Couverts* in the fourth line literally means "covered," but a plausible emendation is *converts,* "converted." If so, the fourth line could be translated as, "The majority will remain outside and will not be converted." That is, despite persecution, most Jews will still refuse to convert to Christianity.

18.

Par les phisiques le grand Roy delaissé,
Par sort non art de l'Ebrieu est en vie:
Luy & son genre au regne hault poulsé,
Grace donnee à gent qui Christ envie.

By remedies the great king abandoned,
By luck, not the Hebrew's art, remains alive:
He and his race raised high in the realm,
Grace given to those that hate Christ.

A reasonably clear prophecy: A sick king will have lost all hope of recovery through conventional remedies. He will recover by chance, not by the skill of a Jewish doctor. Nonetheless, out of gratitude both the doctor and the Jews as a whole will be elevated in the kingdom.

I do not know of any instance in history that fulfills this prophecy. There was the case of Rodrigo López, a Portuguese Jewish physician who was hanged, drawn, and quartered in 1594 for allegedly conspiring to poison Queen Elizabeth I of England—an event that helped feed anti-Semitism at the time and may have inspired Shakespeare's *Merchant of Venice*. But this is exactly the opposite situation of the one Nostradamus predicts.

21.
Quand ceux du polle artiq unis ensemble,
En Orient grand effraieur & crainte:
Esleu nouveau, soustenu le grand tremble,
Rodes, Bisance de sang barbare taincte.

When those of the Arctic Pole are united together,
In the Orient, great fright and fear:
A new one elected, sustained; the great one trembles;
Rhodes, Byzantium stained with barbarian blood.

The first couplet strikingly predicts a situation that would have been hard to foresee in Nostradamus's time: the creation of a great "circumpolar" union. This makes one think of Russia, which holds by far the most "circumpolar" territory. Beginning in the sixteenth century, the Russian Empire expanded rapidly to the east, eventually bringing all of Siberia under its dominion. This expansion did not stop until the nineteenth century and could legitimately be said to have brought "fright" to the Orient.

The fourth line, like many passages in Nostradamus, predicts fighting in the Levant. Also like a number of passages in Nostradamus, however, it seems to foretell a Christian attempt to reconquer the Ottoman Empire, which did not happen in Nostradamus's time (cf. I.8, IV.39). Rhodes was held by the Ottomans until 1912. At this point it was taken by Italy, which in turn held it until 1943. After brief occupations by the Germans and British, Rhodes became part of the Greek state in 1948.

22.

Dedans la terre du grand temple celique,
Nepveu à Londres par paix faincte meurtry,
La barque alors deviendra scismatique,
Liberté faincte sera au corn & cry.

Inside the land of the great heavenly temple,
Nephew murdered in London by false peace:
The bark then shall become schismatic,
False liberty will everywhere be proclaimed.

No good candidate has emerged for the "nephew murdered in London." As for "the great heavenly temple," the most famous Temple in London is the district that was once occupied by the Knights Templar and is now the site of the Middle Temple and the Inner Temple, two of the four Inns of Court. A British lawyer must be admitted to one of these Inns of Court in order to practice as a barrister. The Temple Church, built by the Templars in 1185 and modeled on the Church of the Holy Sepulchre in Jerusalem, is the only round church in London. If Nostradamus has this church in mind, perhaps he is associating its roundness with that of the dome of heaven. But being the site of secular courts, it is not a

terribly "heavenly" temple—if indeed "heavenly" is the right translation for the cryptic word *celique* (usually taken as derived from
the Latin *caelum,* "heaven").

In any event, the most interesting part of the verse is the second
couplet, which is much more transparent in meaning. The "bark"—
that is, "St. Peter's bark," or the Vatican—will become schismatic, and
a false liberty will be proclaimed everywhere. If one were a tradition-
alist Catholic, no doubt one would be tempted to apply this to the
reforms of Vatican II. Another interpretation might take this verse as
an allusion to the suppression of the Templars in 1312 by a "schismatic" papacy that expropriated their lands.

24.

Mars & le sceptre se trouvera conionct,
Dessoubz Cancer calamiteuse guerre:
Un peu apres sera nouveau Roy oingt,
Qui par long temps pacifiera la terre.

Mars and the scepter will find themselves conjunct
Under Cancer, calamitous war:
A little while after will a new king be anointed,
Who for a long time will pacify the earth.

Many of Nostradamus's predictions are astrologically motivated.
Here he is talking about a situation where Mars and Jupiter ("the
scepter") are conjunct in Cancer. The astrological reasoning is
fairly clear. Mars means war, while Jupiter acts to magnify and
increase: hence "calamitous war." Furthermore, Jupiter, which astrologers call the "great beneficent," is exalted in Cancer, which
would point to the coming of a new ruler who will bring peace.

Such conjunctions are not one-time events, but recur periodically. According to *The American Ephemeris,* this particular conjunction took place most recently on July 2–3, 2002. For the United
States, it certainly augured war. The incursion into Afghanistan
had been launched that spring, to be followed by the invasion of

Iraq in the spring of 2003. As of this writing in June 2005, it is still unclear whether the prophecy of a "new king" who will bring long-lasting peace will be fulfilled.

25.

Par Mars contraire sera la monarchie,
Du grand peycheur en trouble ruyneux:
Jeune noir rouge prendra la hierarchie,
Les proditeurs iront iour bruyneux.

By Mars the monarchy will be contrary,
Of the great fisherman in ruinous trouble.
Young black-red will take the hierarchy;
The traitors will move on a foggy day.

This verse is widely taken to refer to Napoleon's coup d'état against the French Directory on the Eighteenth Brumaire, 1799 ("Brumaire," meaning "foggy," was the name for November in the French Revolutionary calendar). Some commentators read *noir,* "black," in the third line as a sort of anagram for *roi,* "king," so that we would have "the young red [i.e., revolutionary] king" as a reference to Bonaparte.

A similar takeover would bring Louis Napoleon, Bonaparte's nephew, to power as dictator of France in 1851; the next year, Louis Napoleon would proclaim himself Emperor Napoleon III. In *The Eighteenth Brumaire of Louis Napoleon,* Karl Marx characterized this event as a seedy imitation of Bonaparte's original coup. Although Marx's title is ironic, Louis Napoleon's takeover also took place in a "foggy" time of year: on December 2.

27.

Dedans les isles de cinq fleuves à un,
Par le croissant du grand Chyren Selin:
Par les bruynes de l'air fureur de l'un,
Six eschapés, cachés fardeux de lin.

Within the isles of five rivers to one,
By the crescent of the great Chyren Selin,
By the fogs of the air, furor of one,
Six escaped, hidden loads of flax.

This quatrain is chiefly remarkable for its direct link of "Chyren" to "Selin." The reference to the "crescent" reinforces the association with Henri II, who had the moon on his banner. The first line does not fit easily with any known entity. To take it as literally as possible, one might conclude that Nostradamus is talking about a delta, where several streams flow into one body of water. Given the phrase "fogs of the air," Nostradamus is probably imagining some exploits for Henri II in the Low Countries, where a number of rivers run into the North Sea.

33.
Sa main derniere par Alus sanguinaire
Ne se pourra par la mer guarantir:
Entre deux fleuves craindre main militaire,
Le noir l'ireux le fera repentir.

His right hand by sanguinary Alus
Will not be able to protect him by sea:
Between two rivers, fear a military hand,
The wrathful black will make him repent.

"Alus" in the first line is another mysterious Nostradamian name. Some see it as an anagram of "Saul"; for others, it is a future Antichrist, like "Mabus" in II.62. More likely, it derives from the Greek *hals,* "salt"—metaphorically, "sea," an interpretation reinforced by the second line. The verse would then refer to a sea battle. Whoever is involved here—and that is totally unclear—will not be able to protect himself by sea. "Black," *noir,* in the last line is sometimes regarded as an anagram for "*roi,*" "king" (cf. VI.25). More literally, it could apply to the "black" Moors, who fought the Christians on the Mediterranean in Nostradamus's era.

34.

Du feu volant la machination
Viendra troubler au grand chef assiegez:
Dedans sera telle sedition,
Qu'en desespoir seront les profligés.

The machination of the flying fire
Will come to trouble the great chief besieged.
Within there will be such sedition
That the wretches will be in despair.

One of a number of verses in which Nostradamus seems to foresee modern technology, with its "machination of the flying fire." Many commentators see this as a prophecy of aerial bombardment, which fits the line quite well, although it could also refer to attack by artillery—a form of warfare that was used in Nostradamus's day. The rest of the quatrain could apply to any situation in which a besieged force mutinies or tries to treat with the enemy.

37.

L'oeuvre ancien se parachevra,
Du toict cherra sur le grand mal ruyne:
Innocent faict mort on accusera:
Nocent caiché, taillis à la bruyne.

The ancient work will be completed,
From the roof evil ruin will fall on the great one:
An innocent made dead will be accused:
The culprit hidden, grove in the fog.

It is comparatively easy to apply this quatrain to John F. Kennedy's assassination, as several commentators have done. We have ruin falling on a great man from the roof; the accused, Lee Harvey Oswald, innocent (according to various theories) and soon eliminated;

the real culprits hidden in the fog, literal or metaphorical. John Hogue even equates Nostradamus's "grove" with the "grassy knoll" from which several witnesses reported hearing gunshots. If there is any other situation that fits this quatrain better, it is hidden by the fogs of history. If so, it is unfortunate that Nostradamus is so vague about the real culprits.

42.
A logmyon sera laissé le regne,
Du grand Selin qui plus fera de faict:
Par les Italies estendra son enseigne,
Regi sera par prudent contrefaict.

To Logmyon will the kingdom be left
Of the great Selin who will do more deeds;
By the Italies he will extend his banner;
He will be guided by prudent counterfeit.

The chief source of interest here is the enigmatic Logmyon, a figure whose name is often understood as deriving from Ogmios, the ancient Celtic equivalent of Heracles. Dr. de Fontbrune, a French commentator on Nostradamus, modifies this interpretation somewhat. He indicates that Ogmios (or Ogham) is a combination of Hercules and Mercury, the god of communication, and so represents "the force of eloquence." By extension, then, this line predicts the replacement of the French monarchy by a government of "eloquence"—that is, a republic (cf. IX.89).

A more cautious interpretation would equate "Logmyon" with the youngest son of Henri II ("Selin"): François, the Duc d'Alençon, who was originally christened Hercules. Nostradamus appears to be predicting that this son will inherit the throne and extend French territory into Italy, neither of which came to pass. The last line could also be translated, "He will be guided by a prudent cripple," *contrefaict* meaning both "counterfeit" and "deformed."

49.

De la partie de Mammer grand pontife
Subjuguera les confines du Dannube:
Chasser les croix par fer raffe ne riffe,
Captifz, or, bagues, plus de cent mille rubes.

From the party of Mammer, great pontiff
Will subjugate the confines of the Danube,
To chase the crosses with iron, by hook or by crook,
Captives, gold, rings, more than a hundred thousand rubies.

"Mammer" in the first line is usually translated as "Mars," "Mamer" being a name given to the war god by the Sabines, an ancient tribe who lived next to the Romans. This is certainly possible, but an echo of "mammon," *lucre,* may be intended as well. It could also be a pun for *ma mère,* indicating that the pontiff in question is particularly devoted to the Virgin (as John Paul II was).

As Leoni notes, Nostradamus most likely means that a war-like (and possibly greedy) pope will lead a campaign against the Turks in the Danube basin, and will come back with many captives and much treasure. This was plausible in the context of the time—some of the pontiffs did lead armies (for example, Julius II, pope from 1503 to 1513)—but if this is the prophecy, it was not fulfilled.

Some Nostradamian scholars tend to see Hitler whenever "Hister" or the Danube is mentioned, and this quatrain is no exception (cf. II. 24, IV.66, V.29). The third line, which speaks of a cross, an iron, and a hook, is sometimes seen as alluding to the "hooked cross," or swastika, as well as to the Iron Cross, the highest German military decoration. By this reading, the verse is indicating that Hitler will conquer the Danube basin and take many prisoners as well as a great deal of booty. This is plausible only if one overlooks the grotesquery of calling the Nazi dictator a "great pontiff."

51.

Peuple assemblé, voir nouveau espectacle,
Princes & Roys par plusieurs assistans:
Pilliers faillir, murs, mais comme miracle,
Le Roy sauvé & trente des instants.

People assembled to see a new spectacle,
Princes and kings among many at hand:
Pillars to fall, walls, but as a miracle,
The king saved along with thirty present.

This quatrain is said to have helped the Swiss astrologer Karl Ernst
Krafft predict an assassination attempt on Adolf Hitler. Using astrology along with this verse, Krafft warned Hitler of danger from
a bomb exploding in the period of November 7–10, 1939.

On November 8, 1939, Hitler spoke at a celebration of the an-
niversary of his 1923 Beer Hall Putsch in Munich. Contrary to
their habit, Hitler and the top Nazi leaders with him left the event
early. Soon afterward, a bomb exploded, killing seven and wound-
ing sixty-three.

The attempted assassination was very likely a sham; the bomb
was probably planted by Hitler's own orders to eliminate some of
the troublesome old guard in the Nazi Party.[49] Nonetheless, the
prediction brought Krafft to the attention of Joseph Goebbels,
who put the astrologer to work adapting Nostradamus's prophecies
for use as propaganda during World War II.

The propaganda campaign did enjoy some success. In May
1940, the Luftwaffe strewed thousands of pamphlets over Belgium
and France. Containing faked prophecies by Nostradamus, they
announced that flying machines would bring heavy destruction
(cf. VI.34) but that the southeast of France would be spared. The
aim of these pamphlets was to unsettle the traffic around Paris.
Walter Schellenberg, chief of the German espionage services, wrote
in his memoirs, "I never imagined that [these brochures] could

have produced such an effect. All the efforts of the [French] civil and military authorities to prevent a great outpouring of refugees toward the Southeast were fruitless."[50]

Despite these successes, Krafft eventually fell afoul of the Nazi regime and died en route to Buchenwald in 1945.

58.

Entre les deux monarques esloignés,
Los que le Sol par Selin clair perdue:
Simulte grande entre deux indignés,
Qu'aux Isles & Sienne la liberté rendue.

Between the two distant monarchs,
While the Sun through Selin loses its light,
A great clash between two indignant ones,
To the Isles and Siena liberty bestowed.

"Selin" is again Henri II; *Sol,* or "Sun," seems to refer to the Hapsburgs, since both the Holy Roman emperor Charles V and his son, Philip II of Spain, had a rising sun on their coats of arms. Nostradamus is forecasting a conflict between France and the Hapsburg Empire, which will return "liberty" to the "Isles"— presumably Corsica, Sardinia, and Sicily—and to Siena. This prophecy is reasonably straightforward, but it was not fulfilled. Corsica was fighting to break free from Genoa, as we have already seen (III.23), and France at the same time was trying to take it over, but this effort was not successful: after a few years of French occupation, Corsica was returned to Genoa. Sardinia and Sicily remained in Hapsburg hands for centuries afterward. Nor would Siena, an independent state in the Middle Ages, recover its liberty. At the time this prophecy was written, Siena was in the hands of the Spaniards, who in 1557 sold the territory to the grand duchy of Tuscany. It would remain in the possession of Tuscany until the unification of Italy in the 1860s.

63.

La dame seule au regne demouree,
L'unic estaint premier au lict d'honneur:
Sept ans sera de douleur exploree,
Puis longue vie au regne par grand heur.

The lady alone remaining in the kingdom,
The unique one deceased first in the bed of honor.
Seven years she will be tested by grief,
Then long life in the kingdom, with greatness.

A quatrain usually applied to Catherine de' Medici, Henri II's queen. The first two lines indicate that she will survive her husband, who, as we have seen in I.35, died in a freak jousting accident in 1559. She lived to see three of her sons on the throne of France: François I, who died in 1560 after a year of reign; Charles IX, who reigned from 1560 to 1574; and Henri III, who ruled from 1574 to 1589. Henri, her favorite son, detached himself increasingly from her influence during his tenure as king, but Catherine always remained a powerful influence. Henri III himself was assassinated a few months after her death (cf. V.38).

67.

Au grand empire parviendra tout un autre
Bonté distant plus de felicité;
Regi par un issu non long du peaultre,
Corruer regnes grande infelicité.

One completely different will attain the great empire,
Goodness remote more than felicity;
Ruled by one not far from the pallet,
To condemn kingdoms to great unhappiness.

A verse that is sometimes understood as characterizing a coming Antichrist. The second line is ambiguous, and could mean either that the man in question is more remote from goodness than from felicity (that is, good luck), or that he is removed from both goodness *and* felicity. Similarly, the "pallet" in the third line is usually taken as indicating the bed of a whore, although it may also mean someone not far from the cradle—that is, someone very young.

Most commentators see in it a reference to Napoleon, presumably on the grounds that he was under the thumb of Josephine—but it hardly seems correct to picture Napoleon as under anyone's thumb. The most plausible interpretation is that the great empire is, as it was in Nostradamus's day, the Holy Roman Empire, and that this verse is disparaging some future Hapsburg heir who will be governed by the "son of a whore" and will bring great misfortune on his domain.

I do not know of any Hapsburg emperors that fit this description particularly well. The closest is perhaps Karl I, the last Hapsburg emperor, who inherited the throne of Austria-Hungary in 1916, in the middle of World War I. Karl repeatedly tried to negotiate peace with the Allies, largely because of the influence of his pro-Allied wife ("one not far from the pallet"), Princess Zita of Bourbon-Parma. But Karl and his ministers botched the negotiations so badly that no accord was ever reached. When Austria collapsed in defeat in 1918, Karl lost the throne. He died in poverty in 1922, at the age of thirty-four.

72.

Par fureur faincte d'esmotion divine,
Sera la femme du grand fort violee:
Juges voulans damner telle doctrine,
Victime au peuple ignorant imolee.

By the feigned rage of a divine emotion
Will the woman of the great fort be violated.
The judges wanting to condemn such a doctrine.
Victim immolated by the ignorant people.

Usually seen as a reference to Gregory Rasputin (1866?–1916), the sinister Siberian magus who gained almost limitless power over the Empress Alexandra of Russia in the last years of the tsarist regime. Rasputin's entrée to the Romanov court came through his capacities as a healer: he was able to provide relief for Tsarevich Alexis, the heir to the throne, who suffered from hemophilia. Rasputin's healing powers, stemming from his hypnotic abilities, were real enough, but he falsely portrayed himself to the empress as a *starets,* a spiritual elder, though in fact he was a vulgar and ambitious debauchee. In this sense he could be said to have "violated" her, although they apparently did not have sexual relations.

Rasputin's capricious and corrupting influence at a time when Russia was going through the First World War led practically all the government to condemn him, and he was murdered by a conspiracy of noblemen in December 1916. The Romanov dynasty was overthrown two months later, and the imperial family was shot by the Bolsheviks in 1918, victims sacrificed to "the ignorant people."

An alternate translation of part of the second line is, "The wife of the great strong one." *Fort* means "strong" in French, although it is also a now obsolete word for "fort." Since *fort* is also an adverb, yet another possible translation is, "The wife of the great one powerfully violated."

74.
La deschassee au regne tournera,
Ses ennemis trouvés des conjurés:
Plus que jamais son temps triomphera,
Trois & septante à mort trop asseurés.

The exile will return to the kingdom,
Her enemies found among conspirators:
More than ever her age will triumph,
Seventy-three to death too much assured.

Erika Cheetham sees in this a prophecy of Elizabeth I of England, whom it suits fairly well. Imprisoned during the reign of her sister, Mary I, Elizabeth took the throne in the midst of intrigue and conspiracy, which never entirely disappeared in her reign; we have already encountered Rodrigo López's plot (real or imagined) against her in 1594 (cf. VI.18). Certainly the Elizabethan age was one of "triumph" for England; it is still remembered as a high point in national history.

The most obvious reading of the last line is that seventy-three conspirators will be condemned to death: the French participle *asseurés* is masculine plural. Nonetheless, Cheetham sees in it a somewhat garbled prophecy of Elizabeth's own death at the age of seventy in 1603.

75.
Le grand pilot par Roy sera mandé,
Laisser la classe pour plus hault lieu attaindre:
Sept ans apres sera contrebandé,
Barbare armee viendra Venise craindre.

The great pilot will be commanded by the king
To leave the fleet to attain a higher place.
Seven years later he will be proscribed.
Venice will come to fear a barbarian army.

"The great pilot" almost certainly refers to Admiral Gaspard de Coligny; if so, the prophecy proved accurate. During the religious wars of France in the 1560s, Coligny was leader of the Protestant cause, and in 1569, the Protestant King Henri of Navarre (later Henri IV of France) made him commander of the Protestant forces. In 1570, Coligny was one of the negotiators of a short-lived armistice between Catholics and Protestants. He then returned to Paris, where he tried to convince the young King Charles IX to go to war with Spain. Displeased, Catherine de' Medici, the queen mother, allowed the Duc de Guise to assassinate Coligny. Coligny was murdered on August 24, 1572. He was the first victim of the St. Bartholomew's Day Massacre, a vicious nationwide purge of Protestants (cf. IV.47, 62, IX.79).

The last line does not seem related to the rest of the quatrain. To say that Venice would have cause to fear a "barbarian army" at a time when the Venetians were facing constant pressure from the Ottomans did not require any prophetic skill. But the syntax makes the meaning ambiguous: the line could also mean, "Barbarian army will come to fear Venice."

83.
Celuy qu'aura tant d'honneur et caresses,
A son entrée de la Gaule Belgique:
Un temps apres fera tant de rudesses,
Et sera contre à la fleur tant bellique.

He who will have so much honor and so many caresses
Upon his entry into Belgian Gaul,
A while after will show such rudeness
And will be so warlike against the flower.

This quatrain is frequently, and plausibly, taken as a reference to Philip II of Spain. Philip received the Spanish Netherlands (presumably meant here by "Belgian Gaul") as part of his inheritance from his father, Charles V, but he had no fondness for the nation, and was so hostile to its embrace of Protestantism that the Netherlands rebelled in 1568.

Philip II, initially known as "the Prudent King," became more reckless later in his reign. The last line, referring to the "flower," that is, the *fleur de lis,* predicts war with France. Since the two nations were at war at the time of this writing, in 1557, it again did not require a great deal of prognostication to make such a forecast. But many commentators also point to Philip's wars against Henri IV of France in the 1590s as a fulfillment of this verse.

92.

Prince de beauté tant venuste,
Au chef menee, le second faict trahy:
La cité au glaive, de poudre face aduste,
Par trop grand meurtre le chef du Roy hay.

Prince of beauty so elegant,
Led to the head, the second made, betrayed:
The city to the sword, face burned with powder,
Through too much slaughter the king's head hated.

Commentators generally ascribe this quatrain to Louis XVI, the king of France who was overthrown by the Revolution. By this interpretation he was "led to the head" of the nation, then demoted to second place as a constitutional monarch after the upheavals of 1789. The *glaive*, or sword, has been understood metaphorically as a reference to the blade of the guillotine, to which Louis succumbed in 1793.

The chief difficulty with this ascription comes from the first line, since Louis XVI was not a notably handsome man. One could resolve this difficulty by making this line speak, not of Louis himself, but of the voluptuousness and luxury of the court during his reign.

93.

Prelat avare d'ambition trompé,
Rien ne sera que trop viendra cuider:
Ses messagers, & luy bien attrapé,
Tout au rebours voir, qui le bois fendroit.

Greedy prelate fooled by ambition,
There will be nothing that he will come to think too much:
He and his messengers well entrapped,
To see everything reversed, so he will cut wood.

This quatrain has puzzled commentators, who see in it a reference to a pope or prelate whose ambition leads him to overstep his bounds. The reference to cutting wood in the last line has puzzled many.

If one sets aside the word "prelate"—which admittedly does point to someone in the Church—the figure who fulfills this prophecy best is Kaiser Wilhelm II. In 1888, he ascended the throne of a newly unified Germany, which was essentially the creation of the great statesman Otto von Bismarck. Almost immediately, Wilhelm began to undo Bismarck's chief geopolitical strategy, which was to avoid war on two fronts. Wilhelm's saber-rattling led republican France and autocratic Russia into a secret agreement for mutual defense, which would prove to be one of the triggers of World War I.

When Germany collapsed in defeat in November 1918, Wilhelm abdicated and fled to the Netherlands, where he remained until his death in 1941. During his exile, his chief leisure pursuit was sawing wood. Ever a man for doing things on a grand scale, the ex-kaiser chopped down some forty thousand trees on his estate.

97.
Cinq & quarante degrés ciel bruslera,
Feu approcher de la grand cité neufve,
Instant grand flamme esparse sautera,
Quand on voudra des Normans faire preuve.

Forty-five degrees, the sky will burn,
Fire to approach the great new city.
Instantly a great scattered flame will leap up,
When one will want to make proof of the Normans.

Undoubtedly the most celebrated of Nostradamus's quatrains in recent years. Many have seen in it a prediction of the 9/11 disaster in New York, the "new city" (cf. I.87, X.49), which is at 42 degrees north latitude (and hence reasonably close to 45 degrees). "The

Normans" has generally been taken to refer to the aftermath, when the U.S. wanted support from the recalcitrant French in the fight against terrorism.

Did Nostradamus, then, predict the World Trade Center disaster? One way to answer this question would be to look at interpretations of this quatrain from before the actual event.

John Hogue, in a book published in 1997, comments on this verse, "The sky ignites into flames above New York City." He gives possible other interpretations as involving Novyi Byelograd (New Belgrade)—a suburb of Belgrade, Serbia, that, according to Hogue, sits exactly on the 45-degree line—as well as the greenhouse effect.

Erika Cheetham, writing in 1973, interprets the verse thus: "New York county lies between 40° and 45° parallel in the U.S.A. . . . It appears that this attack is very widespread (scattered flame)."

This verse was thus interpreted as foreseeing an attack of some kind on New York before the actual event, and that Nostradamus watchers viewed it as such. So there is something to be said for the idea that he predicted an event like 9/11, although the details are extremely vague.

All this said, the "new city" more likely refers to one of the many French towns named Villeneuve, which means "new city": these generally lie between 44 and 50 degrees north latitude. Or it could mean Naples, originally founded by Greek colonists, who named it Neapolis (also meaning "new city"). Moreover, Naples was ruled by Normans in the Middle Ages. By this interpretation, Nostradamus here is predicting a major fire or a volcanic eruption near Naples. (Mount Vesuvius, whose eruption buried Pompeii and Herculaneum in 79 A.D., is nearby.)

One will have to make up one's own mind about the application of this prophecy to September 11. My own view is that, insofar as we can credit Nostradamus with prophetic ability, it is not in the realm of specific events or situations: as we have already seen so often, when he does this, he is wrong. Personally, I suspect that what Nostradamus at his best managed to accomplish was the creation of something like the interpretations of the hexagrams in the

Chinese oracle known as the *I Ching,* or "Book of Changes." The verses of the *I Ching* do not predict specific events that will happen one time only, but rather set out archetypal situations that can apply to many circumstances. I believe that this ultimately will be the most profitable and intelligent way to approach Nostradamus.

The only other thing I should add here is that there are some spurious Nostradamian verses that have circulated about 9/11, chiefly on the Internet. Here are some examples:

In the City of God there will be a great thunder,
Two brothers torn apart by Chaos,
while the fortress endures, the great leader will succumb.
The third big war will begin when the big city is burning.

Two steel birds will fall from the sky on the Metropolis.
The sky will burn at forty-five degrees latitude.
Fire approaches the great new city.
Immediately a huge, scattered flame leaps up.

Within months, rivers will flow with blood.
The undead will roam earth for little time.

In the city of York there will be a great collapse,
two twin brothers, torn apart by chaos,
while the fortress falls, the great leader will succumb,
the third big war will begin when the big city is burning.

In the year of the new century and nine months,
From the sky will come a great King of Terror . . .

The sky will burn at forty-five degrees.
Fire approaches the great new city . . .

No doubt there are others. As should be clear, these verses are all either imitations of Nostradamus, cobbled-together pieces of this quatrain and others (notably X.72), or both. They are in fact urban legends, and I have found many of them on David Emery's "Urban Legends and Folklore" column on the Web site About.com and similar sources.

100.

LEGIS CANTIO CONTRA INEPTOS CRITICOS

Quos legent hosce versus mature censunto,
Profanum vulgus & inscium ne attractato:
Omnesq: Astrologi Blenni, Barbari procul sunto,
Qui aliter facit, is rite, sacer esto.

LEGAL SONG AGAINST INEPT CRITICS

Let those who read these verses think maturely;
Let them not attract the profane and ignorant crowd.
Let all blind astrologers, barbarians stay away.
Who does otherwise, acts rightly; may he be holy.

This quatrain is written in Latin. In fact it is plagiarized almost word for word, as Peter Lemesurier has noted, from Petrus Crinitus's warning to lawyers in a 1504 work entitled *De honesta disciplina* ("On Honest Discipline"). As often in Nostradamus, there are errors and misprints: *cantio* ("song") in the title should no doubt be *Cautio* ("warning"); *quos* ("whom") in the first line should be *qui* ("who").

The verse is a warning against misinterpretation by the vulgar. It is more of a literary pose than a genuine admonition. Such statements frequently occur in works emulating Greek and Latin literature, in which poets often pretended to be expounding some esoteric doctrine that would be misunderstood by common minds. The most famous of these passages appears in Horace's *Odes* III.1, which begins, "*Odi profanum vulgus et arceo,*" "I hate and abhor the vulgar crowd"—echoed in the second line of Nostradamus's quatrain.

The Greek and Latin poets were in turn imitating the masters of the ancient mystery schools, in which certain rites and doctrines were revealed only to initiates. Nostradamus is trying to give his own work the same patina of esoteric exclusivity, but the stance is so common—not to say commonplace—in the literature of his time that it cannot be taken too seriously.

Century VII

7.

Sur le combat des grans chevaulx legiers,
On criera le grand croissant confond.
De nuict ruer monts, habitz de bergiers,
Abismes rouges dans le fossé profond.

On the fight of the great light horses,
The great crescent will be proclaimed to be overwhelmed.
At night, climbing mountains, shepherds' clothing,
Red chasms in the deep ditch.

"The great crescent" leads most commentators to take this verse as
a prediction of some great Muslim defeat. But the verse is actually
rather ambiguous: "the great crescent" is *said* to be defeated, but
is it actually?

John Hogue interestingly relates this quatrain to the Soviet invasion of Afghanistan in 1979. The Soviets marched rapidly into
the country and installed a puppet government. They soon found
themselves facing a long war of attrition fought by mountain guerrillas clad in the traditional clothing of the herdsmen of the region.

Remaining in the valleys as much as possible, the Red Army endured enough bloodshed to prompt them to evacuate in 1988, as the Soviet Union itself was beginning to collapse.

11.

L'enfant Royal contemnera la mere,
Oeil, piedz blessés, rude, inhobeissant:
Nouvelle à dame estrange & bien amere,
Seront tué des siens plus de cinq cens.

The royal child shall disdain his mother,
Eye, feet wounded, rude, disobedient.
News strange and very bitter to the lady,
Of hers over five hundred will be killed.

The two women with whom this quatrain are most often associated both have the surname de' Medici. The first we have already encountered: Catherine de' Medici, who at the time of this writing in 1557 was queen of France and—after the death of her husband, Henri II, in 1559—the queen mother. She dominated two of her sons who succeeded to the throne, but the third, Henri III, pushed her aside, particularly in the last years of her (and his) life in the 1580s.

Théophilus de Garancières, a seventeenth-century commentator on Nostradamus, suggests another choice: Marie de' Medici (1573–1642), queen of France under Henri IV. Upon his death in 1610, she served as regent for their son Louis XIII, who ruled from 1610 to 1643. In the early years of Louis's reign, Marie held virtually unlimited power in the realm, but in 1617 Louis began to assert himself. He engineered the assassination of his mother's favorite, the devious and corrupt Concino Concini. Garancières says that more than five hundred of the queen's favorites died in this purge. I have not been able to corroborate this claim, but Concini's wife was also beheaded and burned for sorcery.

After Concini's fall, Marie was forced into exile, but she was reconciled with Louis in 1622. In 1630, following her attempt to overthrow the king's powerful adviser, Cardinal Richelieu, she fled to the Spanish Netherlands, where she lived until her death, in 1642—only a year before her son's.

16.

Entrée profonde par la grand Royne faicte
Rendra le lieu puissant inaccessible:
L'armee des trois lyons sera deffaicte,
Faisant dedans cas hideux & terrible.

The deep entrance made by the great queen
Will make the mighty place inaccessible.
The army of the three lions will be defeated,
Making situations hideous and terrible within.

This seems to refer to the fortification of the port of Calais on the northern coast of France by Mary I of England: Calais was in English hands at the time. In 1558, only a short time after this prophecy was written, the Duc de Guise of France would take Calais, making this a successful prediction. The third line alludes to the three lions on the English royal coat of arms.

25.

Par guerre longue tout l'exercite expuiser,
Que pour souldartz ne trouveront pecune:
Lieu d'or d'argent, cuir on viendra cuser,
Gaulois aerain, signe croissant de Lune.

By a long war, exhausting all the army
For soldiers they will not find money.
In place of gold, of silver, leather will be minted,
Gallic brass, sign crescent of Moon.

The general thrust of this quatrain is that an exhausted army will be paid in scrip—remarkably, one made out of leather. The reference to the crescent, a common motif in Nostradamus, as usual can have two meanings: the crescent of Henri II or that of the Muslims. The last line makes it more likely that Henri II is indicated.

Actually, in those years it was the Spanish monarchy, with its restive and far-flung empire, that faced the greatest fiscal stress. Nostradamus may be alluding to the decree of January 1, 1557, in which the Spanish state declared bankruptcy. In his circuitous way, he could be implying that financial difficulties will lead the Spaniards to capitulate to France and reconfigure their finances on French terms ("Gallic brass"). This did not happen. Spain won its war with France and extracted itself from its fiscal plight thanks to huge loans from the financial dynasties of the Fuggers and the Medici.

The reference to leather money may seem puzzling, but in fact leather has occasionally been used as a material for scrip and banknotes in many eras, including that of Nostradamus. During the German currency crisis in the early 1920s, some issues of *Notgeld* ("money of need") were made of leather. One specimen I have come across is for 50 million marks—in that era of hyperinflation, a nearly worthless sum. If one wishes to apply this quatrain to more modern times, that era in Germany, when the ruinous reparations demanded by the victorious Allies caused the currency to collapse, would be a good candidate.

33.
Par fraude regnes, forces expolier,
La classe obsesse, passaiges à l'espie:
Deux fainctz amiz se viedront rallier,
Esveiller hayne de long temps assoupie.

By fraud kingdoms, powers to despoil,
The fleet blockaded, passage watched by spies.
Two pretended friends will again come to ally,
To awaken a hatred for a long time asleep.

A quatrain that, along with the one immediately following, is often taken to presage the fall of France in 1940 and the subsequent German occupation. John Hogue connects the verse above with an episode in July 1940, when a British task force sank the French fleet in the port of Mers-el-Kebir at Oran in Algeria. The battle came at the end of a long and fruitless negotiation between the British and French about what to do with the latter's navy after the French capitulated to Hitler. In the end the two sides could reach no agreement, and the British, acting under Churchill's orders, sank the French fleet to keep it from falling into the hands of the Germans. Nearly 1,300 French sailors were killed, stirring rancor against the British.

The British commander, Vice Admiral Sir James Somerville, later said the action at Mers-el-Kebir was "the biggest political blunder of modern times and will rouse the whole world against us." The Nazis made great play of the incident to stir up anti-British sentiment in occupied France.

34.
En grand regret sera la gent Gauloise,
Coeur vain, legier, croira temerité:
Pain, sel, ne vin, eaue, venim ne cervoise,
Plus grand captif, faim, froit, necessité.

The Gallic folk shall be in great sorrow;
It will reckon a heart empty, light, to be bold.
Bread, salt, nor wine, water; poison, not beer;
The greatest one captive, hunger, cold, want.

Like VII.33, above, this is often seen as a prediction of the fall of France as a result of misplaced faith in its civilian and military leadership ("it will reckon a heart empty, light, to be bold"). The verse also evokes the German occupation of France between 1940 and 1945. Certainly all the conditions listed in this quatrain applied to the situation. The hardships visited upon the French by their occupiers were enormous; daily rations at certain times were below starvation level.

By this interpretation, "the greatest one captive" could refer to Marshal Henri-Philippe Pétain, the former World War I commander who took over as premier of France after the collapse and signed a humiliating treaty of surrender with Hitler. Pétain agreed to head the puppet government in Vichy and gave his full support to the Nazi regime. After the war, he was tried and condemned for treason. He died in 1951, at the age of ninety-five, while serving a sentence of life imprisonment.

CENTURY VII ENDS ABRUPTLY *with quatrain* 42. *We do not know why: no reason is given either by Nostradamus or by his pupil and editor Chavigny.*

Century VIII

I.

PAU, NAY, LORON plus feu qu'à sang sera,
Laude nager, fuir grand aux surrez.
Les agassas entrée refuser.
Pampon, Durance les tiendra enserrez.

PAU, NAY, LORON more fire than of blood shall be;
The great one to swim the Aude, flee to the enclosures.
The magpies to refuse entrance.
Pampon, Durance will keep them locked up.

This impenetrable verse is chiefly interesting for the phrase "PAU, NAY, LORON" in the first line. Pau, Nay, and Loron are towns in Béarn in southwestern France, but as the printing in all capitals suggests, this is quite possibly an anagram. Many interpreters unscramble it to read napaulon roy, "Napoleon the king," who was more a man of "fire than of blood." This presumably means that Napoleon's warlike nature outstripped his relatively humble background as the scion of minor Corsican nobility.

"Magpies" in the third line is usually thought to allude to the representatives of one of the popes called Pius, whose name in French, "Pie," is a homonym for *pie*, "magpie"; *agassa* is Provençal for *pie*. Napoleon would imprison both Pius VI and Pius VII. On the other hand, the syntax for this line is so broken and obscure that it is difficult to make anything of it. The application to Napoleon seems highly forced. At its core the quatrain seems to be about a failed escape by someone who seeks help from the Vatican but is refused and ends up incarcerated again.

4.

Dedans Monech le coq sera receu,
Le Cardinal de France apparoistra
Par Logarion Romain sera deceu
Foiblesse à l'aigle, & force au coq naistra.

Within Monaco the cock will be received,
The cardinal of France will appear.
By Logarion a Roman will be deceived.
Weakness to the eagle, and strength to the cock shall grow.

This quatrain relates to the tiny Mediterranean principality of Monaco, which in Nostradamus's time was a protectorate of Spain. In 1641, Spanish dominance came to an end when Honoré III of Monaco signed a treaty assuring his country of "the protective friendship of France," whose national symbol is the cock. (The "eagle" refers to the Spanish Hapsburgs.) In 1861 the principality regained its independence, which it retains to this day, although its ties to France are extremely close. If the reigning Grimaldi family (currently represented by Prince Rainier III) ever dies out, Monaco will become an autonomous state of France.

"Logarion" in the third line is mystifying. Lemesurier emends it to "Logmion," which makes the verse interesting in that, as we have seen (VI.42), Ogmios was the Hercules of ancient Gaul, and Hercules was closely associated with Monaco; its name may derive from an ancient epithet of the Greek hero: "Heracles Monoikos,"

"Hercules Alone." Monaco's main port is the Port of Hercules. In 1793, the French Republic would annex Monaco, renaming it "Fort Hercule."

The first man that comes to mind in relation to the "cardinal of France" is the formidable Cardinal Richelieu, Louis XIII's adviser, not to say master. It was Richelieu's negotiations that led to the aforementioned treaty of protection in 1641.

All in all, this is one of Nostradamus's more intriguing and impressive prophecies. It is comparatively easy to tie this quatrain to Monaco and to its eventual drift away from Spain to France.

4 (ALTERNATE).

Beaucoup de gens voudront parlementer,
Aux grand Seigneurs qui leur feront la guerre:
On ne voudra en rien les escouter,
Helas! Si Dieu n'envoye paix en terre.

Many people will want to confer
With the great lords who will make war on them.
No one will want to hear anything of them.
Alas! If God does not send peace on earth!

This quatrain is an alternate to the one above (there are alternatives to the first six quatrains in Century VIII). It is so clear, in fact, that its authenticity, like that of the other alternates, is seriously doubted; they first appear in an edition of 1605, almost forty years after the magus's death. If they are genuine, they may have been early drafts or rejects of Nostradamus's that were later discovered and printed.

Regardless, the message of this verse is worth heeding. Essentially it says that the people do not want war; it is the "great lords" who inflict it upon them. The people will protest, of course, but "no one will want to hear anything of them." It would be impossible to connect this quatrain with any specific situation; rather, it seems to be an all-too-accurate reflection of politics and society in all ages. The last line suggests that Nostradamus—or whoever wrote this verse—can see no way out of this dilemma through human means alone.

9.

Pendant que l'aigle & le coq à Savone
Seront unis Mer Levant & Ongrie,
L'armee à Naples, Palerne, Marque d'Ancone,
Rome, Venise par Barb' horrible crie.

While the eagle and the cock are at Savona,
The sea, Levant, and Hungary shall be united.
The army at Naples, Palermo, Ancona,
Rome, Venice with horrible barbarian cry.

As we have seen (VIII.4), the "eagle" is the Hapsburg Empire and the "cock" is France. Savona was at the time in the Republic of Genoa. Figuratively this could point to French and Spanish struggles in that region, in which the French were trying (unsuccessfully) to loosen Genoa's grip on Corsica and take it for themselves. In the meantime, "the [Mediterranean] sea, Levant, and Hungary shall be united" under the sultan of Turkey. This was already more or less true at the time this verse was written. Hungary was mostly under Ottoman rule; "the Hapsburgs paid tribute for the small buffer strip they retained," as Edgar Leoni notes.

The quatrain is stating one of Nostradamus's principal messages: that the warfare between France and Spain was pointless and dangerous while the threat of Muslim Turkey loomed over Europe. Ultimately, the Christian alliance led by Spain would stop the Turkish fleet in its westward push, and the Poles, Hungarians, and Austrians would stanch the Ottoman onslaught in southeastern Europe, but Turkey was a formidable and at the time still growing power, and Nostradamus's warning was not a foolish one.

16.

Au lieu que HIERON *feit sa nef fabriquer,*
Si grand deluge sera & si subite,
Qu'on n'aura lieu ne terres s'attacquer
L'onde monter Fesulan Olympique.

In the place where HIERON built his ship,
There will be so great and sudden a deluge,
That one will not have land or space to attack;
The wave to climb Olympic Fiesole.

HIERON, like practically every word that Nostradamus has in all capitals, is a source of dispute among his aficionados. One theory holds
that the word should read IESON—that is, the ancient Greek hero
Jason—but this seems forced. Taking the name at face value leads us
to Hieron, the name of two tyrants of Syracuse in the fifth and third
centuries B.C., when that city was a medium-sized naval power.

In this case, Nostradamus would be predicting a tremendous
flood that will engulf Syracuse, on the east coast of Sicily, going all
the way up to Fiesole in central Italy, even possibly to Mount
Olympus in Greece (although *Fesulan Olympique* could just be a
poetic epithet, in the sense of "majestic Fiesole"). Nothing of this
kind has happened yet, although, like certain other quatrains (II.3,
VI.5), to the modern mind it suggests the possible consequences
of global warming.

17.

Les bien aisez subit seront desmis
Par les trois freres le monde mis en trouble.
Cité marine saisiront ennemis,
Faim, feu, sang, peste, et de tous maux double.

Those well at ease will suddenly be put down;
By three brothers the world put in trouble.

Enemies will seize a maritime city,
Hunger, fire, blood, plague, and all evils doubled.

A quatrain chiefly of interest because of its mention of three brothers, who are sometimes seen—for example, by Erika Cheetham—as
the Kennedys (John, Robert, and Edward; cf. IX.36). In this case,
the "world put in trouble" would refer to the Cuban Missile Crisis
of 1962, which brought the world closer to nuclear warfare than it
has ever been before or since. But this is not very convincing. While
John and Robert were intensely involved with this incident, Edward was not. Moreover, it would hardly be fair to pin the blame
on the Kennedys alone, since they were merely reacting to a Soviet
deployment of nuclear warheads.

Edgar Leoni notes that this verse probably points to the same
three brothers that are mentioned in paragraph 13 of the *Epistle to
Henri II,* which indicates that not all of these three brothers have
the same father, and moreover that the youngest will in some way
"augment the Christian monarchy," which is impossible to apply
to Edward Kennedy in any fashion. The section in the *Epistle*
points to a European context, and one closer to Nostradamus's
own time. It is not clear whom he may have meant. To all appearances, this prophecy has not been fulfilled at all.

19.

A soubstenir la grand cappe troublee
Pour l'esclaircir les rouges marcheront.
De mort famille sera presque accablee
Les rouges rouges le rouge assomeront.

To sustain the great troubled cape,
To clarify it, the reds will march.
A family will be nearly overcome by death.
The red reds the red will fell.

Certainly the reddest of all quatrains. *Cappe* in the first line is literally cape (in the sense of a garment), although Lemesurier sees it

as a veiled equivalent for *pape,* "pope"—a reasonable conjecture given that "reds" in Nostradamus often refer to cardinals.

Taken as a reference to Vatican intrigues, however, the verse is quite obscure. Instead it is customarily taken as a prediction of the French Revolution. *Cappe* in the first line then becomes "Capet," the surname of Louis XVI, by which he was called after his downfall. (Under ordinary circumstances, no monarch will endure the indignity of having to use his surname.) The "reds" then become the revolutionaries. Red was not a color symbolizing revolution in that period (except as part of the tricolor cockade of red, white, and blue), but it could be taken as an allusion to the blood that was spilled.

The last two lines fit the French Revolution well enough. The king and queen were executed in 1793, and their son, the dauphin, died in prison in 1795. The "red reds" versus the "red" in the last line would then reflect a conflict between the moderate Girondists and the extremist Jacobins during the Reign of Terror.

On the other hand, apart from the first line, with its presumed reference to the Capets, the prophecy fits the Russian Revolution as well or better (cf. I.3). We have the family of the tsar exterminated, and the "red reds," the Bolsheviks, gaining ascendancy over the more moderate "reds," the Mensheviks. (The grammar of the French makes it clear that the "red reds" will prevail.) Indeed many Mensheviks were purged in the early years of the Soviet regime.

28.
Les simulachres d'or et d'argent enflez,
Qu'apres le rapt au lac furent gettez
Au decouvert estaincts tous & troublez.
Au marbre script prescripts intergetez.

The imitations of gold and silver inflated,
Which after the theft were thrown into the lake.
By the discovery, all are frightened and troubled.
On the inscribed marble, prescriptions intermixed.

Lemesurier connects this verse to the discovery of pagan ritual objects in the sacred lake at Names in 1557, which is reasonable. Like many learned men of his era, Nostradamus was fascinated with the artifacts of Greco-Roman antiquity that were constantly being unearthed at the time. *Prescripts* is ambiguous, but it would seem likely to mean "prescriptions" more in the ethical or legal sense than in the medical sense.

This would all be merely of mild interest to the modern reader, except that this quatrain has often been interpreted—and backed up with dubious translations—to suggest a forecast of monetary collapse in our own day. The first line fits in with this to some degree, but the rest of the quatrain does not. The last line has sometimes been translated, "All scrips and bonds will be wiped out," which is so tenuously connected to the original that I find it hard to understand how anyone could have seen this meaning in it.

I cite this instance here because many instances in which Nostradamus supposedly predicted events in modern times are based on equally dubious readings of his work. The obscurity of his verses makes it easy to bend the meaning to whatever purposes one likes. Few of his commentators have avoided this temptation entirely.

37.
La forteresse aupres de la Tamise
Cherra par lors le Roy dedans serré,
Aupres du pont sera veu en chemise
Un devant mort, puis dans le fort barré.

The fortress near the Thames
Will fall when the king is locked inside.
Near the bridge he will be seen in a shirt.
One in front dead, then in the fort barred up.

A quatrain applied to King Charles I of England. The "fortress near the Thames" is read as Windsor Castle, which is near that river.

After Charles was taken prisoner by the forces of Parliament during the English Civil War, he was imprisoned there. On January 16, 1649, he was removed from that location to stand trial. After his conviction, he was beheaded on January 30. Charles famously said before his execution, "Let me have a shirt more than ordinary, by reason the season is so sharp as probably make me shake [*sic*], which some will imagine proceeds from fear. I would have no such imputation." After his execution, Charles's body was exposed to public view for many days "that all men might know that he was dead," according to one contemporary source. He was buried in St. George's Chapel in Windsor Castle.[51]

The connections are intriguing, but as most interpreters have had to concede, there are many inexactitudes. Windsor Castle did not "fall" with Charles in it; it was already in the hands of Parliament. Moreover, he was not seen near the bridge in a shirt. The only bridge in the city at the time was London Bridge, and Charles's execution took place near the Banquetting House, Whitehall—a site two miles away. Nevertheless, Charles I fits this quatrain better than anyone in Nostradamus's own day, when England, ruled by Mary Tudor, did not even have a king.

41.

Esleu sera Renard ne sonnant mot,
Faisant le saint public vivant pain d'orge
Tyrannizer apres tant à un cop.
Mettant à pied des plus grans sus la gorge.

The fox will be elected not saying a word,
Playing the saint in public, living on barley bread,
To tyrannize after, so much at one blow,
Putting his foot on the throats of the greatest.

This quatrain is often applied to Napoleon III of France, who first was elected as president of France in 1848, then made himself dictator with a coup in 1851, and finally proclaimed himself emperor the next year (cf. IV.65; VI.25). "Living on barley bread" would mean to affect austerity. In this connection the nineteenth-century Nostradamus commentator Anatole Le Pelletier quotes the emperor's steward as saying, "Napoleon III eats only barley bread."

John Hogue connects this verse with Maximilien Robespierre, the chief instigator of the 1793 Reign of Terror who also made a pretense of virtue and was even nicknamed "the Incorruptible." In fact it is not difficult to apply this quatrain to any historical figure who affects virtue but practices tyranny.

43.
Par le decide de deux choses bastars
Nepveu du sang occupera le regne
Dedans lectoyre seront les coups de dars
Nepveu par peur pleira l'enseigne.

By the fall of two bastard things
Nephew of blood will occupy the realm.
Within Lectoyre will be blows of darts.
Nephew by fear will fold the ensign.

Like VI.41 above, this quatrain is frequently applied to Napoleon III. The reasoning: the "two bastard things" would be the July monarchy of Louis-Philippe (who ruled from 1830 to 1848) and the National Assembly of 1848, or the Second Republic, which replaced him. The "nephew of blood" is Napoleon III, great-nephew of Napoleon I.

By this reading, *Lectoyre* yields an interesting result. This word is an anagram of "Le Torcey" or "Le Torcy," a suburb of Sedan, a French town near the Belgian border, where the decisive battle of the Franco-Prussian War took place in August-September 1870 (cf. I.92). The battle was a disaster both for France and for Napoleon III himself, who fell from power. Writing about it immediately afterward, the German chancellor Otto von Bismarck observed, "Yesterday and the day before cost France 100,000 men and an emperor."

Anatole Le Pelletier, in a work published in 1867, predicted something similar in regard to this verse, saying that this might portend "a check to the imperial arms." Thus (as with VI.97 and its alleged prediction of 9/11) such an interpretation of this verse cannot be entirely dismissed as hindsight.

51.

Le Bizantin faisant oblation,
Apres avoir Cordube à soy reprinse:
Son chemin long repos pamplation,
Mer passant proy par la Colongna prinse.

The Byzantine making oblation,
After having retaken Córdoba for himself.
His road long, rest, vine cutting,
Sea, passing prey taken by the Pillar.

This verse seems to predict a reconquest of Spain by the Muslims—in this case, the Turks. "The Byzantine" is a strange way of referring to them, however: actually the Byzantine Greeks at Constantinople were overcome by the Turks in 1453. But there is no better way of understanding it, since the Byzantines never held Córdoba at any point and thus could not retake it. In any event, up to today no such reconquest has taken place.

The last line seems to indicate corsair piracy in the vicinity of the Pillars of Hercules, i.e., Gibraltar. Here again Nostradamus is predicting something that was already a constant feature of his time.

56.

La bande foible la tertre occupera
Ceux du hault lieu feront horribles crys,
Le gros trouppeau d'estre coin troublera.
Tombe pres D. nebro descouvers les escris.

The feeble band shall occupy the mound.
Those of the high place will make horrible cries.
The great outer band will trouble the corner.
Tomb near D. Nebro, writings discovered.

The chief item of interest in this quatrain is the interpretation given to the mysterious "D. Nebro" in the last line. Lemesurier relates it plausibly to the Ebro River in Spain, so that the line would mean the discovery of some ancient inscriptions near the Ebro (cf. VIII.28).

As long ago as the eighteenth century, however, another interpretation has been offered for this enigmatic place name: it is a pun for "Edinburgh," and predicts the Battle of Dunbar in 1650, in which the forces of the future King Charles II were routed by Oliver Cromwell's Parliamentary army. Dunbar is on the Scottish coast, some twenty-five miles east of Edinburgh. In this battle, Cromwell's forces were outnumbered, but managed to occupy the high ground, assuring themselves of victory; hence, "The feeble band shall occupy the mound." The last line supposedly refers to the fact that the victorious Parliamentary army captured the records of the Scottish War Office.

Like many such interpretations, this one is only tenuously related to what was written. The first three lines could refer to any number of battles in which a weaker force wins by virtue of a superior emplacement. To take an example almost at random, in the 1775 siege of Boston during the American Revolution, the rebellious Americans drove the British out of the city by placing captured artillery on the surrounding hills. As for the records of the Scottish War Office, the interpretation is ingenious but not convincing, since no tomb was involved.

59.
Par deux fois hault, par deux fois mis à bas
L'orient aussi l'occident foyblira

Son adversaire apres plusieurs combats,
Par mer, chassé au besoing faillira.

Two times high, two times brought low
The East, as well as the West, shall weaken.
Its adversary, after many battles
By sea, pursued in a time of need, shall fail.

Another prophecy of the struggle between East and West. By far the most reasonable application would be to the drawn-out battle between the Catholic forces of the Mediterranean (Spain, Venice, Genoa, and the Papal States) and the Muslim Turks. The verse predicts, accurately enough, a great seesawing of dominance between the two. The last two lines could presage the Battle of Lepanto in 1571, which, as we have seen (II.79, III.1, V.23), marked a turning point in the struggle and served as the high-water mark of Turkish naval power in the Mediterranean. The Christian fleet was later reproached for failing to follow up on its victory and pursue the Ottomans (perhaps echoed in the last two lines), but inasmuch as half of its own men were out of action at that point, it probably did not have much choice.

More wide-ranging interpretations of this verse suggest that "two times high, two times brought low" refers to the two Muslim invasions of Europe, the first by the Saracens and Moors, the second by the Turks. This is certainly plausible: Nostradamus would then be prophesying that the Ottoman onslaught on Europe would fail, as it eventually did.

It is a mark of how much the geopolitical situation has changed of late that up to about 1990, the most obvious interpretation of this verse would view the East in terms of the Soviet bloc. Now, as of this writing in 2005, one would be more likely to think of the "East" as the Muslim Middle East. This does not necessarily confirm Nostradamus's prescience or suggest that the events fore-shadowed here are going to happen in our own future. Even so, it is striking that we in the early twenty-first century are more likely to view global politics as Nostradamus did than would someone reading this verse thirty years ago.

60.

Premier en Gaule, premier en Romanie,
Par mer & terre aux Anglois & Parys
Merveilleux faitz par celle grande mesnie
Violant terax perdra le NORLARIS.

First in Gaul, first in Romania,
By sea and land to the English and Paris,
Marvelous deeds by that great band.
Violent monster shall lose NORLARIS.

NORLARIS in the last line is usually taken to be an (inexact) anagram of "Lorraine." In that case, which transfer of that much disputed territory is at issue here? At the time Nostradamus was writing, the Holy Roman Empire held Lorraine, so it is reasonable to suppose that this is what he means. Peter Lemesurier suggests that the "violent monster" is Emmanuel Philibert, Duke of Savoy and commander-in-chief of the imperial forces at the time.

On the other hand, the second line seems to imply that the English and French are allied at that point, which was not the case in Nostradamus's time and was rarely, if ever, the case until the mid-nineteenth century.

Taking the quatrain as much as possible at face value, we would go to the twentieth century. At the beginning of World War I, Germany held Lorraine, which it had taken as part of the spoils of the Franco-Prussian War of 1870–71. The German army did indeed perform impressively in World War I, forcing the British and French to a deadlock on the Western Front and overcoming Romania soon after it entered the war on the side of the Allies in 1916. In the end, however, the "violent monster," who in this case would be Kaiser Wilhelm II, ended up losing the war, and Germany had to give Lorraine back to France under the Versailles Treaty. Except for the Nazi occupation during World War II, France has held it to this day.

65.

Le vieux frustré du principal espoir,
Il parviendra au chef de son empire:
Vingt mois tiendra le regne à grand pouvoir,
Tirant, cruel en delaissant un pire.

The old man, disappointed in his principal hope,
Will attain to the head of his empire.
Twenty months he will hold the realm with great power,
Tyrant, cruel, leaving behind one worse.

Marshal Henri-Philippe Pétain, whom we have already encountered in VII.34, is often seen as the subject here. Presumably "disappointed" in his greatest hope—of keeping France independent—he attained the headship of the French "empire," which at that time was a republic. He was named premier in June 1940, and in July became head of the puppet Vichy government in unoccupied France. When the Germans occupied the entire country in November 1942 in response to the Allied invasion of North Africa, Pétain was reduced to the role of a figurehead, making his effective tenure a total of twenty-eight months. "One worse" is sometimes identified with Pierre Laval, the collaborationist who was Pétain's vice premier.

This is all plausible, except that Pétain's role in the occupation of France conveys the impression of weakness, apathy, and old age rather than cruelty. His strategy seems to have been to try to preserve an independent role for France, and to retain her overseas empire, in the Nazi world order that he believed was coming.

66.

Quand l'escriture D.M. trouvee,
Et cave antique à lampe descouverte,
Loy, roy, & Prince Ulpian esprouvee,
Pavillon Royne & Duc sous la couverte.

When the inscription "D.M." is found,
And ancient cave by lamp discovered,
Law, king, and Ulpian prince proven,
Pavilion, king and queen under the cover.

Another of Nostradamus's predictions of the discovery of an ancient Roman tomb. "D.M." is a standard ancient Roman inscription for *diis manibus,* or "to the divine ghosts." The early Romans conceived of the Di Manes as the undifferentiated spirits of the dead; later on they were identified with the family ancestors. In the period of the empire it was customary to write on a tombstone *D.M. Sacrum,* that is, "sacred to the divine ghosts," followed by the name of the deceased. Thus the letters "D.M." are extremely common on Roman tombs. It is as if Nostradamus were to predict the discovery of a modern tombstone bearing the letters "R.I.P."

In this case the Roman is presumably Emperor Marcus Ulpius Traianus, usually known as Trajan, who reigned from 98 to 117 A.D. The only other notable figure to have this name is Domitius Ulpianus, usually known as Ulpian, who lived in the third century A.D. and was one of the most distinguished jurists in Roman history. Because Ulpian is called a "prince" here, it is more likely that Nostradamus has Trajan in mind.

Trajan's tomb lies at the base of Trajan's Column, which is still standing in Rome. The base of the column consists of a massive cube containing a number of small rooms, the innermost of which was Trajan's tomb chamber. Two holes drilled in the rear wall of the room are thought to have held the funerary urns of Trajan and his wife Plotina.

All of this is comparatively simple, but it is also puzzling, since it was fairly obvious where Trajan would have been buried, even in Nostradamus's time. He may be suggesting that the real site of the emperor's remains lies elsewhere.

70.

Il entrera vilain, meschant, infame,
Tyrannisant la Mesopotamie,
Tous amys fait d'adulterine d'ame,
Tertre horrible noir de physiognomie.

He will come in a villain, cruel, infamous,
Tyrannizing Mesopotamia,
All friends made by the adulteress of the soul.
Horrible mound, black in countenance.

In this quatrain Nostradamus is most likely predicting the coming of some future Antichrist. "Mesopotamia" would seem clear enough as a reference to the land between the Tigris and the Euphrates in what is now Iraq. This is the most likely interpretation here, even though Nostradamus sometimes applies this term to any place that lies "between two rivers," including French towns such as Lyon and Avignon. Nostradamus probably intended this verse as a prophecy of some rather nebulous apocalyptic figure, but John Hogue sees in it a reference to Saddam Hussein, who fits it well enough.

The third line probably alludes to the Whore of Babylon from Revelation: "And I saw a woman sit upon a scarlet coloured beast, full of names of blasphemy, having seven heads and ten horns. And the woman was arrayed in purple and scarlet colour, and decked with gold and precious stones and pearls, having a golden cup in her hand full of abominations and filthiness of her fornication: And upon her forehead was a name written, MYSTERY, BABYLON THE GREAT, THE MOTHER OF HARLOTS AND ABOMINATIONS OF THE EARTH" (Rev. 17:3–5).

Most translators, incidentally, see the word *d'ame* in the third line, which literally means "of soul," as a misprint for *dame,* "lady," but I have rendered it as it appears. In textual criticism it is standard practice, when confronting a disputed word, to tend to adopt the *less* common reading as the more likely one. This is because if a scribe or a printer is going to make an error, he has a greater chance of mistaking a less common word for a more common one. In this instance, *d'ame* is a less common usage than *dame.* Consequently, while the printer could easily have mistaken *d'ame* for *dame,* it is comparatively unlikely that he would have done the reverse. This is one of the basic principles of textual criticism, and it is worth keeping in mind when scrutinizing texts such as Nostradamus's, which are full of both intentional ambiguities and ordinary mistakes.

71.
Croistra le nombre si grand des astronomes
Chassez, bannez & livres censurez,
L'an mil six cens & sept par sacre glomes
Que nul aux sacres ne seront assurez.

The number of astronomers shall grow so great;
Chased, banned, books censored,
In the year 1607 by sacred crowds,
So that nothing will be safe for the sacred ones.

A prophecy that Nostradamus's interpreters generally write off as a failure. I am not so sure. It is quite true that, as far as anyone can tell, no prominent astronomer fell afoul of the ecclesiastical authorities in 1607. If we set aside the date, however, we come up with two astronomers in that era who had to face the Inquisition.

The first is Giordano Bruno (1548–1600). Bruno began his career as a Dominican, but left the order when his ideas proved too radical for the Catholic Church of the day. He had similar difficulties with the Lutherans and the Calvinists. In 1593, he was denounced to the Inquisition in Venice and was extradited to Rome. He remained in the dungeons of the Inquisition for six years before being granted a trial. He was convicted and burned at the stake in 1600.

Bruno was so radical a thinker, and so obnoxious personally, that it is hard to single out one particular idea that earned him this dismal fate. He is chiefly remembered as a Renaissance magus of a type that included Nostradamus himself, but it would not be dishonest to characterize him as an astronomer. Building upon Copernicus's heliocentric theory of the solar system, he postulated the idea of an infinite universe—one of the first Western astronomers to suggest such an idea.

A more celebrated figure is Galileo Galilei (1564–1642), one of the greatest scientists of all time. Galileo, like Bruno, embraced Copernicus's heliocentric theory, which was denounced as a heresy in 1616; at this time Copernicus's text was put on the Church's Index of Forbidden Books. In 1633 Galileo came to the attention of the Inquisition, which convicted him of heresy for his scientific views and ordered him to house arrest in Siena, where he remained until his death.

In terms of this quatrain, Nostradamus was wrong in applying the date 1607 to this persecution of astronomers. Viewed on a broader scale, however, his prophecy unfortunately proved correct.

76.

Plus macelin que Roy en Angleterre,
Lieu obscur nay par force aura l'Empire:
Lasche sans foy, sans loy saignera la terre,
Son temps s'approche si pres que je souspire.

More a butcher than a king in England,
Born in an obscure place, he will have the empire by force.
Slack, faithless, lawless, he will bloody the earth;
His time comes so close that I gasp.

Since the seventeenth century, this verse has been applied to Oliver
Cromwell (1599–1658), Lord Protector of England. By birth he was
a minor landowner, and in his early years he earned no distinction.
In the 1630s, however, he underwent a religious conversion and
became a Puritan. Elected to Parliament, he turned into one of the
most formidable political figures England has ever produced.
Leading the Parliamentary forces in the long and bloody English
Civil War of the 1640s, he signed the death warrant for King
Charles I in 1649. For the next nine years, until his death, he ruled
the nation as king in fact, though not in name.

Cromwell remains the best candidate to fit this verse. But he
does not fit it all that well. No doubt by the standards of the time,
which put such a premium on loyalty to king and Church, he might
have been "lawless and faithless," but he had an intense religious
faith and single-handedly created a rough semblance of constitutional republican government in an age of the divine right of Kings.
By no account could he be called "slack" (*lasche*): his inflexible will
was perhaps his salient trait. Even the detail about his time coming
soon was not really true. This quatrain was first published in 1558;
Cromwell would not come to power for another ninety years.

77.

L'antechrist trois bien tost annichiliez,
Vingt & sept ans sang durera sa guerre,
Les heretiques mortz, captifs, exilez,
Sang corps human eau rogie gresler terre.

The Antichrist: three very soon annihilated.
His war shall last twenty-seven years, blood.
Heretics dead, captive, exiled,
Blood, human body; reddened water to hail upon earth.

In the *Epistle to Henri II* (§23), Nostradamus speaks of a coming
Antichrist whose empire will include the former realms of Xerxes,

king of Persia in the fifth century B.C., and of Attila the Hun, whose hordes swept over southeastern Europe in the fifth century A.D. No such figure has yet emerged, although his imminent coming, like the Second Coming of Christ, has been proclaimed now for hundreds of years.

If we set aside the reference to the Antichrist—for whom innumerable candidates have been suggested, ranging from Napoleon and Hitler to Henry Kissinger and George W. Bush—what we see here is a sobering prophecy of the Thirty Years' War, which raged across Europe from 1618 to 1648. The war cast such ruin over the continent that the Treaty of Westphalia, which ended the conflict, was nicknamed "the Peace of Exhaustion."

It is common in the annals of prophecy to find reasonably accurate predictions of some oncoming disaster, combined with the mistaken conclusion that this will bring on the final apocalypse. We find something of this kind in what is called "the Apocalyptic Discourse" or "the Little Apocalypse" in the Gospels (Matt. 24; Mark 13; Luke 21), where Christ seems to be predicting the coming destruction of Judea by the Romans, to be followed by the end of time. The destruction of Judea did take place, in the Jewish War of 66–73 A.D., but although it marked the end of an era for both Judaism and Christianity, it did not constitute the end of the world.

So here with Nostradamus. He may have had some premonitions of the great war between Catholics and Protestants that would engulf Europe in the next century, and for which he had ample evidence in the religious warfare of his own day. And he may have concluded—understandably, though incorrectly—that so calamitous an event could only be a prelude to the end of time itself.

80.

Des innocens le sang de vefve & vierge.
Tant de maulx faitz par moyen se grand Roge.
Saincts simulachres trempez en ardant cierge
De frayeur crainte ne verra nul que boge.

The blood of innocents, of widow and virgin.
So much evil done by means of the great Red.
Holy images soaked in burning wax.
From terror, fear, he will see none who budges.

A quatrain frequently associated with the Russian Revolution, chiefly because of its mention of "the great Red." The Protestants certainly destroyed sacred images in Nostradamus's time, and it is hard to imagine that he did not at least have them in the back of his mind when he wrote this. But given that "red" often refers to cardinals in Nostradamus (cf. VI.10, VIII.19), it is hard to give this verse an interpretation that is contemporary with his own time. The Russian Revolution and subsequent civil war, with its wholesale slaughter and its desecration of churches and icons, fits this quatrain as well as anything.

92.

Loin hors du regne mis en hazard voiage
Grand ost duyra pour soy l'occupera,
Le roy tiendra les siens captifs ostrage.
A son retour tout pays pillera.

Far away from the kingdom, sent to a dangerous journey,
He shall lead a great host, shall take it for himself;
The king will hold his own captives hostage.
Upon his return he will pillage the whole country.

To view the situation of Nostradamus's own time, this quatrain most plausibly speaks of the revolt of the Spanish Netherlands, a long-standing struggle of the Low Countries to liberate themselves from the rule of Spain that took place roughly between 1558 and 1618. Essentially the struggle was about religion: Philip II of Spain wanted to wipe out Calvinism, which had taken deep hold of the Netherlands, and the Dutch wanted a policy of religious tolerance.

The figure mentioned in the first two lines is the Duke of Alva, sent by Philip II to suppress the revolt. Hence the third line: "The king will hold his own [as] captives hostage"—that is to say, he will make captives of his own subjects. The word *ostrage* is curious. It is usually taken as equivalent to *otage,* "hostage," but it also resembles *outrage,* "outrage." If we assume that this is not simply an error, it might be a portmanteau word attempting to combine the meanings of "outrage" and "hostage."

Although the Duke instigated a reign of terror, he failed in his efforts to wipe out Protestantism. The struggle continued actively until 1609, when a twelve-year truce was signed, effectively confirming the existence of the United Provinces of the Netherlands as an independent entity. The nation's status would be confirmed by the Treaty of Westphalia in 1648, but by then the Netherlands had long been independent and had entered its zenith of power, wealth, and cultural magnificence.

Some commentators, such as John Hogue and Erika Cheetham, see in this verse a reference to more modern figures, including Charles XII of Sweden, Napoleon, and Mao Zedong. Of these, the last is probably the most convincing, as Mao and his army were forced into a long retreat by the Nationalist forces of Chiang Kaishek in 1934. In an epic, year-long journey that came to be known as the Long March, Mao not only consolidated his control of the Communist Party but also brought its cause to the attention of the Chinese masses. It was the beginning of Mao's march to triumph, culminating in the expulsion of the Nationalists in 1949.

As for the last two lines, which speak of captivity and pillage: Mao attempted to impose total control upon hundreds of millions of Chinese, thus "making his own people captive." In 1958, he initiated the Great Leap Forward, a massive push to industrialize China that produced unmitigated disaster. Estimates of the deaths resulting from this effort range from 4 million to 40 million; the ensuing famine is sometimes said to have been the largest in history. In its wake, Mao himself had to go into temporary retirement.

96.

La synagogue sterile sans nul fruit
Sera receu entre les infideles
De Babylon la fille du porsuit
Misere & triste luy trenchera les aisles.

The sterile, fruitless synagogue
Shall be received among the infidels.
From Babylon the daughter of pursuit,
Wretched and sad, will cut his wings.

The first two lines are as clear as one finds anywhere in Nostrada-mus: the Jews, persecuted in practically all of Christendom, will find refuge among the Ottoman Turks. This was happening in Nostradamus's time and was more a statement of current fact than a glimpse of the future. The reference to the "fruitless synagogue" possibly alludes to Christ's cursing of the fig tree (Mark 11:12–24; in Jewish tradition, the fig tree is often used as a trope for the Torah). The last two lines suggest that this is an unholy compro-mise, and that the Jews will pay for it in the end.

In this context, it is important to remember that anti-Semitism was the standard attitude in the day. Although Nostradamus was the descendant of Jewish converts, there is little if any evidence that he had any residual fondness for the religion of his ancestors. Verses like this one suggest that he did his best to distance himself as much as possible from them.

99.

Par la puissance des trois rois temporelz,
En autre lieu sera mis le saint siege:
Où la substance de l'esprit corporel,
Sera remis & receu pour vray siege.

By the power of three temporal kings,
The Holy See shall be moved to another place,

Where the substance of the bodily spirit
Shall be restored and received for the true seat.

Peter Lemesurier takes this verse to apply to the Council of Trent,
which was summoned in 1545 as a response to the Protestant Reformation and which reaffirmed the Catholic doctrine of the "Real
Presence" of Christ in the Eucharistic Host (implied in the last two
lines of this quatrain). This interpretation is credible, given that
the council, which met intermittently in the years between 1545
and 1563, had to move several times because of opposition by the
temporal powers. In regard to the future, however, Nostradamus
was wrong, given that he was writing around 1558. Pope Pius IV
ordered the reopening of the council at Trent itself at Easter 1561,
the objections of the French notwithstanding. In this sense, the
location of "the Holy See" did not change.

On the other hand, it is peculiar to refer to the site of the council as "the Holy See." Some commentators see in it a prophecy that
the Papacy will have to move again, as it did during its "Babylonian Captivity" at Avignon in the fourteenth century. No doubt
Nostradamus had something of the sort in mind, but this has not
happened up to now.

100.

Pour l'abondance de larme respandue
Du hault en bas par le bas au plus hault
Trop grande foy par ieu vie perdue,
De soif mourir par habondant deffault.

For the abundance of tears shed,
From high to low, from low to higher:
Too great a faith for the game, life lost;
To die of thirst by abundant deficiency.

This quatrain is often dismissed as hopelessly opaque. But if it is,
as Lemesurier suggests, a premonition of the wars of religion that

were beginning in Nostradamus's time, it is hauntingly poignant. The second line would then be speaking of the reversals of national fortune that they would engender, reducing Spain, for example, to a third-rate power.

"Too great a faith for the game" implies that it is an excess of faith that causes the folly of religious warfare. The paradoxical last line may be alluding to those with so much faith that they will die for it—and yet missing the central teaching of Christianity, which is after all a religion of love.

Century IX

3.
La magna vaqua à Ravenne grand trouble.
Conduitz par quinze enserrez à Farnese:
A Romme naistre deux monstres à teste double
Sang, feu, deluge, les plus grands à l'espase.

The big cow at Ravenna, great trouble.
Led by fifteen, enclosed in the Farnese,
At Rome to be born two double-headed monsters;
Blood, fire, flood, the greatest ones on the loose.

This quatrain is a hodgepodge. The first two lines are somewhat garbled. *Magna vaqua,* literally meaning a "big cow," presumably alludes to Magnavacca, a port near Ravenna, now called Porto Garibaldi. The "Farnese" in the second line is most likely the Farnese Palace in Rome, built by one of the city's great families between 1530 and 1546. The last line resembles many in the *Prophecies;* I suspect that Nostradamus tended to invoke "blood, fire, flood," and so on when he needed an extra line to fill out a quatrain.

The third line is the most interesting part of this verse. The "double-headed monsters" at Rome could hint at some ecclesiastical conspiracy, but it could be taken literally as a prediction of mutant births, which in Nostradamus's time were a source of much fascination; he often speaks of them himself. (I have left out most of these quatrains, since they are of limited interest to the modern reader.) In his day such mutations were taken as portents of coming troubles, possibly the end of the world itself.

Times have not changed as much as we may think. Today we do not regard mutations as omens in the old-fashioned sense, but still we see them as signs that something is wrong: pollution, nuclear radiation, genetic manipulation. No doubt this is a more informed perspective, but the upshot is the same: the human mind reacts to such deviations from the norm with an instinctual abhorrence and grasps at any meaningful explanation for them, whether it is to be found in biological causes or the will of God.

8.

Puisnay Roy fait son pere mettre à mort,
Apres conflit de mort tres inhoneste:
Escrit trouvé soubson donra remort,
Quand loup chassé pose sus la couchette.

The younger one made king, his father put to death,
After a deadly conflict most dishonest.
Writing found, suspicion will cause regret,
When the hunted wolf rests on the cot.

This verse describes an extremely unusual situation: a young man made king while his father is still alive (since his father is to be put to death). Normally, of course, a man inherits the crown only after his father's demise. In Nostradamus's time the most prominent example of a son inheriting a kingdom while the father was still alive was the abdication of Emperor Charles V of the throne of Spain in favor of his son, Philip II, in 1556. In 1558, shortly before his death, Charles would hand over his German and Austrian domains to his brother, Ferdinand I. Charles's motives appear to have lain in his advancing age and the difficulty of governing a discontinuous realm that stretched from Hungary to the Atlantic. Some have also attributed it to religious reasons, to the desire to prepare for the *buen morir,* the "good death."

The most likely meaning of this verse, then, is that once Philip has his hands on the crown, he will use intrigue to make sure his father is out of the way for good. Since there was little love between France and the Hapsburg domains at this time, it was natural for Nostradamus to expect the worst for the Hapsburgs in the immediate future. At any rate, this outcome did not emerge. Charles V died of natural causes in 1558, on good terms with his son.

17.

Le tiers premier pys que ne feit Neron,
Vuidez vaillant que sang humain respandre:
R'edifier fera le forneron,
Siecle d'or, mort, nouveau roy grand esclandre.

The third first, worse than Nero ever did,
Emptied, brave, how human blood shall spill.
He will have the oven rebuilt,
The Golden Age dead, new king, great scandal.

"The third" in this verse is frequently understood to refer to the *tiers état,* the Third Estate in France, consisting of the common people (the first two estates being the church and the nobility). "The third first" would then mean that the Third Estate will come to dominate, which came true during the French Revolution in 1789. At this point, the people will be guilty of worse crimes than the psychopathic Roman emperor Nero. This prophecy is thus applied to the Reign of Terror in 1793.

As for the "oven" in the third line, John Hogue connects it with the Tuileries Palace in Paris, where Louis XVI and his family were kept under house arrest during the Revolution. ("Tuileries" literally means a kiln for baking tiles, which is what stood on that spot before the palace was built.) The "Golden Age" now "dead" would be the glorious eras of Louis XIV, XV, and XVI; the "new king" would be Napoleon, whose comparatively humble birth would constitute a "scandal."

All this makes a certain amount of sense, at least from a monarchist perspective. On the other hand, the pre-Revolutionary era was hardly a Golden Age to the commoners on whom burdensome taxes and rents were levied to pay for the splendors of the aristocracy (who were themselves exempt from taxation). Moreover, taken all in all, the quatrain is remarkably vague about all the details except bloodshed—a feature so common to Nostradamus's era, and to practically all other eras before or since, that it does not help make this prophecy more precise. Like many Nostradamian interpretations, this one hangs chiefly on one word—in this case *tiers,* or "third"—and on the frail supposition that it refers to the rise of the Third Estate.

18.

Le lys Dauffois portera dans Nancy
Jusques en Flandres electeur de l'empire,
Neufve obturee au grand Montmorency,
Hors lieux provez delivre a clere peyne.

The Dauphin lily will carry in Nancy
Elector of the empire as far as Flanders.
New blockage for great Montmorency,
Away from known places delivered to clear pain.

One of Nostradamus's most famous verses, at least in France. The last two lines have been interpreted as a remarkable forecast of the fate of the fourth Duc de Montmorency during the reign of Louis XIII. In 1632, Montmorency, with the aid of some 3,000 German cavaliers, led an uprising in Languedoc. The uprising was crushed, and Montmorency was beheaded. Étienne Jaubert, a seventeenth-century commentator on Nostradamus, says the executioner was named "Clerepeyne" (as in the fourth line here), but this is unsubstantiated.[52]

"The Dauphin lily" is thus said to refer to Louis XIII, allegedly the first to hold the title of dauphin (heir to the French throne) since the death of Nostradamus. The reference to Nancy, a city in the east of France, refers to Louis's occupation of the city in 1633. It had been previously ruled by France's archenemy, the Hapsburg Empire.

The "Elector of the empire" would be Philip Christoph von Sötern, who as archbishop of Trier was one of the electors of the Holy Roman Empire. Rulership of the Holy Roman Empire was not hereditary (though the Hapsburgs tried to make it so); rather the emperor was chosen by some half-dozen electors representing the sacred and secular powers of this domain, which included most of Central Europe. During the Thirty Years' War, Sötern accepted protection from the French against the Hapsburgs, but he was captured by the latter in 1635 and spent ten years in prison until he was liberated by the French in 1645.

What, then, does this interpretation amount to? In the end it mostly seems to be a jumble of facts of French history in the 1630s and 1640s fit disjointedly into Nostradamus's verse—which is itself somewhat disjointed. I discuss it at such length because it is regarded—improbably—as one of Nostradamus's most remarkable prophetic successes.

As usual, a more compelling interpretation (at least of the second half of the verse) keeps us closer to Nostradamus's own time. When he was writing this verse, "Montmorency" could mean only one person: Anne de Montmorency (who, despite his given name, was a male), Constable of France. Montmorency defended St. Quentin against the Spaniards in 1557, but the latter won, and Montmorency was captured (cf. IV.8). He would remain incarcerated until the French and Spanish signed a peace treaty in 1559. When Nostradamus wrote this verse, in 1557–58, it was no doubt already known that Montmorency was a prisoner, which is certainly a form of "clear pain."

20.

De nuict viendra par la forest de Reines,
Deux par vaultorte Herne la pierre blanche.
Le moine noir en gris dedans Varennes
Esleu cap. cause tempeste feu, sang tranche.

At night he will come through the forest of Reines,
Two by Vaultorte, Herne, the white stone.
The black monk in gray within Varennes
Elected cap. causes tempest, fire, slices blood.

The standard interpretation of this quatrain, like IX.17, hangs on a single word—in this case "Varennes," a small town in northeastern France whose moment in history came on June 21, 1791. On this date, during the French Revolution, Louis XVI and Marie Antoinette, along with their children and some attendants, were apprehended trying to flee the country. According to one account, Louis was recognized when a villager compared his face to the image on a piece of paper money. The royal family was taken back to Paris, which they never left alive: the king and queen were beheaded in 1793 ("slices blood"), and their son, the dauphin, died of tuberculosis and neglect in prison in 1795 (cf. VIII.19).

To pursue this interpretation further, the king is called a "monk" because he suffered from phimosis (a condition in which the foreskin of the penis cannot be retracted), which made him incapable of siring children during his first seven years of marriage. Sometimes it is said to allude to the sober attire he was wearing when captured. "Elected cap." means "Elected Capet": Capet was the king's surname (cf. VIII.19), and he was "elected" in the dubious sense that the revolutionary National Assembly tried without success to make him into a constitutional monarch.

The place names in the second line, notes Peter Lemesurier, are in Maine, a province southwest of Paris, nowhere near Varennes. On the other hand, the forest of "Reines," or Rennes, is fifty miles southeast of Varennes, and the royal family would not have passed through it on their abortive escape. To confuse matters further, as Edgar Leoni observes, there are twenty-six towns in France named Varennes, so even the presence of that name hardly proves anything.

In short, the whole application of this quatrain to the flight to Varennes—possibly including the word "Varennes" itself—is extremely tenuous. The verse is worth discussing chiefly because it casts light on how Nostradamus's inscrutable and often ungrammatical verses can be creatively adjusted to fit historical situations that they only dimly resemble.

The most interesting exploration of this quatrain appears in a 1984 essay by Georges Dumézil, the great scholar of comparative religion. Entitled " . . . *Le moyne noir en gris dedans Varennes*" ("The Black Monk in Gray Inside Varennes"), it gives an elaborate mock-philological reading of this verse. "Forest of Reines," for example, literally "forest of queens," refers to Louis's escape through a concealed door in the queen's apartments. "Vaultorte" is a composite of *vaulx*, "valley," and *torte*, "tortuous," referring to the tortuous route Louis took from Paris to Varennes.[53] Dumézil intended the essay as a game, an indulgence in intellectual sport, as indicated by the title of the English translation, "A Nostradamian Farce," but many supposedly earnest readings of Nostradamus are far more preposterous.

Lemesurier claims that this verse actually applies to one Antoine du Plessis, a defrocked Franciscan monk of Nostradamus's time who ended up as an exceptionally cruel commander of harquebusiers during the French wars of religion. (Franciscans wore gray robes and were often known as Greyfriars.) The claim is an interesting one, but I have been able to turn up nothing on du Plessis.

28.

Voille Symacle port Massiliolique,
Dans Venise port marcher aux Pannons:
Partir du gouffre & sinus Illirique
Vast à Socile, Ligurs coups de canons.

Allied fleet, port of Marseille,
In the port of Venice to march to Pannonia.
Departure from the gulf and the Illyrian bay.
Ruin to Sicily, Ligurian cannon shots.

The "allied fleet" in all probability refers to the Holy Alliance of Spain, Genoa, Venice, and the Papal States, combined to fight the Turks. To say that this fleet will put in at Marseille on the southern coast of France was not necessarily reassuring, since France was generally at odds with the Holy Alliance for most of that period. But Nostradamus here seems to be saying that France will join the Alliance and that these combined forces will march into Hungary (Pannonia; cf. III.58, V.13, IX.28), presumably to free it from the Turks, who in turn will devastate Sicily. The repercussions will reach as far as Portugal (Liguria).

This theme makes its appearance in Nostradamus from time to time. He seems to have viewed events of his time through the lens of a devout Catholicism. Evidently he felt that France was making a mistake in its frequent alliances with the Muslim Turks against the Catholic Hapsburgs, and that it would reverse its position, eventually to drive the Turks from Europe.

The rulers of France never took his advice. Despite many twists and turns, the French grand strategy was remarkably clear and consistent in this era: at all costs to prevent encirclement by the Hapsburgs, who ruled Spain, Germany, Austria, and the Netherlands. To achieve this aim, in the sixteenth century the French would join with the Muslim Turks, and, in the Thirty Years' War of the next century, with the Protestant powers of Europe. As often happens in world events, realpolitik consistently overcame ideology.

33.
Hercule Roy de Romme & d'Annemarc,
De Gaule trois Guion surnommé,
Trembler l'Italie & l'unde de sainct Marc
Premier sur tous monarque renommé.

Hercules king of Rome and Annemarck,
Of tripartite Gaul, surnamed Guion.
Italy and the wave of St. Mark to tremble,
First renowned above all monarchs.

This quatrain has inspired marvelous bouts of creativity among Nostradamus's interpreters. In all likelihood, "Hercules" is François, the Duc d'Alençon, who was originally christened Hercules. He was the youngest son of Henri II and Catherine de' Medici, for whom Nostradamus incorrectly foresees a dazzling future (cf. VI.42). "Tripartite Gaul" is an allusion to the famous first line of Julius Caesar's *Gallic War: "Omnis Gallia est divisa in partes tres,"* "The whole of Gaul is divided into three parts." "Annemarc" has required some ingenuity. The two most frequently voiced suggestions are that it is a pun for Denmark—*Danemark* in French—and that it refers to Hungary and Bohemia, which in 1526 were brought into the Hapsburg domains by the marriage of Anne, sister of the deceased king of Hungary, to the brother of Charles V.

In this instance I prefer the latter suggestion, since, along with "Rome," it would then be a cryptic way of describing the Holy Roman Empire, of which "Hercules" will be the head. If this is the correct interpretation, the prophecy did not come true, since "Hercules" died in 1584 at the age of thirty without acquiring any of these honors.

John Hogue sees the last three lines of this verse as a reference to Charles de Gaulle, leader of the Free French Army in World War II and president of France from 1958 to 1970. This is ingenious but far-fetched, since it involves an arbitrary detachment of the last three verses from the first.

Monarchist interpretations of Nostradamus see this verse, like others with similar import, as a prediction of a coming king of France who will restore the monarchy and inaugurate an era of world peace, echoing the myth of the universal ruler that we have already encountered (cf. I.4). This viewpoint has a certain amount of truth to it in that Nostradamus seems to have held this view himself. Whether one believes this could still happen will depend, of course, on one's own expectations about the future. To me it does not seem likely.

36.

Un grand Roy prins entre les mains d'un Joyne,
Non loing de Pasque confusion coup cultre:
Perpet. captifs temps que fouldre en la husne,
Los que trois freres se blesseront & murtre.

A great king taken between the hands of a young one,
Not far from Easter, confusion, blow, knife:
Perpet. captives, weather with lightning on the mizzen,
While three brothers wound and kill one another.

As in VIII.17, "three brothers" here is sometimes taken to mean the Kennedys. And as in VIII.17, this interpretation is not plausible. It depends on mistranslating the reflexive verb in the last line so that the line reads, "While three brothers are killed and wounded," which is not justified by the original. Whatever opinion one holds of the Kennedys, it is not right to claim that they did damage to one another: their mutual relations seem to have been remarkably harmonious. Moreover, John F. Kennedy was assassinated in November, Robert in June—neither of which is close to Easter.

This verse probably refers to the mysterious "three brothers" mentioned in the *Epistle to Henri II,* 13–14, though Le Pelletier connects it to François II, Charles VIII, and Henri III, the three sons of Henri II who succeeded him to the throne. Even this, though, is not terribly plausible, since struggle among the brothers was not a major factor in the Valois dynasty at the time.

44.

Migres, migre de Genesve trestous
Saturne d'or en fer se changera.

Le contre RAYPOZ *exterminera tous,*
Avant l'a ruent le ciel signes fera.

Flee, flee, all from Geneva:
Saturn shall change from gold to iron.
The adversary RAYPOZ will exterminate all;
Before his coming the sky will show signs.

A warning to flee from Calvinist Geneva. The second line has an astrological import, probably meaning that Saturn will move out of a favorable aspect with the sun ("gold") to an unfavorable aspect with Mars ("iron"). Astrologers link hard aspects between Saturn and Mars with various misfortunes, especially war.

RAYPOZ is usually taken as an anagram for "Zopyra." Edgar Leoni says this is a name chosen by King Philip II of Spain for one of his heraldic devices, after the name of an ancient Persian hero. The verse would then prophesy an invasion of Protestant Geneva by the arch-Catholic Hapsburgs—a plausible supposition in the era, but one that was never fulfilled.

45.
Ne sera soul jamais de demander,
Grand Mendosus obtiendra son empire,
Loing de la cour fera contremander,
Pymond, Picard, Paris, Tyron le pire.

There shall never be a single one to ask.
The great Mendosus will have his empire.
Far from the court he will have countermanded
Piedmont, Picardy, Paris, Tyrrhenia the worst.

Most commentators see "Mendosus" in the second line as an anagram for "Vendosme," the house from which Henri of Navarre stemmed. If this is true, then the prophecy has some accuracy to it, since Henri won the throne of France in 1589.

Nostradamus evidently made this prophecy about Henri in another context. Supposedly, in 1564 he was presented to the ten-year-old Henri and predicted his future kingship by the somewhat peculiar method of reading the moles on his body. This prediction apparently did take place; Henri was fond of relating it years afterward, and there is even a painting of the event by a nineteenth-century French artist named Louis-Joseph Denis-Valverane, which is sometimes reproduced in books about Nostradamus.

Given this interpretation, the rest of the quatrain does not hold up well. The epithet "Mendosus" is contemptuous, meaning "deceitful" in Latin. And the last two lines are full of dark presentiments: *Tyron* is sometimes read as *tyran,* or "tyrant." These do not fit Henri, one of the most beloved monarchs in French history. Another interpretation of this verse takes Henri out of the picture entirely and applies it to the future Antichrist, whoever he or she may be.

49.
Gand & Bruceles marcheront contre Envers
Senat de Londres mettront à mort leur roy
Le sel & vin lui seront à l'envers,
Pour eux avoir le regne en desarroy.

Ghent and Brussels will march against Envers;
Senate of London will put their king to death.
Salt and wine for him shall be adverse,
For them to have the kingdom in disarray.

The second line of this verse marks one of Nostradamus's most signal prophetic successes: a clear and understandable forecast of the execution of Charles I of England by the Puritan-controlled Parliament in 1649. (Those with a taste for numerology also like to point out that this verse is numbered 49.) "Salt and wine" are sometimes interpreted as signifying wit and strength, respectively, or as an indication of difficulties over taxes, which were generally levied on these two commodities in Nostradamus's time.

The last line would then suggest that the regicide will leave the kingdom of England in disarray—an understandable sentiment from a monarchist's perspective, although in fact the Protectorate (so called from the title of its leader, Oliver Cromwell, Lord Protector) governed England capably until Cromwell's death in 1658 (cf. IV.62, VIII.56, 76). At that point it collapsed under the rule of his incompetent son Richard, and two years later Charles I's son, Charles II, was restored to the throne in reasonably good order.

51.

Contre les rouges sectes se banderont,
Feu, eau, fer, corde par paix se minera.
Au point mourir ceux qui machineront,
Fors un que monde sur tout ruynera.

Against the reds sects shall form,
Fire, water, iron, rope will pine for peace.
On point of death those who will machinate,
Save one who above all will ruin the world.

The "reds," as we have already seen, probably refer to cardinals, so that the "sects" would be the innumerable Protestant groups that were springing up at the time. The second line would then point to the wars of religion that were beginning to plague France when this verse was written in the late 1550s. The third line predicts an evil fate for these heretics, except for their leader, John Calvin, who remains safe in his Geneva stronghold. This is a plausible reading of this verse and makes sense in the context of Nostradamus's time, although it would then directly contradict IX.44.

A twentieth-century interpretation, favored by Leoni and Cheetham, applies this verse to the various combinations of nations and states against the Soviet Union in the wake of the Russian Revolution. (The British and Americans even launched an unsuccessful invasion of Soviet Russia through the Arctic port of Archangel in 1918–19.) By this view, this attempted "combination" against the Communist Reds would leave Europe open to fascism, since the fascists often claimed to be saving their nations from Communism. The last line would refer to Hitler.

Although this view is intriguing, it makes more sense to see this verse in light of the religious warfare of the sixteenth century, which left such an enormous mark on that era and which would have been very much in the mind of any educated person of the time. The word "sects" lends itself better to a religious rather than to a political application.

55.
L'horrible guerre qu'en l'occident s'apreste
L'an ensuivant viendra la pestilence,
Si fort horrible que jeune, vieulx, ne beste,
Sang, feu, Mercure, Mars, Jupiter en France.

The horrible war that is being prepared in the West,
The following year will come the pestilence,
So powerfully horrible that neither young, nor old, nor beast
    [will survive];
Blood, fire, Mercury, Mars, Jupiter in France.

A quatrain that is customarily applied to the Spanish influenza epidemic that erupted worldwide in 1918–19, in the wake of World War I. The pandemic killed between 20 million and 40 million people in a single year—more than the war itself; the effects of the flu in the U.S. were so great that the average life span was reduced by ten years. Inasmuch as this was the greatest epidemic in history and followed a world war, it is a remarkably good candidate for fulfilling this quatrain. The last line seems to refer to a conjunction of Mercury, Mars, and Jupiter (which happens reasonably often), but it is not clear what sign he means when speaking of "France."

To view this verse in a more pedestrian light, plague and pestilence were an unrelenting feature of daily life in Nostradamus's time; as we have seen, he himself had lost his first family to an epidemic around 1534. The French city of Besançon, for example, reported forty outbreaks of the plague between 1439 and 1640. These epidemics were unimaginably severe by modern standards, and could double or triple the already high death rate. According to the French historian Fernand Braudel, the biological climate of the era was characterized by "a number of deaths roughly equivalent to the number of births; very high infant mortality; famine; chronic undernourishment; and formidable epidemics."[54] To predict a pestilence following a great war—which would worsen an epidemic by increasing the chances of contagion and depleting the food supply—was, from a prophetic point of view, unremarkable.

60.

Conflict Barbar en la Cornere noire.
Sang espandu trembler la d'Almatie,
Grand Ismaèl mettra son promontoire
Ranes trembler secours Lusitanie.

Barbarian conflict in black headdress.
Bloodshed, Dalmatia to tremble.
Great Ishmael shall send his promontory.
Frogs to tremble, Lusitanian help.

A quatrain on Turkish incursions in the Balkans (Dalmatia is on the coast of the former Yugoslavia). Ishmael, the eldest son of Abraham, is associated with the Arabs and the Muslims in general. The last line would indicate that the French (the frogs; cf. V.3) will be uneasy about this development, but that Spain will come to the aid of Christendom. Lusitania is a well-known name for Portugal, but perhaps it serves here as a veiled reference to Spain, which Nostradamus would have had to be extremely careful about mentioning in a positive light.

If this is the interpretation, it is a more or less correct reading of the situation in Nostradamus's time, when the Turks occupied most of the Balkans up as far as Hungary. The trembling frogs would constitute another veiled warning to the French to avoid keeping the Turks as political bedfellows, while Spain could be expected to provide help—as it did in containing Turkish maritime power in the Mediterranean.

To give this quatrain a modern application, one could see it as a premonition of the Bosnian conflict of the 1990s, when Dalmatia and its vicinity did "shake" with grievous ethnic strife. The "promontory" of "Ishmael" would then refer to the largely Muslim state of Bosnia, while the last line would allude to the European powers' initial dithering, followed by their intervention.

65.

Dedans le coing de luna viendra rendre,
Ou sera prins & mys en terre estrange,
Les fruitz immeurs seront à grand esclandre
Grand vitupere à l'un grande louange.

Within the corner of Luna he will come to give up,
Where he will be taken and sent to a strange land.
Unripe fruit will be a great scandal;
Great blame for one, great praise.

"Luna"—the moon—in the first line has led a number of commentators to connect this verse with the moon landing of 1969 and the space program that made it possible. Applying such a reading, Erika Cheetham suggests that "unripe fruit" in the second line means that the rocket boosters are not yet ready for such an intense flight. Making a similar interpretation, John Hogue claims that "unripe fruit" indicates the defective rocket boosters in the space shuttle *Challenger* of 1986, causing it to explode.

This is certainly a far-fetched interpretation, but this is a quatrain for which no more obvious meaning in the context of Nostradamus's time presents itself. All in all, I find that the first two lines fit the moon landing better than the last two fit the *Challenger* disaster: there does not seem to me to be a terribly close resemblance between "unripe fruit" and defective rocket boosters.

73.

Dans Fois entrez Roy ceiulee Turban
Et regnera moins revolu Saturne
Roy Turban blanc Bizance coeur ban
Sol Mars, Mercure pres la hurne.

In faith enters the king of the blue turban,
And will reign less than a revolution of Saturn.
The king of the white turban, Byzantium heart ban,
Sun, Mars, Mercury near the Urn.

This quatrain, with its reference to the whites versus the blues, is clearly connected to II.2. As we saw in that verse, "white turbans" indicate Sunni Turks, the "blue turbans" Persian Shi'ites. "*Fois*" is sometimes understood as the French town of Foix near the Spanish border, sometimes as the Moroccan city of Fez, but it may simply mean that the Sunnis, the "blue turbans," will have the upper hand as a whole in the faith ("*foi*") of Islam.

76.

Avec le noir Rapax & sanguinaire
Yssue de peaultre de l'inhumain Neron,
Emmy deux fleuves main gauche militaire,
Sera murtry par Joyne chaulveron.

With the rapacious and bloody black,
Issued from the pallet of the inhuman Nero,
Between two rivers, left hand military,
He will be murdered by the young bald one.

Peter Lemesurier suggests that "the young bald one"—*Joyne chaulveron*—in the fourth line means the Reformer John Calvin. Lemesurier then takes this quatrain to refer to Michael Servetus, a Spanish theologian who committed the cardinal theological crime (for that era) of denying the divinity of Christ. Hounded by the Inquisition in the Catholic countries, Servetus made his way to Geneva, where he was burned at the stake by Calvin in 1553. The reference to Calvin in the fourth line is plausible, but the first two lines seem to apply more to some sort of despot or brigand than to a heretic, unless we take them as a generic form of deprecation.

79.
Le chef de classe par fraude stratageme,
Fera timides sortir de leurs galleres.
Sortis murtris chef renieur de cresme,
Puis par l'embusche luy redront les saleres.

The head of the fleet by fraud, stratagem,
Will make the timid come out of their galleys.
Emerged, murdered, the chief denier of chrism,
Then by ambush shall they pay him his salary.

As both Leoni and Hogue note, this quatrain can apply to Gaspard de Coligny, admiral of France. His role as leader of the Protestant Huguenots (presumably the "timid" hiding in "their galleys") would lead Nostradamus to call him "the chief denier of chrism," chrism being the holy oil used in Catholic sacraments such as confirmation. The last line is also grimly accurate, since Coligny was murdered in his house on August 24, 1572. As we have seen (cf. IV.47, 62; VI.75), this event triggered the St. Bartholomew's Day Massacre, in which an unknown number of Huguenots (one estimate from 1581 says fifteen thousand) were slaughtered across France. By this interpretation, this quatrain is one of Nostradamus's most accurate and comprehensible prophecies.

89.

Sept ans sera Philip, fortune prospere,
Rabaissera des Arabes l'effaict,
Puis son mydi perplex rebors affaire
Jeusne ogmyon absymera son fort.

Seven years will Philip be, prosperous fortune;
He will bring down the Arabs' effects.
Then his south perplexed, contrary matter,
Young Ogmion will crush his strength.

The obvious reference here is to Philip II of Spain, for whom Nostradamus predicts a short stint of good fortune, particularly against the Arabs of North Africa. Then he will have difficulties to the south of his domain, and Ogmion, who resurfaces here, will bring him down.

This prophecy has only the roughest relation to what actually happened early in Philip's reign. He suffered more setbacks than successes in his early struggles against the Turks and the Arabs of North Africa. In 1561 the Mediterranean island of Djerba was taken by the Turks; the Spaniards lost ten thousand men. In 1568, he indeed found "his south perplexed" when the Moriscos revolted in the southern part of the Iberian peninsula (cf. III.20). In 1571, the Spaniards and their allies defeated the Turks decisively at Lepanto. The king of France ("young Ogmion") had little involvement with these events.

Le Pelletier in the nineteenth century applied this verse to Louis-Philippe, the "bourgeois king," who took the French throne in 1830, the last of the Bourbon dynasty. Popular or at least tolerated in his early years, he became more authoritarian as his reign progressed. By 1848, he had managed to alienate almost all sectors of society and was deposed in favor of the Second Republic. If we take de Fontbrune's interpretation of "Ogmios" as meaning republican government (cf. VI.42), the quatrain has some application to Louis Philippe, but only in the most indirect way.

90.

Un capitaine de la grand Germanie
Se viendra rendre par simulé secours
Un Roy de roys ayde de Pannonie,
Que sa revolte fera de sang grand cours.

A captain of the great Germany
Will come to appear in feigned assistance.
A king of kings, help of Pannonia.
How great a flow of blood will be caused by its revolt!

Another verse that has a dual interpretation, one modern, one contemporary to Nostradamus. The latter would indicate the Hapsburg Holy Roman emperor ("king of kings"), who ruled Germany
and Austria, and who would come to the help of Hungary ("Pannonia"; cf. III.58, V.13, IX.28) in its revolt against the Turks. In
Nostradamus's time, the Hungarian defeat at Mohács in 1526 had
led to the nation's absorption by the Ottoman Empire in 1541.

By this interpretation, the prophecy is fairly accurate. The intermittent wars between the Turks and the Holy Roman Empire would recommence in the late seventeenth century: in 1683
the Turks surrounded Vienna, and were driven off only by the
intervention of King John III of Poland. The war that followed
ended in the Ottomans' defeat at the Battle of Zenta in 1697
by Hapsburg forces. In 1699, Hungary passed from Turkish into
Hapsburg hands, where it would remain until the collapse of
the Hapsburg Empire in 1918.

The modern interpretation takes us to the Second World War,
in which Hitler is the German "king of kings" who comes in
"feigned assistance" to Hungary. During World War II, Hungary
was an ally of Germany. Hungarian forces fought alongside the
Germans on the Russian front; in January 1943, the Russians annihilated the Hungarian Second Army at Stalingrad, killing an
estimated forty thousand soldiers. In 1944, the Germans occupied
Hungary and installed a fascist government. The deportation of

Hungarian Jews to the death camps commenced, and nearly half a million Hungarian Jews were killed. In short, Hungary would suffer a "great flow of blood" during this war—but as a result of its alliance with the Third Reich, not from any revolt against it.

In sum, this quatrain is reasonably successful as a prophecy about Hungary, but as usual, the interpretation that stays closest to Nostradamus's time is the more convincing of the two.

99.

Vent Aquilon fera partir le siege,
Par murs geter cendres, chauls, & pousiere.
Par pluye apres qui leur fera bien piege
Dernier secours encontre leur frontiere.

North wind will make the siege depart,
Over the walls throwing cinders, coal, and dust;
By rain afterward, which will make a good trap for them.
Final aid against their frontier.

This verse has been assigned a number of historical applications, all of which hinge on the detail of the north wind in the first line. Some connect it with Napoleon's disastrous retreat from Russia beginning in October 1812 (cf. I.60, IV.12, V.26). The army found relief only when it escaped the borders of Russia back into the Grand Duchy of Warsaw, at that time a client state of Napoleon's empire.

One might also link the quatrain with Hitler's offensive against the Soviet Union, launched in June 1941. The attack—an utter surprise to the Soviets, who had signed a nonaggression pact with the Nazis in 1939—rapidly penetrated far into the Russian heartland. At one point that autumn, it seemed that both Moscow and Leningrad would fall to the Germans. "General Winter," Russia's greatest ally, struck back in November. Hitler, arrogantly assuming that his forces would have defeated the Soviets by then, had not even had winter outfits issued for his army. The German general

Heinz Guderian lamented how his "insufficiently clothed, half-starved men" faced the "well-fed, warmly clad and fresh Siberians, fully equipped for winter fighting."[55] The Soviets turned back the invasion and would bear the brunt of the fighting against the Third Reich for much of the next four years.

All this said, the details of this quatrain are fairly general, except for the inexplicable reference to the "cinders, coals, dust" flung over the walls. Consequently these lines could be applied to the lifting of practically any siege as a result of winter cold followed by heavy spring rains.

Century X

2.

Voille gallere voil de nef cachera,
La grande classe viendra sortir la moindre.
Dix naves proches le tourneront poulser,
Grandes vaincues unies à soy joindre.

Galley sail will hide ship's sail.
The great fleet will come out as the lesser.
Ten ships nearby will return to repulse them,
Great losers united to join with themselves.

Generally taken as a prophecy of the defeat of the Spanish Armada, which attempted to invade England in July 1588 but was defeated by the English in a battle off Gravelines. The Spanish commander, the Duke of Medina-Sidonia, was determined to return to Spain, but since the English Channel was blocked, the armada had to sail around Scotland and Ireland, where storms destroyed about three-quarters of its number. Consequently, the expedition returned to Spain in humiliation.

The quatrain fits this situation, but as usual somewhat cumbrously. In the key battle at Gravelines, the numbers of English and Spanish ships were more or less equal at about sixty. The last line is grammatically broken and difficult to make out: it sounds as if the defeated fleet ends up joining with another, but this did not happen. In fact the armada failed in part because Medina-Sidonia did *not* succeed in joining up with the Duke of Parma, who was commanding a fleet based in the Spanish Netherlands.

4.

Sus la minuict conducteur de l'armee
Se saulvera, subit esvanouy,
Sept ans apres la fame non blasmee,
A son retour ne dira oncqu ouy.

Under midnight the leader of the army
Will save himself, suddenly vanished.
Seven years later, his fame not blemished,
To his return no one will say anything but yes.

The nineteenth-century commentator Charles A. Ward connected this quatrain with the Battle of Worcester on September 3, 1651, in which Charles II of England attempted to regain the throne of England lost by his father, Charles I, who had been executed two years earlier. At Worcester, Charles II faced Oliver Cromwell's Parliamentary forces and lost disastrously. Of this battle the historian Mark Kishlansky writes, "Cromwell obliterated what was left of the royalist forces at Worcester. Charles II escaped the battlefield with little more than his life. His dignity was left in the hollow of an oak tree, where he hid from the victors."[56] Charles had to flee to France in disguise. Cromwell would rule England as Lord Protector until his death, which coincidentally took place seven years to the day after this battle. Charles was restored to the throne two years later, in 1660. It would be simplistic to say that "no one said anything but yes" to his return, but he ruled successfully until his death in 1685.

Accepting this interpretation, we can regard this as one of Nostradamus's more successful predictions.

10.

Tasche de murdre enormes adulteres,
Grand ennemy de tout le genre humain:
Que sera pire qu'ayeulx, oncles, ne peres,
En fer, feu, eau, sanguin & inhumain.

Stained with murder, enormous adulteries,
Great enemy of all the human race:
He will be worse than his ancestors, uncles, and fathers;
In iron, fire, water, bloody and inhuman.

This verse could be connected to any one of the monsters of human history. The second line was applied to Napoleon by a contemporary Venetian ambassador named Mocenigo. But it makes most sense as a general prophecy of some coming Antichrist.

12.

Esleu en Pape, d'esleu sera mocqué,
Subit soudain esmeu prompt & timide:
Par trop bon doux à mourir provocqué,
Crainte estainte la nuit de sa mort guide.

Elected as pope, by the elected one he will be mocked,
Sudden, hasty, moved, prompt and timid.
By too much sweetness provoked to die,
Extinct fear guides the night of his death.

The seventeenth-century commentator Théophilus de Garancières connected this verse to one Cardinal Santa Severina, who died of grief two months after his elevation to the Papacy in 1591 was ruled illegal, but I have not been able to verify this claim.

John Hogue plausibly links it with Pope John Paul I, who served as pontiff for little more than a month in 1978 before his sudden and mysterious death. He was found on the morning of September 28 sitting up in bed, his face in a grimace: he had died sometime in the night. The officially cited cause was a heart attack, but some have suspected that the pope was poisoned because he was about to initiate widespread reforms and clean up the Vatican's finances, which would eventually lead to the Vatican Bank scandal of 1981.

Another theory holds that the culprit was an actual heart attack rendered fatal by incompetent on-site medical staffing in the Vatican, which had previously harmed the health of popes Pius XII and Paul VI. In any case, the Vatican did not permit an autopsy for John Paul I, and a considerable amount of suspicion remains about his death. This verse fits him at least to the degree that he was occasionally "mocked" (probably unjustly) for being too simple and naive for the job and that he was known for his "sweetness," which won him the nickname of "the Laughing Pope."

18.

Le ranc Lorrain fera place à Vendosme,
Le hault mys bas & le bas mys en hault.
Le filz d'Hamon sera esleu dans Rome,
Et les deux grands seront mis en deffault.

The rank of Lorraine will give way to Vendôme,
The high put low and the low put on high.
The son of Hamon will be elected in Rome,
And the two great ones will be put in default.

This quatrain has been called one of Nostradamus's clearest and most successful. In essence it is saying that the House of Lorraine will lose out for the throne of France to the House of Bourbon: the Bourbon claimant, Henri of Navarre, was also Duc de Vendôme. As we have seen (IX.45), he would take the throne as Henri IV in 1589. The "two in default" would then be the dukes of Guise and Mayenne, of the House of Lorraine.

"The son of Hamon" is widely understood to refer somehow to the heretical faith of the Protestant Henri, who will nonetheless be accepted by "Rome," that is, the Vatican. (In fact Henri did convert to Catholicism upon becoming king; cf. V.85.) The name "Hamon" is taken as alluding to Ammon, an ancient Egyptian god equated by the Romans with Jupiter, or to Amon, a king of Judah who "did that which was evil in the sight of the Lord" (2 Kings 21:20). It might just as well be connected with Ammon, a nation with whom the Israelites frequently fought in the days of the Judges, or for that matter with Haman, the villainous grand vizier in the Book of Esther. But rather than referring to Henri, the line seems to be saying that some future monster or heretic will be chosen as pope.

In regard to the glory evidently predicted here for the House of Valois, Edgar Leoni raises an extremely interesting issue: what, then, are we to do with the other quatrains that predict even more stunning futures for Henri II and his offspring (e.g., IV.77 and V.80)? This leads us to a curious possibility: that Nostradamus, in his cunning way, was inserting prophecies with alternative futures into his quatrains so that his predictions would be vindicated no matter how events turned out. In all fairness to Nostradamus, I should point out that he was at least correct in predicting ultimate triumph for the Valois rather than for their rivals of the House of Lorraine. If the reverse were true, the prophecy would have been a palpable failure.

22.

Pour ne vouloir consentir au divorce,
Qui puis apres sera cogneu indigne,

Le roy des Isles sera chassé par force
Mis à son lieu que de roy n'aura signe.

For not wishing to consent to the divorce,
Who afterward will be recognized as unworthy,
The king of the Isles will be chased by force.
Put in his place one who will have no sign of a king.

This quatrain is almost universally connected to the dramatic abdication of King Edward VIII of Britain in order to marry the American divorcée Wallis Simpson in 1936. Indeed the verse fits this situation in some tantalizing details. Edward VIII was later "recognized as unworthy" because of his unappetizing sympathies for the Third Reich. (Upon his accession to the throne, Edward sent a cable to Hitler saying that he regarded an alliance between Britain and Germany as "an urgent necessity.") Edward was replaced on the throne by his brother George VI, whose diffident manner, accompanied by a nervous stammer, did indeed give "no sign of a king." Actually, George went on to become a remarkably effective and inspiring monarch during the painful years of World War II.

These details, which do not fit any situation in Nostradamus's own day—England was ruled by a queen at the time—should not blind us to certain difficulties with this interpretation. As is common in Nostradamus, the syntax is broken and deliberately obscure. *Who* is not willing to consent to the divorce? In the case of Edward VIII, it was Parliament and British public opinion as a whole, but to take the quatrain at face value, it appears that the king himself is not willing to consent. Moreover, it is not really accurate to say that Edward VIII was chased from the throne "by force." The process, although dramatic, was peaceful. Although he was yielding to pressure from both the public and his own family, Edward abdicated voluntarily. Edward and Wallis, as Duke and Duchess of Windsor, went on to live comfortable lives as leaders of the international smart set until their deaths in 1972 and 1986, respectively.

26.

Le successeur vengera son beau frere,
Occuper regne souz umbre de vengeance:
Occis obstacle son sang mort vitupere,
Long temps Bretaigne tiendra avec la France.

The successor will avenge his brother-in-law,
To occupy a kingdom under the shadow of revenge.
Obstacle killed, his blood, vicious death.
For a long time Brittany will hold to France.

It is strange that this verse is frequently connected with the Kennedy brothers, like other verses mentioning brothers (cf. VIII.17, IX.36). Here, however, it is not even a question of brothers as such, but brothers-in-law, which is the meaning of the French *beau frère*. Even if we set this aside, it is hard to see how Robert Kennedy "avenged" the death of his brother John. Moreover, Robert did not "occupy a kingdom" in any sense: he never became president, being assassinated himself in 1968. Rather, the verse seems to refer to some unidentified episode in which a man avenges his brother-in-law's murder and occupies the throne under a shadow.

The last line is ambiguous: *Bretaigne* can mean either "Brittany" or "Britain." "Brittany" is the more obvious choice in the context of Nostradamus's time: Britain and France were not allied then, nor would they be for hundreds of years. Brittany, in medieval times a semi-independent duchy over which England and France had long contended, had only been formally absorbed into France in 1531. Here Nostradamus is predicting that this relationship will last a long time, as it has up to the present.

27.

Par le cinquieme et un grand Hercules,
Viendront le temple ouvrir de main bellique,

Un Clement, Jule, & Ascane recules,
Lespe, clef, aigle n'eurent onc si grand picque.

By the fifth and a great Hercules,
They will come to open the temple with a warlike hand.
A Clement, Julius, and Ascanius put back,
Sword, key, eagle never had so great a quarrel.

This quatrain raises the issue of "retroactive prophecies" by Nostradamus. Most commentators see this as a reference to the sack
of Rome by the troops of Emperor Charles V ("the fifth and a great
Hercules") on May 6, 1527, some thirty years before this was written. The "temple" then is figuratively the Church. Clement VII
was pope at this time. Julius Caesar and Ascanius, the son of Ae-
neas, the legendary ancestor of the Roman people, both point to
Rome's heroic past, "put back" by this disaster. The "key" would
be the key of Peter; the "eagle" is the Hapsburg emblem; the
"sword" has its usual signification of conflict.

   This interpretation for the quatrain is so neat that it leaves us
with only one question: why would Nostradamus make a prediction for something that already happened? It is clear that Nostradamus mined historical incidents to inform his prophecies, but it
does not leave us with any real idea of why he might have done
this. Probably he associated these events with certain astrological
configurations and simply concluded that when these returned,
something similar would happen.

   I do not know what he might have seen astrologically. Casting a
chart for Rome on May 6, 1527, I see Mars in Sagittarius opposing
both the sun and Venus (in Taurus and Gemini, respectively), and
the moon in Leo opposing Saturn in Aries. (These are all unfortunate
aspects, balanced to some degree by a favorable aspect between Jupiter, the planet of empire, and Saturn, the planet of hardship.) Sagittarius rules religion and Mars rules war, so this could point to a war
of religion, but none of these aspects is so remarkable or rare, either
separately or in combination, to point strikingly to such a disaster.

31.

Le saint empire viendra en Germanie,
Ismaelites trouveront lieux ouverts.
Anes vouldront aussi la Carmanie,
Les soustenants de terre tous couverts.

The holy empire will come to Germany.
Ishmaelites will find open spaces.
Asses will also want Carmania,
The supporters all covered by earth.

As noted in the commentary on III.58, Nazi propagandists used this verse to foretell ultimate triumph for Germany in World War II. The last line is then translated, "The strongholds on land all covered," to mean that Britain will lose all her overseas possessions.[57] While Britain did give up practically all her overseas possessions after the war, it was not because of a German victory, which fortunately never took place.

Taken on its own, the quatrain is puzzling. To say "the holy empire will come to Germany" is baffling, since in Nostradamus's time the "holy empire," presumably the Holy Roman Empire, was *centered* in Germany. The only plausible interpretation is that the Holy Roman Empire will have to retreat back to Germany, its stronghold, while the Muslims, the "Ishmaelites," will find open terrain, stretching their empire as far as "Carmania," an antique name for a part of Persia located at the north of the Strait of Hormuz. Since Persia was already Muslim at this point, it required no great insight on Nostradamus's part to state this.

Often, indeed, as one looks at Nostradamus's verses, one confronts the possibility that he may simply have been indulging in a learned joke. To say that the Holy Roman Empire will be in Germany and to say the Muslims will extend their empire to a region they already control point to a sensibility that takes pleasure in stating very obvious points in very obscure ways. I am reminded of VIII.66, where he makes the portentous but unastonishing prediction that a tomb will be discovered displaying the ancient Roman equivalent of "R.I.P." Ironically, this may well be a tactic that has led Nostradamus's more credulous readers to hold him in such high esteem.

34.

Gaulois qu'empire par guerre occupera,
Par son beau frere mineur sera trahy:
Par cheval rude voltigeant trainera,
Du fait le frere sera longtemps hay.

The Gaul who will occupy the empire by war
By his minor brother-in-law will be betrayed.
He will draw along by a rude, cavorting horse;
By this deed the brother will long be hated.

This verse has been applied to Joachim Murat, the commander of Napoleon's cavalry. Murat, known for his vanity and dash, was one of Napoleon's most capable generals and in 1804 was rewarded by marriage to Napoleon's sister Caroline. In 1808 Napoleon made him king of Naples. In 1813–14, fearing betrayal by Napoleon, Murat turned on him first in return for guarantees by Austria that he would keep his throne. Murat proved to be a poor player of the power game, however, and soon went back to Napoleon's cause. After Napoleon fell in 1815, Murat was captured and shot. He himself gave the order to fire.

This quatrain fits Murat quite well, and overall is better suited to Napoleon's time than to Nostradamus's, when France did not have an empire. The third line could obscurely reflect Murat's career as a cavalry commander.

39.

Premier fils vefve malheureux mariage,
Sans nuls enfants deux Isles en discord,

Avant dixhuict incompetent eage,
De l'autre pres plus bas sera l'accord.

First son, widow, unhappy marriage,
Without any children, two isles in discord.
Before eighteen, immature age,
Lower will be the arrangement of the other nearby.

This verse is notable in that in Nostradamus's own day, it was taken to presage the death of young King François II in 1560 (cf. X.50). François, then sixteen, had a fainting spell in November of that year. "Each courtier recalls now the thirty-ninth quatrain of Century X of Nostradamus and comments on it under his breath," wrote the Venetian ambassador, Michele Suriano, at the time. "Widow" would then refer to François's young bride—Mary, Queen of Scots—who returned to her homeland after her husband's death. The couple had no children.

In this case, the last line would refer to Charles IX, François's brother, who inherited the throne upon the latter's death in December 1560. Charles, then only ten years old, was indeed promised in marriage to Elizabeth of Austria in that year.

40.

Le jeune nay au regne Britannique,
Qu'aura le pere mourant recommandé,
Iceluy mort LONOLE donra topique,
Et à son fils le regne demandé.

The young one born to the Britannic realm,
Whom the dying father will have recommended—
That one dead will give LONOLE cause to talk,
And from his son the kingdom asked.

This verse is sometimes taken to refer to Edward VIII, whose abdication I have already discussed in relation to X.22. But this is hard to see: Edward VIII was forty-one when he ascended the throne—hardly a "young one." "LONOLE" is then taken as an allusion to London, but this is forced; it is not an anagram and does not sound much like "London" or the French name for London, *Londres.* Nor did Edward have any sons or indeed any children.

The nineteenth-century commentator Charles A. Ward gives a more intriguing interpretation for this verse. He applies it to Charles II of England, who was nineteen when his father was executed in 1649. Lonole, says Ward, is Oliver Cromwell, who was nicknamed "Old Noll." The two words sound similar enough—given the pronunciation differences between English and French—to make this a striking hit for Nostradamus.

"And from his son the kingdom asked" is ambiguous but equally fascinating. One could see it as Old Noll, the Lord Protector, "asking the kingdom" from Charles II, the legitimate heir. Or one could see it as a reference to Richard Cromwell, Oliver's son, who took over from his father as Lord Protector when the elder died in 1658 ("Whom the dying father will have recommended"). Richard's ineptitude led the English people to ask for the kingdom back, as it were (cf. IX.49), and they bestowed it on Charles II in the Restoration of 1660.

42.

Le regne humain d'Anglique geniture,
Fera son regne paix union tenir:
Captive guerre demy de sa closture,
Long temps la paix leur fera maintenir.

The human kingdom of English geniture
Will make its kingdom hold peace, union.
War half captive by its closure,
For a long time will have them maintain peace.

The interpretation here hinges on the meaning of the word *Anglique* in the first line, which I have translated as "English." Although the customary French word is *Anglais,* it is common for Nostradamus to bend the forms of words to his own tastes and purposes. By this rendition, the verse would refer to the long Pax Britannica—which was not something that it would be obvious for Nostradamus to predict, since the nation was then, as it had long been, an enemy of his own. Most commentators apply the quatrain to the century between the Napoleonic Wars and World War I, when Europe was by and large peaceful and Britain was the world's most powerful nation.

Some interpreters, however, translate *Anglique* as "angelic," although the customary French word for that is *angélique.* This speculative reading is not as unlikely as it may sound: after all, it makes some sense as a contrast to "human," and would then make the first line read, "The human kingdom of angelic geniture." In this case Nostradamus would be predicting a long reign of millennial peace through the cooperation of the angels with humans. "Geniture" then might contain an echo of Genesis 6:2, which speaks of the "sons of God" taking wives of the "daughters of men," and in fact the cohabitation of divine beings and humans is a common theme in mythology.

49.
Jardin du monde au pres de cité neufve,
Dans le chemin des montaignes cavées,
Sera saisi & plongé dans la Cuve,
Beuvant par force eaux soulfre envenimées.

Garden of the world near the new city,
In the path of the hollowed-out mountains,
Will be seized and plunged in the tank,
Forced to drink sulfur-poisoned waters.

A quatrain that, like I.87 and VI.97, is often connected to New York because of its mention of the "new city." The "garden of the world" would then be New Jersey, which styles itself "the Garden

State." "The path of the hollowed-out mountains" would point to the skyscrapers of Manhattan, even possibly, as John Hogue indicated in 1997, the World Trade Center. Hogue believes the third line reflects Nostradamus's attempt to describe the terrorists concocting explosives, so he links it to the attempted explosion of the buildings by Islamic terrorists in February 1993. "Forced to drink sulfur-poisoned waters" would refer to motorists caught in the Holland Tunnel between Manhattan and New Jersey, who would be submerged in tainted waters that would pour in as a result of this disaster.

The matter is probably better understood in a somewhat more prosaic manner. As Edgar Leoni points out, this quatrain, like VI.97, probably predicts an eruption of Mount Vesuvius on the Campanian plain near Naples, whose name, as we have seen, means "new city." Nonetheless, as with VI.97, an application of this quatrain to New York seems less ridiculous than it might have seemed several years ago. Certainly it would be hard for most Americans today to read this verse without thinking of 9/11, its precursors, and its possible successors.

55.
Les malheureuses nopces celebront,
En grande joye, mais la fin malheureuse:
Mary & mere nore desdaigneront,
Le Phybe mort, nore plus piteuse.

The unhappy ones will celebrate a marriage
In great joy, but the end unhappy.
Husband and mother will despise the daughter-in-law.
The Phybe dead, daughter-in-law more piteous.

This is usually applied to Mary, Queen of Scots, and her husband, François II of France, son of Henri II and Catherine de' Medici (cf. X.39). Mary was one of the more tragic figures of her time. She was less than a year old when she was crowned queen of Scotland upon the death of her father, James V, in 1543. Henry VIII of England took advantage of her minority to invade his northern neighbor, and for her safety Mary was removed to the French court, where she grew up. She was married to François in 1558, when he was fifteen and she sixteen. Upon the death of Henri II in 1559, François became king of France and Mary became queen. But François (presumably "the Phybe," or "Phoebus," the sun god and so figuratively the king) died the next year. Catherine, the queen mother, did not want the young widow in the country, so Mary was sent back to Scotland. She reigned there ineptly until 1567, when the Protestant faction forced her to abdicate. She fled to England, where Queen Elizabeth I held her imprisoned for the next nineteen years. Implicated in a plot to kill Elizabeth, Mary was executed in 1587.

This quatrain fits Mary's situation so well that Nostradamus's more skeptical investigators have wondered whether the verse was doctored. Although it was written around 1558, the earliest surviving edition comes from 1568, after Nostradamus's death. Some have suspected that his acolyte Chavigny sculpted the prophecy afterward to better fit the actual facts, but this cannot be proved one way or the other.

John Hogue sees in this verse a prophecy of the equally unhappy fate of Princess Diana, scorned both by her mother-in-law, Queen Elizabeth II, and by her husband, Prince Charles. The disdain Diana experienced jibes with the verse. On the other hand, the last line implies that the husband will die before the wife, and Diana was killed in an automobile accident in 1997, while Charles is still alive at this writing. At any rate, the quatrain could fit almost any situation in which the mother and son combine against the daughter-in-law, an Oedipal situation that is probably as common among monarchs as it is among ordinary people.

66.

Le chef de Londres par regne l'Americh,
L'isle d'Escosse tempiera par gellee:

Roy Reb auront un si faux antechrist,
Que les mettra trestous dans la meslee.

The head of London, by the kingdom of Americh,
Will temper the Scottish isle with ice.
King Reb will they have, an Antichrist so false
That he will put all of them into the fray.

This quatrain contains a tantalizing reference to someplace that
sounds very much like America, a place that Nostradamus rarely says
much about directly; no doubt he regarded it much as a person today
thinks of Antarctica. Usually this verse is taken as having some future
application—and of course no one can firmly say it will not.

Actually, the historical figure that fits this verse the best is again
Oliver Cromwell (cf. VIII.76), as was noted as long ago as 1672 by
Théophilus de Garancières. Cromwell was "head of London" and
did rule over the nascent English colonies in America. "King Reb"
would indicate one who was both a king and a rebel (*rebelle* in
French). "The Scottish isle" is, of course, customarily taken as
Scotland, but I wonder if the truth is not a bit more subtle. Scotland is not on an island by itself: along with England and Wales,
it is on the island usually known as Great Britain. *Ireland,* on the
other hand, was anciently known as Scotia. This interpretation
would fit neatly with Cromwell's suppression of the Catholic revolt in that nation in 1649–50, which was so brutal that it became
a common Irish oath to say, "The curse of Cromwell upon you."

72.
L'an mil neuf cent nonante neuf sept mois,
Du ciel viendra un grand Roi d'effrayeur:
Ressusciter le grand Roy d'Angolmois.
Avant apres Mars regner par bon heur.

The year 1999, seven months,
From heaven will come the great king of fright,

To revive the king of the Angolmois,
Before, after March, to rule with happiness.

Among the most famous of Nostradamus's verses, this contains one of his very few specifically dated prophecies (cf. X.91). Before 1999 came and went, this quatrain was generally expected to portend some apocalyptic disaster—a nuclear war, a descent of some celestial forces, a reign of terror. Some samples: a "gloomy prediction of the coming of the Third Antichrist in July, 1999" (Erika Cheetham, writing in 1989); "a King of Terror descending from the skies in July 1999" (John Hogue, in 1997); "1999, the seventh month (July 1999), a great frightening chief will come by the path of the skies" (Dr. de Fontbrune, in 1946).

To take the wording as literally as possible, we get "seven months," which would mean seven months had *passed,* leading us to August 1999. In that month we find the most significant astrological event of that year: a total solar eclipse on August 11 combined with a grand square of several planets including Saturn, Mars, Uranus, and the sun. This is an extremely tense configuration. Terrestrially it could be associated with the 7.4 earthquake that took place in Kocaeli, Turkey, on August 17, 1999, but little else. Moreover, Nostradamus could not have known of this grand square, as it involves Uranus, which was not discovered until more than two hundred years after his death. In any event, neither the aspects nor the events of that month add up to anything that would have been worth mentioning almost 450 years in advance.

Peter Lemesurier says the quatrain has to do with the miraculous healing of François I of France in 1525 after his disastrous defeat at Pavia by Emperor Charles V. Lemesurier points out that a number of planets—Jupiter, Mars, Venus, Mercury, and the moon—were in the same signs then as in July 1999, so Nostradamus was predicting the glorious coming of a universal monarch at the end of the twentieth century from the House of Valois-Angoulème, of which François was a member. Lemesurier is correct in his astrological calculations, but it is hard to see why this configuration should have served as a harbinger for a millennial king. For François himself, it was inauspicious to say the least. Defeated and captured, to gain his release he had to sign the humiliating Treaty of Madrid, in which he promised to cede a third of his kingdom to Charles.

What, then, was Nostradamus actually predicting? "Angolmois" is sometimes taken as a fudged anagram of "Mongolois," indicating a revival of the Mongols (or, by extension, the Chinese), but it most likely alludes to the House of Valois-Angoulème that ruled France in his day. Nostradamus appears to have been predicting the restoration of this dynasty in our time. Up to now this has not occurred; certainly it did not occur in 1999. France remains firmly a republic.

73.

Le temps present avecques le passé
Sera jugé par grand Jovialiste.
Le monde tard luy sera lassé,
Et desloial par le clergé juriste.

The present time along with the past
Will be judged by the great Jovialist.
The world will at last be tired of him,
And disloyal by the clerical jurists.

Sometimes taken as a prophecy of the Last Days, this verse is also often applied to John Calvin (cf. IX.51, 76). This is plausible enough, if one takes "Jovialist"—a worshipper of Jove, or Jupiter—as a reference to Protestants. This could be either because Nostradamus thought Protestantism would lead to paganism or because Jupiter is the planet of law, and the Protestants, with their strong emphasis on the Old Testament, seemed "Jovialistic" in this regard. Nostradamus mentions the Jovialists in §34 of the *Epistle to Henri II*, but the reference there is not so clear as to be of any use in interpreting this verse. The last line suggests the irony of

clerical jurists who had once sworn loyalty to the Church reneging
on their oath.

In any event, the quatrain seems unlikely to be referring to the
long-awaited universal monarch, as some contend, since the last
two lines are suffused with ironic deprecation.

74.

Au revolu du grand nombre septiesme
Apparoistra au temps Jeux d'Hecatombe,
Non esloigné du grand eage milliesme,
Que les entres sortiront de leur tomb.

At the turning of the great seventh number
It will appear at the Games of Hecatomb,
Not far from the great millennial age,
That those who entered will leave their tomb.

Very likely a prophecy of the Last Days, this verse is best understood in light of the long-standing idea in Christian apocalyptic
that the world will last seven thousand years (cf. I.48). The first six
thousand years are those of secular history, to parallel the six days
of creation (on the theory that one day to God equals a thousand
years to us; see Ps. 90:4). Afterward will come a seventh millennium, during which Satan will be bound "for a thousand years."
Then he will be "loosed a little season" preceding his ultimate fall
(Rev. 20:2–3). Finally, there will be a general resurrection and judgment (Rev. 20:5).

Exactly when this seventh millennium is supposed to commence
is, of course, the great question. Traditional biblical chronology
places the creation of the world at around 4000 B.C. Nostradamus
himself, in §40 of the *Epistle to Henri II*, dates the creation at 4173
B.C., putting the commencement of the seventh millennium at 1827
A.D. On the other hand, in his *Preface to César,* §19, he says his own
prophecies extend to 3797 A.D., so he cannot have imagined that

time would come to an end in the nineteenth century, or even in the twenty-ninth.

Such confusion in predictions of the Apocalypse cannot be pinned solely on Nostradamus: it is due to ambiguities in the Bible itself. The person who takes the Bible literally (as most Christians did in Nostradamus's time) has to reconcile cryptic and often inconsistent references in Daniel, Revelation, 1 Thessalonians, and the Gospels themselves—not an easy task. Christ's declaration that "of that day and hour knoweth no man" (Matt. 24:36) has not deterred countless of his followers from trying to figure out that very day and hour. The results have not been impressive.

The reference to the "Games of Hecatomb" in the second line is puzzling. In ancient Athens, the Panathenaic Festival, which included games, was held in the month Hekatombaion—roughly equivalent to July in the Athenian lunar calendar. If this is connected with the "seventh month" in X.72, it would suggest that Nostradamus was expecting the millennium to begin at the end of the twentieth century. Other interpreters see in this line a reference to the hecatomb, a ritual slaughter of one hundred oxen in ancient times, and so by extension any great slaughter. The line thus would most likely mean that this event either will take place in the summer or will be preceded by the killing of many people.

86.

Comme un gryphon viendra le Roy d'Europe,
Accompagné de ceux d'Aquilon,
De rouges & blancz conduira grand trouppe,
Et iront contre le Roy de Babylon.

Like a gryphon will come the king of Europe,
Accompanied by those of Aquilon,
Of reds and whites he will lead a great troop,
And they will go against the king of Babylon.

Another reference to the universal Christian monarch who had been expected for more than a millennium even in Nostradamus's time. This king will march against the king of Babylon, accompanied by forces from the north ("Aquilon" is the North Wind). Babylon in Mesopotamia could be equated with Islam, the religion of that area in Nostradamus's time as in ours. As the quintessential symbol of spiritual corruption (cf. VIII.70), Babylon was also associated with Rome by the Protestants. If Nostradamus had secret Protestant sympathies, they might have inclined him to see the universal monarch as coming to overthrow the corrupt Papacy.

John Hogue, writing of this verse in 1997, says, "This is either about the Gulf War of 1991 against Saddam Hussein of Iraq (the King of Babylon), or it augurs a future Gulf War in which the leaders of the European Union, accompanied by the United States (those of the North), return to the oilfields of the Middle East in a second, far more violent clash with Saddam Hussein."[58] If the second Bush administration had been more successful in acquiring allies for its 2003 invasion of Iraq, this prophecy might have appeared to be fulfilled. But then George W. Bush cannot by any stretch of the imagination be described as "the king of Europe."

91.
Clergé Romain l'an mil six cens & neuf,
Au chef de l'an feras election
D'un gris & noir de la Compagne yssue
Qui once ne feut si maling.

Roman clergy, the year 1609,
At the head of the year you will have an election
Of a gray and black issued from the Companion.
Never was there one worse.

This is the only verse in the *Prophecies* that is not rhymed. Like X.72, it is another dated prophecy, and another one that does not fare well in retrospect. In 1609, Pope Paul V was in the fourth year of his reign. Elected in 1605, he would hold the chair of Peter until 1621.

The "gray" and "black" refer to the habits of the Franciscans and Dominicans, respectively, so this individual would presumably reach the Papacy either as a member of one of these orders or by some combined machination of the two. Since the two orders were bitter rivals, the latter seems unlikely.

Compagne literally means "companion," as in "mistress." So Nostradamus is probably saying that this unfortunate choice for a pope will literally be a bastard. Some commentators connect the name with Champagne in France or Campania in Italy, or it could be a portmanteau word evoking some combination of these.

96.

Religion du nom de mers vaincra,
Contre le secte fils Adaluncatif.
Secte obstinee deploree craindra,
Des deux blessez par Aleph & Aleph.

Religion of the name of the sea will conquer
Against the sect, son Adaluncatif.
Sect obstinate, deplored will fear;
Both of them wounded by Aleph and Aleph.

This verse has attracted much attention from Nostradamus's commentators chiefly because of the mysterious name "Adaluncatif" in the second line. It is generally connected with the Muslims for various reasons, including its Arabic sound. The interpretation that makes most sense to me is Dr. de Fontbrune's. He notes that the word is an anagram (exact for once) of *an du califat,* "year of the caliphate." The caliph, from the Arabic *khalifa,* or successor, was the heir to the Prophet's mantle, so the "sect" would be Islam.

The "religion of the name of the sea," Lemesurier suggests, means the Marranos (a pun on the French *mer,* "sea"), Spanish Jews who converted to Christianity. From all this it would appear that Nostradamus is predicting strife between Jews and Muslims, and that the Jews will win in the end.

The second two lines indicate that the struggle will be a bitter one. The deplored, obstinate sect in all likelihood refers to the Jews themselves, who "will fear" as a result of the conflict. The frequent rebuke from the Old Testament—"thou art a stiff-necked people" (Deut. 9:6)—was flung at them by Christians for their "obstinate" refusal to accept Jesus as the Messiah.

"Aleph and Aleph" in the last line is often emended to "Aleph and Alif," the first letters of the Hebrew and Arabic alphabets, respectively. Nostradamus—who assiduously sought to distance himself from his Jewish ancestry—appears to be saying that for all their quarreling, the two are essentially indistinguishable.

This verse has held up well with the passage of centuries. This was not an obvious prediction to make in Nostradamus's time, when Jews were generally treated better in the world of Islam than in Christendom. Conflict between Judaism and Islam did not reach its current level of acrimony until the Jews began to form the state of Israel in the early twentieth century.

98.

La splendeur claire à pucelle joyeuse
Ne luyra plus long temps sera sans sel:
Avec marchans, ruffiens loups odieuse,
Tous peste mesle monstre universal.

The bright splendor for the joyous maiden
Will not shine anymore, will be for a long time without salt.
With dealers, ruffians, odious wolves,
All plagues mix a monster universal.

"The joyous maiden" in the first line is usually linked to Joan of Arc (*La Pucelle d'Orléans,* "the maid of Orleans"), who since her own day in the fifteenth century has been a national heroine of the French. But it is hard to see Joan as a "joyous" figure, given her martial exploits and her death by burning at the stake. More likely the "maiden" is a generalized personification of the same ideal as "splendor." "Salt" is a symbol of intelligence and spiritual purity: "Ye are the salt of the earth," as Christ told his disciples (Matt. 5:3). Nostradamus is forecasting an era of spiritual desolation, when "salt" and spiritual light will seem to be absent from the human race.

This interpretation is reinforced by the last two lines, which point to Nostradamus's Antichrist and reveal an important fact about this figure. These lines say that this "universal monster," this Antichrist, is the creation of all the crimes and follies of humanity. Rather than an individual, it is a creature of the collective. If the concept of the Antichrist has any meaning or value today, I believe it lies in this idea.

100.

Le grand empire sera par Angleterre,
Le pempotam des ans plus de trois cens:
Grands copies passer par mer & terre,
Les Lusitains n'en seront pas contents.

The great empire will be for England,
All-powerful for over three hundred years.
Great forces to pass over sea and land.
The Lusitanians will not be glad about it.

Nostradamus's commentators have remarked that his prophecies are often clearer and more accurate for England than for his own country. Certainly this is a remarkable quatrain to end the *Prophecies,* especially given the long-standing enmity between England and France. Remarkably, it came true. It would be hard to pinpoint exactly the three hundred years he mentions, but roughly speaking, England began its long ascent in the reign of Elizabeth I, in Nostradamus's own time. By the early eighteenth century its naval power had put it in the ascendant over other European powers such as France and Spain, a position it held until the world wars, which eroded Britain's power and ended with the primacy of the United States.

The last line is curious and, taken in its most literal sense, totally incorrect. "Lusitanians" means the Portuguese, and the Portuguese have had a long-standing alliance with Britain that has lasted for more than six hundred years. Dating back to 1373, when the two nations fought together in a battle against Spain, it has been one of the most durable alliances in world history.

"Lusitanians" could be taken more broadly to refer to the Spaniards as a seagoing power. In Nostradamus's time, Spain, with its powerful Mediterranean navy and its far-flung colonies in America and the Philippines, was at the zenith of its naval might. The disaster of the Spanish Armada in 1588 would mark the beginning of Spain's long decline on both sea and land into the status of a third-rate power, from which it has never really emerged.

Nostradamus
and the Uses
of Prophecy

Having taken a look at Nostradamus's life and prophecies, we are now faced with two main questions: Could Nostradamus foretell the future? If not, why have his prophecies been so perennially popular?

By now the answer to the first question should be obvious. While Nostradamus did have a few remarkable hits, overall his predictions, no matter how generously interpreted, have not had a high rate of accuracy. Even prophecies of his that do resonate with later events—such as the ostensible prediction of 9/11 in VI.97—are on shaky ground. Admittedly some of his interpreters saw this verse as a forecast of an aerial attack on New York even before that disaster struck. On the other hand, we also have the strong probability that Nostradamus was thinking of an entirely different place, the "new city" being not New York but Naples or Villeneuve. Furthermore, as the debunkers like to stress, there was nothing in the prophecy that would enable anyone to pinpoint it in advance, and an open-ended prophecy is almost as worthless as no prophecy at all. (I can say today almost infallibly that the stock market will rise, but if I do not say when or by how much, the prediction has no value whatsoever.) Nostradamus's warning—if such is what it was—saved no one from the calamity at the World Trade Center.

In cases where Nostradamus did try to be specific, his record is abysmal. The most obvious instance was the great event predicted in 1999, when we were supposed to see the advent of "the great king of fright" (X.72). Nothing happened—nothing, at any rate, of the apocalyptic magnitude that Nostradamians had been expecting. Some have resorted to special pleading. One interpreter contended that the verses should be dated not from the birth of Christ but from the Council of Nicaea in 325 A.D. Even apart from the total arbitrariness of this choice, it is not clear that such adjustments would improve the record much or at all.

To view his prophecies in a broader perspective, as I have mentioned in my biographical chapter, he was generally correct in forecasting war in the immediate future for his own time. Even setting aside the constant dynastic struggles that afflicted Europe's monarchies in this era, it was reasonable to expect that the religious conflicts that were brewing at the time in France would erupt into open warfare.

Yet here too his record is uneven. Taking his inspiration from an apocalyptic tradition that goes back to the works of a seventh-century writer named Pseudo-Methodius (so called because his text was originally falsely attributed to one St. Methodius), Nostradamus foresaw a massive Muslim invasion of Europe that would be repelled by a universal Christian monarch who, he hinted, would be Henri II or some scion of the House of France.

Pseudo-Methodius refers to this monarch as "the king of the Greeks, i.e., the Romans," a reference to the Byzantine emperor (the Byzantines spoke Greek but called themselves *Romaioi,* "Romans"). A tenth-century monk named Adso changed this "king of the Romans" to the "king of the Franks" to buttress the claims of Charlemagne's descendants to the legacy of the Roman Empire.[59] Nostradamus knew this tradition from a 1523 compilation called the *Mirabilis liber*, which speaks of "the king of the Romans" and predicts that the race that will conquer the "sons of Ishmael" (the Arabs, who traced their ancestry to Abraham's son Ishmael, and more generally the Muslims) will "emerge from Gaul."

This was an understandable prediction to make in his day, in the light not only of Christian apocalyptic tradition but of constant pressure from the Ottoman Turks in both the Mediterranean and southeastern Europe. As I have already noted, the archetype of the universal monarch was vividly alive in the consciousness of Christendom in that age. It was natural for Nostradamus, a Frenchman, to suggest that this universal "king of the Romans" would come from "Gaul"—that is, France.

The actual outcome of this struggle, if dramatic, was considerably less apocalyptic. The Christian European powers managed to hold the Turks at bay for the next century, at which point the Ottoman Empire began a long, slow decline. (Some historians set the beginning of its decline earlier, at the death of the sultan Suleiman the Magnificent in 1566, coincidentally also the year of Nostradamus's death.) In this struggle, France gave its coreligionists no palpable support; in fact, France tended to ally with the Turks against the Catholic Hapsburgs—something Nostradamus warned against frequently. By the 1850s the Ottoman Empire had decayed to the point where it was nicknamed "the Sick Man of Europe." France and Britain would fight the Crimean War to prop it up against encroachments by tsarist Russia. The Ottoman Empire received its fatal blow from World War I, after which it was replaced by today's secular, democratic Turkey.

Some may want to extend the time line further and see Nostradamus's prophecies coming to fulfillment now, with the increasing tension between the West and the Islamic world. By this theory, the Muslim powers will invade Europe sometime in the near future.

Only then will the universal monarch arise and save the day. Some even associate the large-scale migration of Arabs, Turks, and North Africans to Western Europe as a harbinger of this trend.

It is as foolish to state definitively that something will *not* happen in the future as to state it will, so I will not step into the trap of asserting that such an outcome is impossible. Yet I daresay that, even if world events were to play out in such a way over the next century, I doubt they will take a form that would be recognizable from anything in Nostradamus. The immigration of Muslims into Europe has been peaceful: they have come not as invaders but as supplements to the labor force.

To put the matter still more bluntly, I would not base any of my future plans or expectations on anything Nostradamus predicted or is imagined to have predicted. In this I am not being unduly rationalistic, and I hope no one will mistake me for a "skeptical inquirer." As a matter of fact, I am quite convinced—both theoretically and through personal experience—that the future can be known, at least in certain instances, for reasons I will explore below. But I do not believe Nostradamus was able to predict the future well enough to deserve the (admittedly somewhat spotty) reputation he has enjoyed for five hundred years.

We then come to the second question I posed at the outset of this chapter: why have Nostradamus's prophecies attracted so much attention from his day to ours?

In the first place, Nostradamus was a master of his art. With some exceptions, he avoided the greatest mistake a prophet can make: setting definitive dates. It is true that he made some references to years such as 1607, 1702, and 1999—none of which were to see the events he predicted for them—but even here he was clever enough to point to dates that were well past his own lifetime. In saying that his prophecies extended to the year 3797, he managed to ensure that they would attract attention for many generations to come.

Nostradamus's dating showed another stroke of genius. Unlike practically every Christian prophet before him (including Jesus himself, if we are to place any faith in the historicity of the Apocalyptic Discourse in the Gospels; see my comments on VIII.87), he did not yield to the temptation of saying that the end was at hand. Although he foresaw tremendous upheavals in the near future, he did not make the mistake of believing they would usher in the Last Judgment. By implying that history as we know it would continue at least into the fourth millennium, he forestalled the criticism that could be leveled against most other apocalypticists, who have been proclaiming the world's imminent demise for the last two thousand years.

Nostradamus also proved to be a master of oracular language. He was not a good, or even competent, stylist in prose. The fashion of the era called for writing in ornate, complex sentences in imitation of the classical authors, especially Cicero. While this style can have an intricate beauty in the hands of someone with real talent, when used by a second-rate writer such as Nostradamus, the clauses become tangled and the grammatical structure of the sentence sometimes collapses under its own weight.

In poetry it was different. Nostradamus ignored the poetic conventions of the day. He wrote in short, rhymed quatrains that are elliptical, mysterious, and often broken in grammar. This method brought him criticism from the men of letters in his own time, who judged everything by classical models, but it worked remarkably well for his purposes. With his quatrains, he created a world of bizarre and disjointed but gripping images; had he lived in the twentieth century, he might have been hailed as a master of surrealism. Using this dark language, he could appear to say a great deal while saying very little in actuality. With an artful use of archaic and often garbled place names, he managed to make his verses still more evocative and still more obscure.

In short, Nostradamus wrote in oracular language, and oracular language is traditionally ambiguous. One of the most famous instances of this ambiguity comes from the sixth century B.C. Croesus, king of Lydia in Asia Minor, twice inquired of the Delphic Oracle in Greece about whether he should engage Cyrus, king of Persia, in war. According to the Greek historian Herodotus, "The judgment given to Croesus by each of the two oracles was the same, to wit, that if he should send an army against the Persians he would destroy a great empire." Croesus, taking this to augur success for his enterprise, went to war with Cyrus and suffered a disastrous defeat, losing his own kingdom. When he indignantly inquired again, the oracle replied, "It behoved him, if he would take right counsel, to send and ask whether the god spoke of Croesus' or Cyrus' empire. But he understood not that which was spoken, nor made further inquiry: wherefore now let him blame himself."[60]

Nostradamus, too, inserted disclaimers into his work. In the *Epistle to Henri II,* §12, he says his prophecy is like "seeing in a burning mirror, as with beclouded vision, the sad, prodigious, and calamitous events that approach." In the *Preface to César,* §8, echoing Acts 1:7, he says, "It is not ours to know the times and the seasons." (It is a common tactic among apocalyptic prophets to cite verses like this one, and then to ignore their own advice by attempting to predict those very times and seasons. Nostradamus avoided this trap better than most.)

A final reason for Nostradamus's success as a prophet requires looking at the *Prophecies* in a different light than usual. The customary approach is to connect the quatrains with single, specific events in history. But as I suggested in relation to I.34, at least some of the quatrains seem to relate to universal situations, much like the verses in the *I Ching.* This would go a long way toward explaining Nostradamus's enduring reputation, because his verses could then apply—intentionally or otherwise—to any number of recurring circumstances. The quatrain X.55, for example, could fit many situations in which a woman suffers at the hands of her mother-in-law.

A major difference between Nostradamus's *Prophecies* and the *I Ching,* of course, is that the latter is an overt method of divination:

one draws yarrow stalks or casts coins to determine the hexagram and the interpretation that applies to a given situation. Nostradamus's text has no such divinatory apparatus, and I can see no indication that he intended it to be used that way. If one wanted to do so, the best approach would be through the art of bibliomancy: asking a question, closing one's eyes, opening the book at random, and pointing to a line to find an answer. This technique has been practiced for centuries with the Bible and the works of Virgil, who was regarded as a magus in the Middle Ages.

These aspects of his work suggest why Nostradamus was such a successful practitioner of the art of apocalyptic prophecy. But they do not explain why apocalyptic has such an intense and consistent appeal. This appeal is not universal: it is more or less limited to the Abrahamic religions—Judaism, Christianity, and Islam—and to cultures directly connected to them (such as certain American Indian tribes, which, influenced by Christian missionaries, saw the rise of apocalyptic prophets in the nineteenth century). Hinduism and Buddhism also foresee an end to the world, but the time scale on which they imagine it is immense in relation to human history, spanning billions of years. Moreover, they regard this world as merely one in an endless cycle of similar worlds, so the end of human life and destiny is seen not in historical terms but in transcendent terms—stepping out of the cycle of time through spiritual liberation rather than expecting the Lord to bring it all to a speedy conclusion.

But in the West, apocalyptic has maintained a consistent hold on the popular imagination. Why? Prophecies of an imminent end have all failed over and over again for the last two millennia, so the soundest conclusion is that there is nothing in them. If they remain so popular despite their rate of success, they must serve deeper cultural and psychological needs. Apocalyptic expectations remain so widespread in the United States today that these cultural needs must be alive and well.

Why do people feel such a pressing desire to believe that the end of the world is at hand? Why does every disaster and every war—which are unfortunately among the most recurrent events in human experience—inspire someone to stand up and say that this augurs the Last Judgment? And why, against all evidence, are they so readily believed? The sources of these popular needs are in many ways the most interesting issues raised by Nostradamus's legacy, so they are worth exploring in some detail.

One source of apocalyptic expectation is, I suspect, mere boredom. For many if not most of us, life is a daily exercise in the humdrum. People go to work, pay their bills, pursue their hobbies and entertainments, all the while waiting for some deliverance from the everyday. If there is any genuine excitement, it is of the frightening variety—an illness, the loss of a job, the death of a loved one. Vacations and leisure pursuits offer some relief but often make the return to the routine that much more oppressive.

It seems to me that the role of boredom in human history and culture has long been underestimated. H. L. Mencken observed that this was part of the appeal of war. In an essay written in the wake of World War I, he contended that the American people "delight in war and enjoy its gaudy uproar as a country boy enjoys circus day." And so Mencken's era, like many eras, saw young men flock to the colors. They soon learned that the excitement of war was far outstripped by its hardship, horror, and, ironically, ennui.

Today we are more sophisticated. Television has brought the images of war somewhat closer to home, so people are less naive about its grim actualities. But the oppressiveness of daily life remains with us. We try to palliate it with sports, entertainment, and recreation, even with the frantic busyness that is the hallmark of contemporary America, but it is never far away. Although we have more amusements available to us than any other people in history, these provide us with nothing more than brief and intermittent diversion. The only real remedy would be a sense of purpose and meaning to life—something no amount of entertainment could ever provide.

Consequently, I believe many have unconsciously come to see apocalypse as an escape from the tedium of ordinary life. This dynamic works from several angles. In the first place, the idea that the end is near and that the political upheavals of the present were foreseen long ago by Daniel and the Apostle John adds a sense of excitement and involvement to current events, which frequently seem remote to the ordinary person. In the second place, an end to history provides a *meaning* to history. The Second Coming of Christ, if it were to happen, would give a shape to human destiny that is hard to find in social and political currents as conventionally understood. Finally—and not least—the believer has the comfort of knowing he is on the right side, for no one who believes in apocalypse imagines that he is on anything but the side of goodness and justice. We may assume that fundamentalists who look forward to the Rapture believe they will be taken up in the first batch.

Another element in the allure of apocalyptic is that it will set the scales of justice right. We can see this in the origins of the apocalyptic genre in Palestine in the second century B.C. At the time, the Jewish nation was living under the rule of the Hellenistic Seleucid monarchs, who were heirs to a portion of the empire of Alexander the Great. In 167 B.C., one of these rulers, Antiochus IV Epiphanes, embarked on a program of forced Hellenization of the Jews, setting up an altar, and perhaps an image, of Olympian Zeus in the Temple in Jerusalem.

The outrage of the Jews is reflected in the Book of Daniel, one of the earliest apocalyptic writings and the only one to make its way into the Hebrew Bible. Written during the ensuing revolt against the Seleucids, this book sets up Daniel, a legendary sage of the sixth century B.C., as the mouthpiece of a prophecy that would "foretell" events four hundred years after his time. (The technical term for this practice is *vaticinium ex eventu*, "prediction after the event.") Daniel refers to "a vile person"—Antiochus—who will "pollute the sanctuary of strength, and shall take away the daily sacrifice, and . . . shall place the abomination that maketh desolate" (Dan. 11:21, 31)—that is, the idol in the Temple (cf. 1 Macc. 1:54). The archangel Michael will come to Israel's rescue; the dead will be raised, "some to everlasting life, and some to shame and everlasting contempt." Antiochus "shall come to his end, and none shall help him" (Dan. 11:45, 12:1–2).

What happened in fact was that the Jews rose up under the priestly clan of the Maccabees and won back their religious liberties as well as a measure of political autonomy, but this obviously did not begin the end of time. Antiochus himself did not perish as a result of any obvious divine wrath: he died of natural causes.

Despite its failure as a prophecy, the Book of Daniel set up the basic structure of the apocalyptic genre. Arising during some crisis, a text of this kind predicts that this event is the harbinger of the Day of Judgment, when justice will be done and evildoers will receive their due. The Book of Revelation at the end of the New Testament is much the same: most scholars agree that it is a response to the persecution of Christians by the Roman emperor Domitian in the last decade of the first century A.D.

Clearly such texts provide hope of divine justice at a time when this hope seems very faint. Norman Cohn, whose *Pursuit of the Millennium* is one of the best-known studies of the apocalyptic mentality, argued that this impulse arises among the lower orders of society in response to social and economic oppression. Clearly there is some truth in this idea. The higher a person climbs in the socioeconomic scale and the more control he feels he has over his own destiny, the less likely he is to fear or hope for the world's imminent conflagration. (Admittedly, there are disquieting signs that right-wing political leaders in the U.S. today take such ideas more seriously than one might wish.)

On the other hand, some say Cohn's view is too simplistic. Bernard McGinn, a noted scholar of apocalyptic, observes, "This approach is totally blind to those manifestations of apocalyptic traditions that were intended to *support* the institutions of medieval Christianity rather than to serve as a critique, either mild or violent."[61]

This consideration leads us to another use of apocalyptic: as a means of social control. Most of the authors of Christian apocalyptic prophecies were not members of the poorer classes; like

Nostradamus himself, they were ensconced comfortably in the social order. What motive could they have for constantly harping on the rapid coming of the Last Judgment?

To answer this question, consider this quotation from Girolamo Savonarola, the fiery Dominican preacher who induced the citizens of fifteenth-century Florence to burn their books and artworks as emblems of diabolical vanity:

> I have said to you: "the sword of the Lord will come upon the earth swiftly and soon." Believe me that the sword of God will come in a short time. Do not laugh at this "in a short time," and say that it is the "short time" of Revelation which needs hundreds of years to come. Believe me that it is soon. This belief will not harm you; on the contrary it will give you joy in that it makes you turn to penance and walk on the road to God.[62]

Savonarola's prophecies—which were among the sources Nostradamus used—thus had an ulterior motive. They were meant to prick the consciences of Christians, who would then repent and see the error of their ways. From this point of view, whether or not the end was actually near, the faithful would benefit from their repentance and regeneration. They would return to the Church rather than overturn it. Predictions of the imminent Judgment thus serve as a means of social control. We may wonder about the value of fear and hysteria as goads to moral improvement, but for many centuries it has been found to work well enough. For the preacher who wants to save people from their sins, such warnings are useful regardless of whether they come true.

Yet another reason for the popularity of apocalyptic curiously stems from its very improbability. The culmination of time in a physical descent of Christ to earth is not only unlikely, but rather ridiculous as usually conceived. The rash of novels such as the *Left Behind* series and films such as *The Omega Code* only point up this fact. We can assume the fundamentalist view of the end of time is wrong if only because we can assume God is not the creator of a B-grade movie. One would hope that, however the world ends, it would not be with such a lurid and contrived finale.

Subconsciously, I suspect, even many fervent believers recognize this fact. It is not the certainty of the Last Judgment that they cling to; it is its very remoteness and improbability. By focusing their hopes and fears on this unlikely outcome, they may avoid thinking of an event that is not only likely but certain: their own deaths.

Traditional Christian theology conceives of eschatology—the study of the Last Things—in two ways. There is the end of time as I have been discussing it; in theological language, this is called the "general judgment." But there is also the "particular judgment"— the weighing of the soul that each individual will have to face after his or her death. And it is this event—one's own death—that I believe is being masked by apocalyptic hopes and fears.

Psychologists sometimes speak of "displacement"—the transfer of an unconscious fear onto a remote object so as to make the fear more manageable. I would suggest that this is precisely the role that apocalyptic expectations play for many believers today. By projecting their anxieties about death onto some ever receding apocalypse, they are able to cope with them somewhat better. To think of one's own death seriously—not as a remote apocalyptic event with which one can play all sorts of mental games, but as a reality that faces each of us in no more than a few decades—is not only sobering but often terrifying. It forces us to consider what is truly important in life and what is not. This theme has been examined and explored in art of all kinds and genres. Perhaps the most famous fictional treatment of it is Tolstoy's short novel *The Death of Ivan Ilyich,* whose protagonist, an ordinary bourgeois of his time with a comfortable, conventional life, finds he is dying. He realizes that everything he cherished, everything he thought important, meant nothing. And it is too late to change.

Over the centuries Christianity has put much stress on this theme. In medieval times there was a powerful tradition centered around the axiom *Memento mori*—"Remember death." Devout believers aspired toward the "good death" (which I mentioned in reference to the abdication of Charles V in IX.8), whereby an individual would set aside worldly cares and goals and would turn his mind to prayer and repentance as a preparation for the end. The frequent use of the iconic figure of Death, of skulls and skeletons, in funerary art, has a similar thrust. The most striking instance of it I have seen was in a British cathedral, which had a tomb with a carved stone effigy of a medieval bishop. Unlike most such effigies, which decorously show their subjects in robes or armor, this one represented the bishop as a half-rotted corpse.

Here we are faced with quite a different level of eschatology. It is not a matter of improbable Raptures or of second-rate Antichrists concocted out of figures in the news, but of the ultimate reality that without any question faces every last one of us: physical death. This is not a pleasant prospect, and for many it is a difficult one even to imagine. No wonder, then, that many choose to deal with it at second hand, through apocalyptic imaginings. And while I have focused on the Christian aspect of this displacement because it is most relevant to Nostradamus's legacy, the same dynamic seems to be at play in forecasts of a secular apocalypse, which usually involve nuclear war or ecological cataclysm. These are serious issues and must be dealt with seriously, but, like fundamentalist apocalypses, they are also used as means of displacing more immediate sources of anxiety. Some activists even seem to have an attitude like Savonarola's, believing it expedient to keep people in a state of constant terror for fear that they will do nothing at all. But I myself doubt that negative emotions will produce positive actions.

These considerations lead to what may be the linchpin of the apocalyptic mind-set, and perhaps of much human suffering. It is poorly understood and little discussed, but for that reason all the more worth attention here. It is described most clearly in that peculiar and yet extremely powerful text known as *A Course in Miracles:*

The circle of fear lies just below the level the body sees, and seems to be the whole foundation on which the world is based. Here are all the illusions, all the twisted thoughts, all the insane attacks, the fury, the vengeance and betrayal that were made to keep the guilt in place, so that the world could rise from it and keep it hidden. Its shadow rises to the surface, enough to hold its most external manifestations in darkness, and to bring despair and loneliness to it and keep it joyless.[63]

Without going into the elaborate psychological system of the *Course*, I will simply point here to the notion of the "circle of fear"—a belt or zone of fears, hatreds, and anxieties that lie just below the surface of consciousness. This "circle of fear" is universal: each of us participates in its creation. Probably only the most enlightened human beings are entirely free from its effects. For practically all of us, it sits underneath our experience of reality like a water table. All of us tap into it in our own ways.

This fear is not "about" anything particular; it is not necessarily connected to anything real or substantial; it is simply a nameless, objectless anxiety that can attach itself to anything. It holds tremendous power over each of us precisely because we are usually unconscious of it. We imagine that our fears and anxieties are about something real and justified, but there is something suspect about this belief: no sooner does one anxiety disappear than another pops up to take its place. For some—probably most—people, this anxiety can manifest in fears about their personal future or about society or humanity or the earth as a whole; for others, it is displaced onto a fear of an imminent end of the world.

Some say fear is a healthy and normal emotion, that without it we could not function in the world. So it may be under certain circumstances. If a man finds himself facing a wild animal, his instincts will make him run away. But the kind of fear I am talking about is not healthy. It does not increase our chances for survival in a Darwinian sense; instead it is weakening and debilitating. I would go so far as to say that much of what is regarded as mental dysfunction stems from too close a contact with this circle of fear.

Why does this substratum of meaningless fear exist? This is a complex question that leads us into the deepest issues of psychology and perhaps theology as well. A comparatively simple explanation is that we become connected to it as we experience traumas in the course of life. Hence it may be related to what Eckhart Tolle, in his popular book *The Power of Now,* calls the "pain body." "This accumulated pain is a negative energy field that occupies your body and mind," Tolle observes. "If you look at it as an invisible entity in its own right, you are getting quite close to the truth."[64]

This "circle of fear," or "pain body," is, I suggest, a part of the human character structure as we find it in ourselves. We would be healthier individually and collectively without it, but it remains with us, and I do not see any sign that psychology or religion as a whole has attempted to deal with it or has even acknowledged its existence. In fact, certain segments of society have consciously or unconsciously made use of it, as Savonarola did in Renaissance Florence. Tapping into the circle of fear is the easiest way to manage public opinion, because a fearful person is weakened and so more easily manipulated. Some businesses employ this circle of fear in artful ways: the insurance industry is perhaps the most obvious example. Purveyors of luxury goods make use of status anxiety to get the public to buy their products. Politicians exploit fear with hysterical campaign tactics. Religions make use of it to promote their own doctrines: fear of damnation (personal or collective) is created; then the religion offers itself as the magical remedy to the imagined problem.

Conspiracy theorists may argue that commercial and political interests have constructed these fears as a way of keeping the masses in line. But this is too simple. In the first place, there is no stratum of society whose members are above this level of anxiety. Quite the opposite: the higher one climbs, the greater one's fear of falling becomes, as we see in the paranoia of despots and dictators and even of petulant celebrities. If the circle of fear is made use of by the brutal and cynical powers of the world, it is a weapon that hurts them as much as anyone else.

Furthermore, such a conspiratorial view casts us ordinary citizens in the role of helpless victims. We are no such thing. The circle of fear is a collective creation, and everyone who takes part in it is responsible for it. There is no escape in blaming "them"—whoever "they" are—and hiding behind a false innocence. Indeed the fear of "them" is a symptom of the problem.

Where, then, lies our way out? There is only one way that I can see: to acknowledge these tendencies in ourselves, to face them, and to overcome them. This approach may prove far trickier than it first appears. It has often struck me that the sense of a limited self—which some spiritual traditions call the "ego"—takes much of its sustenance from this subliminal layer of fear. If one chances to stray too far from it through some experience of illumination or delight, the ego has to stop and take counsel with its fear to reassure itself of its own existence. Thus a constant noise of anxiety and dread, sometimes loud, sometimes so low as to be unnoticeable, forms the backdrop of ordinary life as we know it today.

While this is an interior experience, the easiest way to see it externally is in social settings. At a dinner party, say, it may happen that people will have an enjoyable time for much of the evening, but at some point the conversation will settle into a more somber note. The topic may turn to the issues of the day—usually politics in some form or another. If there is a great deal of disagreement among those present, either there will be an argument or, more likely, the topic will be avoided by the tacit consent of all. But if those present are in general agreement (as people in the same social set often are), they will plunge into the matter and rehearse their own anxieties about it until they reach a minor crescendo of fear and anxiety. In these settings, there appears to be no good reason to turn the conversation in that direction—it is neither pleasant nor likely to produce any positive conclusions—but people seem unable to avoid it; it is like picking at a wound that itches or hurts.

I have seen this happen so many times in so many different contexts that it appears to be universal, at any rate in America. Among people with spiritual aspirations or pretensions, the prophecies of Nostradamus himself may come up, inevitably as a warning of grim happenings on the horizon. The result is the same: people are taking counsel with their subliminal fears to reassure themselves of their identity—in this instance, of a group identity. Often in these circumstances the mood of the gathering turns dark and closed in, like that of campers trading ghost stories around a fire. The strange mixture of dread and delight present in such experiences suggests that people take pleasure in feeling part of something larger than themselves, even if it is nothing more than a little group huddling together in self-generated terror of the time to come.

At this point it might be helpful to pick up the initial thread of this discussion and ask where Nostradamus fits in. Was he himself aware of any of these issues? Or was he merely trying to exploit them for his own purposes?

In some ways, the question does not make sense in the context. We sometimes forget how far we are from Nostradamus's time. We in the contemporary West are the children of Descartes, who was born in 1596, thirty years after Nostradamus's death. Descartes based his entire philosophy on doubt, asking himself what he could know for certain even if everything around him was a dream generated by an evil demon. While it would take us too far afield to explore Descartes's own answer, the skeptical stance he took set the tone for the next four centuries of Western history. Whether he knew he was doing so, Descartes was exalting doubt over faith, and this is a stance we still take, whether we recognize it or not.

In Nostradamus's day, doubt was not a virtue. In fact, doubting the fundamentals of the Christian faith was virtually unthinkable. And the bedrock of this faith was that Christ would return to judge the quick and the dead. Although the Bible and the teachings of the Church were often vague and confusing about the details, the essential truth of this outcome was unquestioned.

Hence, Nostradamus was merely following in the footsteps of a long tradition, adding some details of his own, along with his own inimitable oracular style, but not overturning or even revising it in any major respect.

Nostradamus was not a fanatic. He was simply applying and updating prophecies in which everyone was supposed to believe. In the end, despite the aura of magic that hovers about him, he comes across in the end chiefly as an enterprising bourgeois of the early modern era. He had tried his hand at many occupations—medicine, pharmaceuticals, confections—before finally, in his late forties, hitting almost accidentally upon one that brought him enormous success and renown. Like another enterprising bourgeois of two centuries later—Benjamin Franklin—he would first make a name for himself by writing almanacs. Soon afterward, sensing an appetite for prophecy in the uneasy mood of his times, he embarked upon his quatrains. By the usual combination of talent and luck—the latter chiefly consisting of the tremendous appetite for occultism at the French court—he established himself as the premier prognosticator in Europe.

Thus in all probability Nostradamus was not a charlatan or a cynic. Unlike many of his commentators, he does not leave the impression that he is sniggering in his sleeve. As we have seen, the apocalyptic prophecies that he echoed had deep roots in the Christian tradition, going back to the Bible itself. From Nostradamus's point of view, his predictions, even those foretelling degeneracy and hard times for the Church, involved no conflict, inner or outer, with his religion, since similar predictions had been made in so many of his sources. The sincerity with which he very likely practiced would have made his work easier: generally speaking, people are more successful if their success involves little or no conflict with their own deep-seated principles.

ONE FINAL QUESTION REMAINS as I come to the end of this book. What lessons can we draw from all this? What is the best attitude for approaching a future that often seems uncertain or menacing?

As I have suggested, it seems highly doubtful that prophecies such as Nostradamus's have any practical value in helping us see what will happen in either the near or the remote future. Nor are there any other sources that fare any better in this regard; even many of the prophecies in the Bible have proved wrong. Prophecy, then, is of no help. It is more a snapshot of collective hopes and fears than any accurate reflection of what is to come.

Conventional economic and political forecasting, despite its apparently august authority, is not always more reliable. On the whole, these predictions say far more about the ideological and commercial agendas of their practitioners than they do about reality.[65] Even when they make every effort to be objective, they usually say more about the preconceptions of the present than about any likely future. To take one example, the well-known futurologist Herman Kahn produced a work in the mid-1960s entitled *The Year 2000*. Some of his predictions were astonishingly accurate. Kahn forecast the "use of real-time large computers for an enormous range of business information and control activity, including most trading and financial transactions . . . computerized processes for instantaneous exchange of money, using central . . . networks for debiting and crediting accounts," as well as "uses of computers for world communications, medical diagnostics, traffic and transportation control, automatic chemical analyses, weather prediction and control, and so on."

In other areas, Kahn's forecasts were far off the mark. Here is his projection of the social future of the year 2000:

Let us assume, then, with expanded gross national product, greatly increased per capita income, the work week drastically reduced, retirement earlier (but life span longer), and vacations longer, that leisure time and recreation and the values surrounding these acquire a new emphasis. Some substantial percentage of the population is not working at all. There has been a great movement toward the welfare state, especially in the areas of medical care, housing, and subsidies for what previously would have been thought of as poor sectors of the population.[66]

All this made perfect sense in the age of Lyndon Johnson's Great Society. How could Kahn, or indeed anyone else, have foreseen the dismantling of the welfare state in the U.S. (and to some extent in other nations), as well as the *increased* number of hours worked by Americans over recent decades? In the light of his entirely reasonable projections, these developments are incomprehensible.

The predictions above are from what Kahn calls a "surprise-free scenario"—one that assumes no major cataclysms. He devotes some attention to other scenarios. As one might expect, they concentrate on nuclear confrontation between the U.S. and the U.S.S.R., the great haunting fear of that era. And yet the index to this work does not even list the words "Christianity," "Islam," "fundamentalism," or "religion"—again understandably, since no one in the intellectual mainstream of 1967 could have expected such an intense resurgence of these forces.

Those who predict the future face an intractable dilemma. The scientific or quasi-scientific futurologist can base his forecasts only on the continuation of current trends. And yet if we know nothing else about the future, it is that current trends do not continue. There are disruptions, dislocations, surprises. The futurologist cannot foresee these.

The apocalyptic prophet faces no such restrictions. He has no incentive to predict more of the same; who would read him then? Consequently, he is entirely happy to foretell all kinds of upheavals, natural and supernatural—the submerging of continents, the manifestation of extraterrestrials, the shifting of the earth's pole, the return of Jesus Christ. In one sense, he too is right. Cataclysms do occur. But somehow they never occur in the way they were predicted.

I HAVE REMARKED SEVERAL times in the course of this book that I believe the future is knowable. So it is at times. Many—probably most—people have had some kind of precognitive experience: suddenly "knowing" that a distant loved one has died, making a last-minute cancellation on a doomed flight due to some vague premonition, having a hunch about the right move on some business deal. From an esoteric perspective, there are two main theories to account for such events.

The first one holds that there exists a realm of images and forms, which has many names in many traditions. The Kabbalists call it the world of Yetzirah, or "formation"; quite possibly it is what the Australian aborigines call the "dreaming" and what some Western occultists refer to as the "astral" realm. This realm of images does not exist in any physical sense, but all the same it has a reality of its own. If you think of a lightbulb, say, that image has some reality, even some substance, although not physically.

It is also taught that this world of images is *prior to* the physical world in a logical and even a temporal sense. That is, events and things manifest in this realm before they appear in palpable reality. Consequently, someone with reasonably clear access to this realm of images—deliberately, through divination or prophetic contemplation, or spontaneously, through dreams or hunches or intuitions—should be able to have some glimpses of the future.[67]

Readers may wonder what this old theory, beloved of the esotericists of the past and to some degree of the present, may have to do with synchronicity, which is often invoked when people attempt to understand the workings of forms of divination such as the Tarot or the *I Ching*. "Synchronicity" in this sense is a coinage of C. G. Jung's, who defines it as an "acausal connecting principle." Jung gives a case in point: "The wife of one of my patients, a man in his fifties, once told me in conversation that, at the deaths of her mother and her grandmother, a number of birds gathered outside the windows of the death-chamber."[68] Such incidents are common; I can relate similar stories from my own family. For

Jung, the connection between these two events—the death and the appearance of the birds—is not causal; that is, the impending death did not *cause* the birds to come or vice versa. But they are related by what he calls a *"meaningful cross-connection."*[69]

In the final analysis, Jung's attempt to characterize synchronicity as "acausal" appears misguided. He seems to be veering toward a connection that is not acausal in the strict sense but has a hidden cause lying outside the physical dimension. Jung locates this hidden cause in the realm of the archetypes, the psychic forces that underlie the human mind and possibly reality itself. For Jung, "meaningful coincidences . . . seem to have an archetypal foundation."[70]

Granting this much, we are left with a theory very close to that of the Kabbalists. The archetypal world is more or less identical to the realm of Yetzirah, of forms and images; as such it can give rise to two phenomena that have no obvious causal relation (such as a death and the sudden appearance of a flock of birds) and yet seem to be meaningfully connected. Jung made much of being scientific in his methods, and to a great degree he was—but his conclusions in many respects resemble those of the old occultists.

The other major theory about the knowability of the future is based on the highly relative nature of time. Time, as Kant argued, is one of the basic structural components of our experience, but it is a construct that our minds have imposed on reality; as hard as this may be to imagine, time has no absolute reality in itself (a conclusion to which contemporary physics may also point). If so, it may be possible to step past the portals of our own experiential framework and take some measure of events in the future.

Many spiritual traditions speak of a higher Self, a part of our being that stands over and above our selves as we customarily experience them. The names for this Self are countless: the ancient Greeks called it the *daimon*; the ancient Romans, the *genius*; to esoteric Christians, it is the kingdom of heaven or the Christ within. This Self stands outside the personality, the conscious self, and outside the categories of conscious experience, including time. It perceives our lives not as a sequence of events and experiences that span several decades but as a whole; it can see a lifetime as we can see a snapshot.

A famous instance of the workings of this Self, or *daimon*, appears in the *Crito* of Plato. Socrates, under sentence of execution, is urged to escape by his wealthy friend Crito, who assures him that he has bribed the guards and can furnish the necessary getaway. Socrates refuses, saying he has had a dream in which a beautiful woman dressed in white appeared to him and recited a line from the *Iliad*: "On the third day to the fertile land of Phthia thou shalt come."[71] Socrates takes this as a message from his *daimon*, the guiding spirit that has directed him all throughout his life, that he will be executed in three days, and that he should not try to escape. One way of understanding this episode is that the *daimon*, the Self, can see the whole of one's life from start to finish, apart from the linearity of time, and can give appropriate guidance.

Although we often assume that such experiences are the prerogative of great men like Socrates, it is the birthright of every human being to have access to this part of our nature. But we have almost forgotten its existence over the centuries. In dreams and fantasies it can be represented by the Wise Old Man or Woman—seen as a wizard, perhaps, a hermit, a priestess, or a magus such as Nostradamus. To return to a point I made in the introduction, it is a sense of alienation from this Self that helps explain the deep-seated hunger for this archetype that we see in contemporary culture.

Nonetheless, we can never lose our connection with this higher Self entirely; to do so is to die, spiritually if not physically. It is the object of many if not most spiritual practices to open up and reinforce this connection with the higher Self, although even without them it may make its presence felt spontaneously in times of great crisis or opportunity.

At these moments, some glimpse of the future may be granted

to us. These moments of insight are almost always shocking; it is eerie to have a sense that something will inevitably happen that may be months or even years in the future. For this reason, such revelations are rare and fleeting, although, from my experience, it seems that we can increase them and make them more vivid through certain types of inner discipline, including certain forms of meditation. It is in this sense that I mean the future is knowable.

Note, however, that these glimpses usually have to do with one's deeper destiny; it is not a question of picking next week's lottery number or finding hot stocks. While these are in principle no more unknowable than anything else, with some experience one soon discovers that the higher Self is not terribly interested in them—and anyway, how helpful would the knowledge really be? As a matter of fact, I only know directly of one case where someone got this kind of information. A friend of my father's once told me he had been awakened in the middle of the night by the image of some numbers that flashed vividly in his mind. It struck him that they might be lottery numbers and that he should buy a ticket using them, but he never got around to it. Of course they were the winning numbers that week.

This story reveals a common reaction to these flashes of premonition. They are often denied or ignored, even when one is convinced at some level that they are true. This attitude is especially ironic when we consider the credulity with which people often embrace the most absurd predictions (based on Nostradamus among others). Perhaps we clutch at others' false insights because we are too afraid to face our own, genuine ones.

In any event, any glimpses we may get of our own future are likely to remain rare and exceptional. Even the most awakened individuals, I suspect, find themselves confronted with many unexpected blessings and disasters in the course of life. Perhaps these events are concealed from us for the same reason we dislike being told the ending of a thriller: we may be on this earth partly for the sheer entertainment of it, and our pleasure would be greatly reduced if we were to know the outcome in advance.

Whether this is so, we remain firmly rooted in a life where the future is obscure and our footing seems ever tenuous. I very much doubt that we will find the certainty we need in prophecies of any kind. Rather, I suspect, we will discover it only in the deep center of our own being, which possesses the knowledge and the resourcefulness to deal with whatever the future presents to our lives.

Afterword: Nostradamus
and 2012

If you were to take the years that have been earmarked as the due date for the End Times, you would find few over the last two millennia that have avoided this peculiar honor. The twelfth-century Italian prophet Joachim of Fiore contended that the year 1280 would mark the dawn of the Era of the Holy Spirit, the dawn of spiritual freedom for all. William Miller, a self-educated preacher in early nineteenth-century New York state, predicted on the basis of his intricate scrutiny of biblical texts that Christ would return sometime between March 21, 1843, and March 21, 1844. Although his followers were disappointed, they regrouped to form the various Adventist denominations that still survive today. In the late nineteenth century, Charles Taze Russell, a Pittsburgh haberdasher who delved into scriptural mysteries, claimed that 1874 marked the 6000th year of man's creation and would inaugurate the Time of the End. Leaving a forty-year "harvest" period brought the target date to 1914. The events of that year seemed at first to prove Russell right, but, at his death in 1916, the Armageddon-like carnage of World War I was still continuing without any providential rescue. After the war had come and gone, Russell's followers, known as Bible Students, decided that 1914 was the *beginning* of the end. The largest segment of these (renamed Jehovah's Witnesses in 1931) later pointed toward a date of 1975, which their revised calculations indicated was the *real* 6000th year of man's creation. But this year passed without any serious damage to the heavens or the earth. At the end of the twentieth century, Nostradamus's date of 1999 was greeted with some apprehension, but, it too, proved to be like any other year.

New Age prophecy, which has retained the habit of apocalyptic speculation while detaching it from the Bible, is now looking toward 2012. It's curiously appropriate that the best article I have read about the 2012 phenomenon appears on a website called Cracked.com. Written by Luis Prada, it is entitled "The Six Best 2012 Apocalypse Theories (and Why They Are All Bullshit)."[72] Prada writes, "You may have noticed a recent trend of trying to fit every hackneyed doomsday prophecy into the same red-letter year of 2012. The theories are obtuse, their connections are flimsy and the perceived consequences are completely unsubstantiated. Unsurprisingly, these prophecies are enormously popular."

Prada's number one theory is credited to Nostradamus. But as you will realize if you have already read this book, Nostradamus makes no reference to the year 2012 in any of his prophecies. Furthermore, when he does mention dates in the future—1580, 1609, 1703, 1999—they are almost always years in which nothing of any great moment occurred. Why, then, has he been connected with 2012? There is, frankly, no good reason. It is simply that Nostradamus has become associated with apocalyptic prophecies as a whole—as Prada puts it, "No one else in history has caused more people to stockpile Spam in their bomb shelters"—and so has the year 2012, so it was inevitable that the two would be connected.

Then there is the History Channel. Discovering that its most successful shows were not the ones that delved into the saga of the Kentucky rifle or the air tactics of the Third Reich, the network began producing specials on more exotic subjects such as Nostradamus and 2012. Here is the network's own write-up of its show *Doomsday 2012: The End of Days*: "A surprising number of prophets— from ancient oracles to contemporary Internet-crawling software 'bots'— point to December 21, 2012 as the End of Days." And for "Nostradamus 2012," we are told, "December 21, 2012 is bearing down on us with alarming speed. Whether or not we are able to collectively heed the warnings and affect a course to avert disaster may be the defining moment of the modern age."[73] Presumably the "may" provides an out in case we don't have to heed the warnings after all.

These documentaries have, of course, attracted critics. John Major Jenkins, author of *Maya Cosmogenesis 2012*, described the 2006 History Channel program *Decoding the Past: Mayan Doomsday Prophecy* (for which he was interviewed) as "45 minutes of unabashed doomsday hype and the worst kind of inane sensationalism."[74]

I doubt the History Channel will be dismayed by such characterizations—certainly not as long as the ratings hold. I have appeared on some of these shows myself, and I can testify that the producers offscreen asking me the questions sometimes have trouble keeping a straight face.

All this said, these programs would not get such high ratings unless they met a need in the collective psyche. My own views about why they do are set out in the previous chapter, "Nostradamus and the Uses of Prophecy," so I won't rehearse them here, although I might add that the thought of doomsday generates a weird pleasure in those—probably including all of us—who feel a deep ambivalence about advanced civilization. We are the creations of this civilization; we could scarcely survive for a week outside the shade of its umbrella; but it is so exacting and artificial that we often find ourselves hating and resenting it. Fantasizing about apocalypse offers a way, even if it is an unsatisfying way, of reconciling these contradictions in ourselves.

But why 2012? Popularizing this year as a target date for apocalypse (or universal spiritual renewal) was originally the work of Valum Votan, or, as he is more commonly known, José Argüelles, the alleged "closer of the cycle and messenger of the new time."

Argüelles is best known as the prophet of the Harmonic Convergence of August 16–17, 1987, which attracted tremendous attention worldwide and is generally reckoned as the point at which the New Age entered mass culture—an outcome that did not please Argüelles. As he told me in a 1998 interview, "It was the beginning of the New Age as commercial marketing, which was anything but our intention."[75]

At any rate, from his interpretation of the extraordinarily intricate Mayan calendar (or calendars—there are apparently seventeen different ones), Argüelles contended that August 16, 1987, marked the end of a "hell cycle" for this planet and that the next five years would be a time of cleansing in preparation for the dawning of a new era on December 21, 2012. Argüelles explains:

> In 2012, the Earth will be in a condition of rapid, unprecedented evolution and change due to the enlightenment of the human species for having returned to living according to the natural 13:20 cycles of time . . . . The oneness of humanity will be the result of the universal telepathy reawakened by returning to the natural cycles. Because of this fact, there will no longer be any need of government, and humanity will have abandoned industrial technology for the development of spiritual, telepathic fourth-dimensional technologies. Creature comfort needs will be supplied by applications of solar and telepathic crystal technologies. The human race will be living and fulfilling UR, the Universal Religion on Earth. The order of reality will be known as the Dominion of Time. Everyone will be getting ready for the great moment of galactic synchronization, July 26, 2013, Yellow Galactic Seed, the completion of the telepathic construction of Timeship Earth 2013 and the advent of the Planetary Manitou, the galactic brain on Earth.[76]

Argüelles urges the world to adopt the Mayan calendar, which is based on a beneficent "13:20" proportion— the Mayan *tzolkin* cycle is 260 days or 20 times 13—instead of the pernicious "Babylonian" calendar, based on a "12:60" rhythm (with twelve months in a year), which, he contends, has warped and damaged human consciousness.

Argüelles's ideas do not necessarily become clearer with further explanation. A more lucid account is provided by John Major Jenkins, who says that December 21, 2012, will be the day on which the point of the sun's rising at the winter solstice coincides with the "Dark Rift" of the Milky Way, a gap in the galaxy as seen from the earth. The Mayans were aware of this "galactic alignment," as Jenkins calls it, and believed that it portended a renewal and transformation of the age."[77]

Still another 2012 prophet is the late Terence McKenna, who in the 1990s replaced Timothy Leary as the pope of psychedelia. Making his own hypercomplicated calculations using the *I Ching*, he arrived at a date for the dawning of a historic "singularity" in mid-November, 2012, but changed it to the Mayan date when he learned of that.

These speculations dovetail with a widespread expectation that we are entering the age of Aquarius, although the date of this occurrence is far more tenuous. Again, it has to do with the point of the sun's rising—in this case at the vernal equinox. Over the last 2,150 years (this figure is vague, as is its starting point), the sun has risen on March 21 with Pisces in the background. At some point it will rise, or has already started to rise, with Aquarius in the background: that will mark the dawning of the age of Aquarius. The dates for this event are unclear because there is no clear line between the zones of Pisces and Aquarius in the sky. Dates I have seen range from A.D. 1600 to 2500; C. G. Jung, in his work *Aion*, which deals in depth with the symbolism of Pisces, suggested that it might begin in 1997, for intricate astronomical reasons.[78]

A third element that converges in this wave of New Age apocalyptic thought is the Hindu concept of the Kali Yuga, the age of darkness under which, it is widely agreed, humanity now labors. By one fairly standard calculation, this began on January 23, 3012

B.C., although its ending date is, again, a matter of dispute. Most Hindus believe that we are still in the Kali Yuga, although a few say it is over. Sri Yukteswar, teacher of the celebrated yogi Paramahansa Yogananda, argued that it actually ended in A.D. 1699.[79]

The starting date for the Kali Yuga bears a curious—though admittedly far from exact—resemblance to the beginning of the Mayan calendar cycle, which is 5,125.36 years in length. Reckoning back from 2012, this takes us back to August 11, 3114 B.C.—not the same date as that of the commencement of the Kali Yuga by any means, but reasonably close. There is another, though even less exact, resonance with the traditional Jewish calendar, which dates the creation of the world at 3761 B.C. Although these dates span over 700 years, they fall in roughly the same era. Considering that traditional Jewish reckoning assigns a life span of 6,000 years to the world, we come to an ending date of A.D. 2239.

Most people will respond to these arcane reckonings in one of two ways: to dismiss them as too obscure or to embrace them precisely because of their obscurity. Practically everyone who looks forward to the 2012 target date as the deadline for planetary awakening understands the calculations only dimly but somehow believes that they portend an apocalypse of disaster—or is it enlightenment?

It's instructive to see how the 2012 prophecies have been manipulated by mass culture, notably by the History Channel. Nearly all of the 2012 visionaries see the date as a harbinger of a new and enlightened consciousness for humanity, but the wizards of television have transmogrified this vision into something that looks very much like a fundamentalist's Last Judgment. Ironically, this may help explain why the phenomenon has become so popular. The apocalyptic genre has been a vibrant, if corrosive, part of Western civilization since the second century B.C. But today the Western mind has been secularized to the point where many people are likely to laugh at reckonings based on stray verses in Daniel, Ezekiel, and Revelation. At the same time, apocalyptic expectation remains so habitual in the Western consciousness that it still continues to look for signs of doomsday even when it has lost faith in the religions that gave birth to the concept. For the New Ager, or, if you like, the "cultural creative," psychedelic visions, calendars created by the ancient Maya, the utterances of indigenous shamans, and calculations based on the *I Ching*—as well as the pronouncements of Nostradamus—are likely to have much more resonance and authority. Hence 2012.

As I've stressed throughout this book, prophecy is far more significant for what it says about collective needs and wishes than for what it says about the future. And yet I would stop short of dismissing the 2012 prophecies—whether or not they are adorned by gleanings from Nostradamus—as entirely a matter of wish fulfillment. While it seems to me ridiculous to single out specific dates—"of that day and hour knoweth no man"—the general pattern seems to have some significance. As we've already seen, several traditional reckonings date the beginning of the current epoch to sometime around 3000 B.C. And one thing is unquestionably true about this period: it is the watershed between history and prehistory. This period around 5000 years ago marks the beginning of civilization as we know it in Egypt and Mesopotamia and India; of what went before, we know nothing except for fanciful myths and tenuous theories cooked up by archaeologists analyzing pottery shards. The world was not created in 3000 or 4000 B.C., but *our* world, the world of man in history, was indeed created then.

Unfortunately, history is a tale of crimes and follies and failures. Even its brightest moments are faint. A civilization reaches a sublime flowering, and a generation later plunges back into darkness and decadence. A saint emerges to remind humanity of wisdom and goodness; a few decades afterward his followers turn his teachings into an excuse for coercion and violence. On the whole, it is far from an inspiring story, and in a way the prediction that everything will continue as usual is as dark a forecast as the gloomiest mutterings of fanatics. Today we find ourselves saying, with Joyce's Stephen Dedalus, "History is a nightmare from which I am trying to awake."[80] Do the prophecies for 2012, however ludicrous they may seem, underscore a hope that humanity will finally awaken collectively?

I believe they do. More than that I cannot say. I am not a prophet, and as this book proves, I do not believe in prophets. But I do sense that the human race is attempting to shake off a long and terrifying slumber. What will come after is sealed off by as impenetrable a wall as the one that shields us from prehistory.

Richard Smoley
Winfield, Illinois
September 2009

Notes

1. Mary Lynn Carter, *Edgar Cayce on Prophecy* (New York: Paperback Library, 1968), 58–63.
2. For a more extensive treatment of these figures, see my book *Forbidden Faith: The Gnostic Legacy from the Gospels to The Da Vinci Code* (San Francisco: HarperSanFrancisco, 2006), chapter 6.
3. [Valentin Tomberg], *Meditations on the Tarot: A Journey into Christian Hermeticism* (Warwick, N.Y.: Amity House, 1985), 200.
4. In Peter Lemesurier, *The Unknown Nostradamus* (Alresford, Hants., U.K.: John Hunt, 2003), 15.
5. In ibid., 25.
6. Paul Johnson, *A History of Christianity* (New York: Atheneum, 1987), 191–92.
7. Edgar Leoni, *Nostradamus and His Prophecies* (1961; reprint, Mineola, N.Y.: Dover, 2000), 20–21.
8. Nostradamus, *Traité des fardemens et confitures,* book 1, chapter 8, quoted in Lemesurier, *The Unknown Nostradamus,* 31–32.
9. Henry Cornelius Agrippa of Nettesheim, *Three Books of Occult Philosophy,* trans. James Freake, ed. Donald Tyson (St. Paul, Minn.: Llewellyn, 1993), 3.
10. In Lemesurier, 59.
11. In Leoni, 38.
12. Jean Dupébe, ed., *Nostradamus: Lettres inédites* (Geneva: Droz, 1983), introduction, 20–21. My translation.
13. In Lemesurier, *The Unknown Nostradamus,* 84.
14. In Leoni, 25.
15. In Nostradamus, *Les premières Centuries ou Propheties,* Pierre Brind'Amour, ed. (Paris: Droz, 1996), introduction, page l. My translation.
16. In Bernard McGinn, *Visions of the End: Apocalyptic Traditions in the Middle Ages* (New York: Columbia University Press, 1979), 49.

17. In Lemesurier, *The Unknown Nostradamus,* 74.

18. The letter to Morel is quoted *in toto* in Lemesurier, *The Unknown Nostradamus,* 76–78.

19. In C. D. O'Malley, *Andreas Vesalius of Brussels, 1514–1564* (Berkeley: University of California Press, 1964), 287–88, 396–98. For the reference, I am indebted to Miguel J. Faria, "The Death of Henry II of France," *The Journal of Neurosurgery,* vol. 77 (Dec. 1992), 964–69.

20. In Leoni, 30.

21. In ibid., 31.

22. In Jean Maguelonne, *Michel de Nostredame, dit Nostradamus* (Paris: Éditions de Vecchi, 2001), 115.

23. In Lemesurier, 117.

24. In Leoni, 33–34.

25. Lemesurier, *The Unknown Nostradamus,* 140, 143.

26. In Leoni, 51.

27. Ibid., 64–65.

28. For this account I am relying on an article by T.W.M. Berkel, "Nostradamus, the Netherlands, and the Second World War," http://nostredame.chez.tiscali.fr/nberk14.html.

29. Lemesurier, *The Unknown Nostradamus,* 145.

30. Beth Gimmel, "Prophecy 2004," *The Sun,* Feb. 17, 2004, 26.

31. Graham Beaton, "The Nostradamus Chronicles, Part Two: Forbidden Prophecies for the 21st Century," *The Sun,* July 4, 2005, 18.

32. Iamblichus, *On the Mysteries,* trans. with annotations by Emma C. Clarke, John M. Dillon, and Jackson P. Hershbell (Atlanta, Ga.: Society of Biblical Literature, 2003), 147 (III.11).

33. Iamblichus, 149 (III.11).

34. Dante Alighieri, *On World Government,* trans. Herbert W. Schneider (Indianapolis: Bobbs-Merrill, 1949), 9 (I.5).

35. Fernand Braudel, *The Mediterranean and the Mediterranean World in the Age of Philip II,* trans. Siân Reynolds (New York: Harper & Row, 1973), vol. 2, 908–9.

36. Brind'Amour, 69.

37. My references to Nostradamus's *Preface to César* and the *Epistle to Henri II* reflect the section numbering in Leoni.

38. Apuleius XI.24; my translation.

39. Erika Cheetham, *The Prophecies of Nostradamus* (New York: Berkley, 1973), 69.

40. Braudel, 898.

41. Pliny the Elder, *Natural History,* II.205; cf. Brind'Amour, 224.

42. For more on the survival of the Cathars, see my book *Forbidden Faith,* chapter 4.

43. For further discussion of this symbolism, see my *Hidden Wisdom: A Guide to the Western Inner Traditions,* coauthored with Jay Kinney (New York: Penguin/Arkana, 1999), chapter 8. For more on the tripartite structure of human nature, see my *Inner Christianity* (Boston: Shambhala, 2002), chapter 4.

44. Norab, *What Will Happen in the Near Future? The Prophecies of the Ancient French Astrologer Nostradamus and the Present War* (Stockholm: Stockholms Bokindustri Aktiebolag, 1940), 50.

45. Ibid., 61.

46. Braudel, 1179.

47. Manilius, *Astronomica* 4.773–74; my translation. See Brind'Amour, 535–36.

48. Daniel Andreev, *The Rose of the World,* trans. Jordan Roberts (Hudson, N.Y.: Lindisfarne, 1997), 20, 67.

49. William L. Shirer, *The Rise and Fall of the Third Reich: A History of Nazi Germany* (New York: Simon & Schuster, 1960), 652–56.

50. Quoted on the Web site *Prophéties pour temps de crise: Interprétations de Nostradamus au fil des siécles*: www.bm-lyon.fr/expo/virtuelles/nostradamus/index.html; my translation of this French text.

51. David Chandler, "Remember: The Execution and Burial of King Charles I," www.sealedknot.org/knowbase/docs/0082_Execution.htm.

52. See Leoni, 62.

53. Georges Dumézil, "A Nostradamian Farce," in Dumézil, *The Riddle of Nostradamus: A Critical Dialogue,* trans. Betsy Wing (Baltimore, Md.: Johns Hopkins University Press, 1999), 10.

54. Fernand Braudel, *The Structures of Everyday Life,* vol. 1: *Civilization and Capitalism, 15th–18th Century,* trans. Siân Reynolds (New York: Harper & Row, 1981), 91.

55. In William L. Shirer, *The Rise and Fall of the Third Reich* (New York: Simon & Schuster, 1960), 862.

56. Mark Kishlansky, *A Monarchy Transformed: Britain, 1603–1714* (London: Allen Lane/Penguin Press, 1996), 200.

57. Norab, 61.

58. John Hogue, *Nostradamus: The Complete Prophecies* (Rockport, Mass.: Element, 1997), 812.

59. McGinn, *Visions of the End,* 82.

60. Herodotus i.53, 92; in *Herodotus,* trans. A. D. Godley (London: Heinemann [Loeb Classical Library], 1921), 61, 119.

61. McGinn, *Visions of the End,* 29.

62. In ibid., 280.

63. *A Course in Miracles* (Tiburon, Calif.: Foundation for Inner Peace, 1975), Text, 367–68.

64. Eckhart Tolle, *The Power of Now* (Novato, Calif.: New World Library, 1997), 29.

65. The best discussion of this topic that I know of can be found in Max Dublin, *Futurehype: The Tyranny of Prophecy* (New York: Viking, 1989).

66. Herman Kahn and Anthony J. Wiener, *The Year 2000: A Framework for Speculation on the Next Thirty-Three Years* (New York: Macmillan, 1967), 91, 194.

67. For further discussion of this topic, see Smoley and Kinney, 103–6.

68. C. G. Jung, *Synchronicity: An Acausal Connecting Principle,* trans. R. F. C. Hull, 2nd ed. (Princeton, N.J.: Princeton University Press, 1973), 22.

69. Ibid., 11. Emphasis Jung's.

70. Ibid., 24.

71. Plato, *Crito,* 44b. My translation.

72. http://www.cracked.com/article__17445__6-best-2012-apocalypse-theories-are-all-bullshit.html; accessed June 22, 2009.

73. http://shop.history.com/detail.php?a=77314 and http://shop.history.com/detail.php?p=87412&v=All; accessed June 18, 2009.

74. John Major Jenkins, "How Not to Make a 2012 Documentary"; http://alignment2012.com/historychannel.html:; accessed June 18, 2009.

75. Richard Smoley, "The Crisis of the Calendar: The *Gnosis* Interview with José and Lloydine Argüelles," *Gnosis* 49 (fall 1998), 31.

76. Valum Votan (José Argüelles), "Mission Statement of Valum Votan, Closer of the Cycle"; http://earthportals.com/Portal__Messenger/votan.html; accessed June 19, 2009.

77. John Major Jenkins, *The 2012 Story: The Myth, Fallacies, and Truth behind the Most Intriguing Date in History* (New York: Tarcher/Penguin, 2009), 117. See also John Major Jenkins, "Mayan Shamanism and 2012: A Psychedelic Cosmology," in Daniel Pinchbeck and Ken Jordan, eds., *Toward 2012: Perspectives on the Next Age* (New York: Tarcher/Penguin, 2008), 60.

78. C. G. Jung, *Aion: Researches into the Phenomenology of the Self,* trans. R. F. C. Hull (Princeton: Princeton/Bollingen, 1959), 94.

79. Swami Sri Yukteswar, *The Holy Science,* 8th ed. (Los Angeles: Self-Realization Fellowship, 1990), 7–20.

80. James Joyce, *Ulysses* (New York: Random House, 1961), 34.

Suggestions for Further Reading

There is an extensive literature on Nostradamus, and there are many editions of his works. However, most are of uneven quality at best. The books I have found most helpful are:

PETER LEMESURIER, *Nostradamus: The Illustrated Prophecies* (Alresford, Hants., U.K.: John Hunt Publishing, 2003). Contains the text of the *Prophecies* as well as the *Preface to César* and the *Epistle to Henri II*. Lemesurier does not attempt to apply the prophecies to any later occurrences; his references are almost entirely to the sources Nostradamus himself used for his verses. This work is thus extremely valuable in rooting Nostradamus's work in the Christian apocalyptic tradition.

EDGAR LEONI, *Nostradamus and His Prophecies* (Mineola, N.Y.: Dover, 2000). This edition is a reprint of Leoni's *Nostradamus: Life and Literature,* originally published in 1961. Despite its age, it remains probably the best interpretation of Nostradamus's prophecies as applied to the future. While I do not agree with all of Leoni's conclusions, his is the most level-headed treatment of the subject I know of. Leoni is particularly good in his citation of previous interpretations from the seventeenth century to his own time. His concise biography of the seer is also engaging and well-researched.

PETER LEMESURIER, *The Unknown Nostradamus* (Alresford, Hants., U.K.: John Hunt Publishing, 2003). Probably the best biography overall, containing the best and most reliable documentation as well as a minimum of speculation.

BERNARD MCGINN, *Visions of the End: Apocalyptic Traditions in the Middle Ages* (New York: Columbia University Press, 1979). McGinn is one of the nation's most respected scholars of the apocalyptic tradition. This collection unfortunately does not extend up to Nostradamus's time, but it contains many of the sources with which he worked, along with a solid and readable account of Christian apocalyptic after the period of the New Testament.

BERNARD MCGINN, *Antichrist: Two Thousand Years of the Human Fascination with Evil* (San Francisco: HarperSanFrancisco, 1994; reprint, New York: Columbia University Press, 2000). Again, this does not deal specifically with Nostradamus, but it is an excellent account of the idea of Antichrist from Christian origins to the present.

FERNAND BRAUDEL, *The Mediterranean and the Mediterranean World in the Age of Philip II,* translated by Siân Reynolds, 2 vols. (New York: Harper & Row, 1972). This is one of the greatest historical works of the twentieth century. Braudel was a pioneer in using statistical data (such as population figures and shipping tonnage) as a supplement to conventional history. He paints a vivid and remarkably complete image of the world in which Nostradamus lived. Part 3 of this work, "Events, Politics, and People," is particularly useful in giving a portrait of main players in the power struggles of the era.

FERNAND BRAUDEL, *The Structures of Everyday Life,* translated by Siân Reynolds (New York: Harper & Row, 1981). This is the first volume of a larger work entitled *Civilization and Capitalism: 15th–18th Century.* It is also valuable in helping the reader to view Nostradamus in his own context.

Selected Bibliography

Alighieri, Dante. *On World Government*. Translated by Herbert W. Schneider. Indianapolis: Bobbs-Merrill, 1949.

The American Ephemeris: 2001–2010. Edited by Rique Pottenger. San Diego, Calif.: ACS Publications, 1997.

Andreev, Daniel. *The Rose of the World*. Translated by Jordan Roberts. Hudson, N.Y.: Lindisfarne, 1997.

Atlas of World History. Edited by R. R. Palmer. New York: Rand McNally, 1965.

Baudrillard, Jean. *The Illusion of the End*. Translated by Chris Turner. Stanford, Calif.: Stanford University Press, 1994.

Braudel, Fernand. *The Mediterranean and the Mediterranean World in the Age of Philip II*. Translated by Siân Reynolds. 2 vols. New York: Harper & Row, 1972.

———. *The Structures of Everyday Life*. Vol. 1, *Civilization and Capitalism: 15th–18th Century*. Translated by Siân Reynolds. New York: Harper & Row, 1981.

Carter, Mary Lynn. *Edgar Cayce on Prophecy*. New York: Paperback Library, 1968.

Cheetham, Erika. *The Final Prophecies of Nostradamus*. New York: Perigee, 1989.

———. *The Prophecies of Nostradamus*. New York: Perigee, 1973.

Cornelius Agrippa, Henry. *Three Books of Occult Philosophy*. Translated by James Freake. Edited by Donald Tyson. St. Paul, Minn.: Llewellyn, 1993.

A Course in Miracles. Tiburon, Calif.: Foundation for Inner Peace, 1975.

Dublin, Max. *Futurehype: The Tyranny of Prophecy*. New York: Viking, 1989.

Dumézil, Georges. *The Riddle of Nostradamus: A Critical Dialogue*. Translated by Betsy Wing. Baltimore, Md.: Johns Hopkins University Press, 1999.

Dupèbe, Jean, ed. *Nostradamus: Lettres inédites*. Geneva: Droz, 1983.

Festinger, Leon, et al. *When Prophecy Fails*. Minneapolis: University of Minnesota Press, 1956.

Fragonard, Marie-Madeleine, and Éliane Kotler. *Introduction à la langue du XVIe siècle*. Paris: Nathan, 1994.

Greimas, Algirdas Julien, and Teresa Mary Keane. *Dictionnaire du moyen français.* Paris: Larousse, 1992.

Halley, Ned. *The Complete Prophecies of Nostradamus.* Ware, Herts., U.K.: Wordsworth, 1999.

Herodotus. *Herodotus.* Translated by A. D. Godley. 4 vols. London: Heinemann (Loeb Classical Library), 1921.

Hewitt, V. J., and Peter Lorie. *Nostradamus, The End of the Millennium: Prophecies, 1992 to 2001.* New York: Simon & Schuster, 1991.

Hogue, John. *Nostradamus: A Life and Myth.* London: Element, 2003.

———. *Nostradamus: The Complete Prophecies.* Rockport, Mass.: Element, 1997.

Iamblichus. *On the Mysteries.* Translated with annotations by Emma C. Clarke, John M. Dillon, and Jackson P. Hershbell. Atlanta, Ga.: Society of Biblical Literature, 2003.

Johnson, Paul. *A History of Christianity.* New York: Atheneum, 1987.

Jung, C. G. *Flying Saucers: A Modern Myth of Things Seen in the Skies.* Translated by R. F. C. Hull. Princeton, N.J.: Princeton University Press, 1978.

———. *Synchronicity: An Acausal Connecting Principle.* Translated by R. F. C. Hull. 2nd edition. Princeton, N.J.: Princeton University Press, 1973.

Kahn, Herman, and Anthony J. Wiener. *The Year 2000: A Framework for Speculation on the Next Thirty-Three Years.* New York: Macmillan, 1967.

King, Francis, and Stephen Skinner. *The Prophecies of Nostradamus and the World's Greatest Seers and Mystics.* London: Carlton, 1994.

King, Francis X. *Nostradamus: Prophecies Fulfilled and Predictions for the Millennium and Beyond.* New York: St. Martin's Griffin, 1994.

Kishlansky, Mark. *A Monarchy Transformed: Britain, 1603–1714.* London: Allen Lane/Penguin Press, 1996.

Lemesurier, Peter. *Nostradamus: The Illustrated Prophecies.* Alresford, Hants., U.K.: John Hunt Publishing, 2003.

———. *Nostradamus: The Next Fifty Years.* New York: Berkley, 1994.

———. *The Unknown Nostradamus.* Alresford, Hants., U.K.: John Hunt Publishing, 2003.

Leoni, Edgar. *Nostradamus and His Prophecies.* Mineola, N.Y.: Dover, 2000.

Lorie, Peter. *Nostradamus: 2003–2005: A History of the Future.* New York: Pocket Books, 2002.

Maguelonne, Jean. *Michel de Nostredame, dit Nostradamus.* Paris: Éditions de Vecchi, 2001.

Mascetti, Manuela Dunn, and Peter Lorie. *Nostradamus: Prophecies for Women.* New York: Simon & Schuster, 1995.

McCann, Lee. *Nostradamus: The Man Who Saw Through Time.* New York: Farrar, Straus, Giroux, 1941.

McGinn, Bernard. *Antichrist: Two Thousand Years of the Human Fascination with*

Evil. San Francisco: HarperSanFrancisco, 1994; reprint, New York: Columbia University Press, 2000.

———. *Visions of the End: Apocalyptic Traditions in the Middle Ages.* New York: Columbia University Press, 1979.

Norab. *What Will Happen in the Near Future? The Prophecies of the Ancient French Astrologer Nostradamus and the Present War.* Stockholm: Stockholms Bokindustri Aktiebolag, 1940.

Nostradamus. *Les premières Centuries ou Propheties.* Edited by Pierre Brind'Amour. Paris: Droz, 1996.

Pigeard de Gurbert, Max [Dr. de Fontbrune]. *Ce que Nostradamus a vraiment dit.* 1938. Reprint, Paris: Stock, 1976.

Ross, Scarlett. *Nostradamus for Dummies: The Fun and Easy Way to Decipher the Predictions of This Sixteenth-Century Prophet.* Hoboken, N.J.: Wiley, 2005.

Shirer, William L. *The Rise and Fall of the Third Reich: A History of Nazi Germany.* New York: Simon & Schuster, 1960.

Smoley, Richard. *Forbidden Faith: The Gnostic Legacy from the Gospels to The Da Vinci Code.* San Francisco: HarperSanFrancisco, 2006.

———. *Inner Christianity: A Guide to the Esoteric Tradition.* Boston: Shambhala, 2002.

Smoley, Richard, and Jay Kinney. *Hidden Wisdom: A Guide to the Western Inner Traditions.* New York: Penguin/Arkana, 1999.

Tolle, Eckhart. *The Power of Now.* Novato, Calif.: New World Library, 1997.

[Tomberg, Valentin.] *Meditations on the Tarot: A Journey into Christian Hermeticism.* Warwick, N.Y.: Amity House, 1985. Reprint, New York: Tarcher, 2002.

Ward, Charles A. *Oracles of Nostradamus.* Reprint, New York: Modern Library, 1940.

Index

About the Author

Richard Smoley has more than thirty years' experience studying and practicing esoteric spirituality. His books include *The Dice Game of Shiva: How Consciousness Creates the Universe*; *Inner Christianity: A Guide to the Esoteric Tradition*; *Conscious Love: Insights from Mystical Christianity*; *Forbidden Faith: The Secret History of Gnosticism*; and *Hidden Wisdom: A Guide to the Western Inner Traditions* (with Jay Kinney). He is also the former editor of *Gnosis: A Journal of the Western Inner Traditions*. Currently he is editor of *Quest: Journal of the Theosophical Society in America* and of Quest Books.

TARCHER
PENGUIN

FIND YOURSELF IN TARCHER
CORNERSTONE EDITIONS . . .

*a powerful new line of keepsake trade paperbacks that highlight the
foundational works of ancient and modern spiritual literature.*

Tao Te Ching
The New Translation from *Tao Te Ching: The Definitive Edition*
Lao Tzu, translated by Jonathan Star

*"It would be hard to find a fresh approach to a
text that ranks only behind the Bible as the most
widely translated book in the world, but Star
achieves that goal."*
— NAPRA ReView

ISBN 978-1-58542-618-8

The Essential Marcus Aurelius
Newly translated and introduced by Jacob Needleman and John P. Piazza

*A stunningly relevant and reliable translation of
the thoughts and aphorisms of the Stoic philosopher and Roman emperor Marcus Aurelius.*

ISBN 978-1-58542-617-1

www.penguin.com

Accept This Gift
Selections from *A Course in Miracles*
Edited by Frances Vaughan, Ph.D., and Roger Walsh, M.D., Ph.D.
Foreword by Marianne Williamson

*"An invaluable collection from one of the great
sources of the perennial wisdom—a gold mine of
psychological and spiritual insights."*
—KEN WILBER

ISBN 978-1-58542-619-5

The Kybalion
Three Initiates

*Who wrote this mysterious guide to the principles of
esoteric psychology and worldly success? History has
kept readers guessing. . . . Experience for yourself
the intriguing ideas of an underground classic.*

ISBN 978-1-58542-643-0

The Spiritual Emerson
Essential Works by Ralph Waldo Emerson,
introduction by Jacob Needleman

*This concise volume collects the core writings that
have made Ralph Waldo Emerson a key source of
insight for spiritual seekers of every faith—with
an introduction by the bestselling philosopher
Jacob Needleman.*

ISBN 978-1-58542-642-3

The Four Gospels
The Contemporary English Version
Foreword by Phyllis Tickle

Discover and understand the beauty and richness of the Gospels of Matthew, Mark, Luke, and John as never before. Here are the life and teachings of Jesus, as found in the four Gospels of the New Testament— now available in this important new collection from the Contemporary English Version translation with a foreword by bestselling author Phyllis Tickle.

ISBN 978-1-58542-677-5

The Hermetica: The Lost Wisdom of the Pharaohs
Timothy Freke and Peter Gandy

The singularly accessible collection of late-antique esoteric writings historically attributed to the legendary Hermes Trismegistus, venerated as a great and mythical sage in the Greco-Egyptian world and rediscovered during the Renaissance.

ISBN 978-1-58542-692-8

Rumi: In the Arms of the Beloved
Translations by Jonathan Star

"A remarkable new sounding of the poetry of Rumi and "an experience of the Divine that you will treasure for a lifetime."
—JOAN BORYSENKO, PH.D.

ISBN 978-1-58542-693-5

The Aquarian Gospel of Jesus the Christ
Levi H. Dowling

A hugely influential interpretation of the "lost years" of Jesus Christ, in which the Son of Man is seen to travel through the religious cultures of the East, learning and preaching the unifying spiritual ethic behind all religions.

ISBN 978-1-58542-724-6

The Aquarian Conspiracy
Marilyn Ferguson

"A bible of the New Age Movement."
— WILLIAM GRIMES, *The New York Times*

A thorough, detailed document of one of the most powerful cultural movements of our era.

ISBN 978-1-58542-742-0

Seven Years in Tibet
Heinrich Harrer

"[O]ne of the grandest and most incredible adventure stories I have ever read."
— SANTHA RAMA RAU,
New York Times Book Review

The vivid, millions-selling memoir of one of the first Europeans ever to enter Tibet.

ISBN 978-1-58542-743-7

The New Religions
Jacob Needleman

"Of all books published to date on today's 'spiritual revolution,' The New Religions is clearly superior, a brilliant, probing analysis . . . . of enduring worth."

—ROBERT GALBREATH,
The Journal of Popular Culture

ISBN 978-1-58542-744-4

If you enjoyed this book, visit

www.tarcherbooks.com

and sign up for Tarcher's e-newsletter to receive
special offers, giveaway promotions, and
information on hot upcoming releases.

TARCHER
PENGUIN

Great Lives Begin with Great Ideas

New at **www.tarcherbooks.com**
and **www.penguin.com/tarchertalks**:

Tarcher Talks, an online video series featuring
interviews with bestselling authors on everything from creativity and prosperity to 2012
and Freemasonry

If you would like to place a bulk order
of this book, call 1-800-847-5515.